MTLE

Pedagogy: Secondary

SECRETS

Study Guide
Your Key to Exam Success

DEAR FUTURE EXAM SUCCESS STORY

First of all, **THANK YOU** for purchasing Mometrix study materials!

Second, congratulations! You are one of the few determined test-takers who are committed to doing whatever it takes to excel on your exam. **You have come to the right place.** We developed these study materials with one goal in mind: to deliver you the information you need in a format that's concise and easy to use.

In addition to optimizing your guide for the content of the test, we've outlined our recommended steps for breaking down the preparation process into small, attainable goals so you can make sure you stay on track.

We've also analyzed the entire test-taking process, identifying the most common pitfalls and showing how you can overcome them and be ready for any curveball the test throws you.

Standardized testing is one of the biggest obstacles on your road to success, which only increases the importance of doing well in the high-pressure, high-stakes environment of test day. Your results on this test could have a significant impact on your future, and this guide provides the information and practical advice to help you achieve your full potential on test day.

Your success is our success

We would love to hear from you! If you would like to share the story of your exam success or if you have any questions or comments in regard to our products, please contact us at **800-673-8175** or **support@mometrix.com**.

Thanks again for your business and we wish you continued success!

Sincerely,
The Mometrix Test Preparation Team

> **Need more help? Check out our flashcards at:**
> **http://MometrixFlashcards.com/MTLE**

TABLE OF CONTENTS

Introduction

Thank you for purchasing this resource! You have made the choice to prepare yourself for a test that could have a huge impact on your future, and this guide is designed to help you be fully ready for test day. Obviously, it's important to have a solid understanding of the test material, but you also need to be prepared for the unique environment and stressors of the test, so that you can perform to the best of your abilities.

For this purpose, the first section that appears in this guide is the **Secret Keys**. We've devoted countless hours to meticulously researching what works and what doesn't, and we've boiled down our findings to the five most impactful steps you can take to improve your performance on the test. We start at the beginning with study planning and move through the preparation process, all the way to the testing strategies that will help you get the most out of what you know when you're finally sitting in front of the test.

We recommend that you start preparing for your test as far in advance as possible. However, if you've bought this guide as a last-minute study resource and only have a few days before your test, we recommend that you skip over the first two Secret Keys since they address a long-term study plan.

If you struggle with **test anxiety**, we strongly encourage you to check out our recommendations for how you can overcome it. Test anxiety is a formidable foe, but it can be beaten, and we want to make sure you have the tools you need to defeat it.

Secret Key #1 – Plan Big, Study Small

There's a lot riding on your performance. If you want to ace this test, you're going to need to keep your skills sharp and the material fresh in your mind. You need a plan that lets you review everything you need to know while still fitting in your schedule. We'll break this strategy down into three categories.

Information Organization

Start with the information you already have: the official test outline. From this, you can make a complete list of all the concepts you need to cover before the test. Organize these concepts into groups that can be studied together, and create a list of any related vocabulary you need to learn so you can brush up on any difficult terms. You'll want to keep this vocabulary list handy once you actually start studying since you may need to add to it along the way.

Time Management

Once you have your set of study concepts, decide how to spread them out over the time you have left before the test. Break your study plan into small, clear goals so you have a manageable task for each day and know exactly what you're doing. Then just focus on one small step at a time. When you manage your time this way, you don't need to spend hours at a time studying. Studying a small block of content for a short period each day helps you retain information better and avoid stressing over how much you have left to do. You can relax knowing that you have a plan to cover everything in time. In order for this strategy to be effective though, you have to start studying early and stick to your schedule. Avoid the exhaustion and futility that comes from last-minute cramming!

Study Environment

The environment you study in has a big impact on your learning. Studying in a coffee shop, while probably more enjoyable, is not likely to be as fruitful as studying in a quiet room. It's important to keep distractions to a minimum. You're only planning to study for a short block of time, so make the most of it. Don't pause to check your phone or get up to find a snack. It's also important to **avoid multitasking**. Research has consistently shown that multitasking will make your studying dramatically less effective. Your study area should also be comfortable and well-lit so you don't have the distraction of straining your eyes or sitting on an uncomfortable chair.

The time of day you study is also important. You want to be rested and alert. Don't wait until just before bedtime. Study when you'll be most likely to comprehend and remember. Even better, if you know what time of day your test will be, set that time aside for study. That way your brain will be used to working on that subject at that specific time and you'll have a better chance of recalling information.

Finally, it can be helpful to team up with others who are studying for the same test. Your actual studying should be done in as isolated an environment as possible, but the work of organizing the information and setting up the study plan can be divided up. In between study sessions, you can discuss with your teammates the concepts that you're all studying and quiz each other on the details. Just be sure that your teammates are as serious about the test as you are. If you find that your study time is being replaced with social time, you might need to find a new team.

Secret Key #2 – Make Your Studying Count

You're devoting a lot of time and effort to preparing for this test, so you want to be absolutely certain it will pay off. This means doing more than just reading the content and hoping you can remember it on test day. It's important to make every minute of study count. There are two main areas you can focus on to make your studying count:

Retention

It doesn't matter how much time you study if you can't remember the material. You need to make sure you are retaining the concepts. To check your retention of the information you're learning, try recalling it at later times with minimal prompting. Try carrying around flashcards and glance at one or two from time to time or ask a friend who's also studying for the test to quiz you.

To enhance your retention, look for ways to put the information into practice so that you can apply it rather than simply recalling it. If you're using the information in practical ways, it will be much easier to remember. Similarly, it helps to solidify a concept in your mind if you're not only reading it to yourself but also explaining it to someone else. Ask a friend to let you teach them about a concept you're a little shaky on (or speak aloud to an imaginary audience if necessary). As you try to summarize, define, give examples, and answer your friend's questions, you'll understand the concepts better and they will stay with you longer. Finally, step back for a big picture view and ask yourself how each piece of information fits with the whole subject. When you link the different concepts together and see them working together as a whole, it's easier to remember the individual components.

Finally, practice showing your work on any multi-step problems, even if you're just studying. Writing out each step you take to solve a problem will help solidify the process in your mind, and you'll be more likely to remember it during the test.

Modality

Modality simply refers to the means or method by which you study. Choosing a study modality that fits your own individual learning style is crucial. No two people learn best in exactly the same way, so it's important to know your strengths and use them to your advantage.

For example, if you learn best by visualization, focus on visualizing a concept in your mind and draw an image or a diagram. Try color-coding your notes, illustrating them, or creating symbols that will trigger your mind to recall a learned concept. If you learn best by hearing or discussing information, find a study partner who learns the same way or read aloud to yourself. Think about how to put the information in your own words. Imagine that you are giving a lecture on the topic and record yourself so you can listen to it later.

For any learning style, flashcards can be helpful. Organize the information so you can take advantage of spare moments to review. Underline key words or phrases. Use different colors for different categories. Mnemonic devices (such as creating a short list in which every item starts with the same letter) can also help with retention. Find what works best for you and use it to store the information in your mind most effectively and easily.

3

Secret Key #3 – Practice the Right Way

Your success on test day depends not only on how many hours you put into preparing, but also on whether you prepared the right way. It's good to check along the way to see if your studying is paying off. One of the most effective ways to do this is by taking practice tests to evaluate your progress. Practice tests are useful because they show exactly where you need to improve. Every time you take a practice test, pay special attention to these three groups of questions:

- The questions you got wrong
- The questions you had to guess on, even if you guessed right
- The questions you found difficult or slow to work through

This will show you exactly what your weak areas are, and where you need to devote more study time. Ask yourself why each of these questions gave you trouble. Was it because you didn't understand the material? Was it because you didn't remember the vocabulary? Do you need more repetitions on this type of question to build speed and confidence? Dig into those questions and figure out how you can strengthen your weak areas as you go back to review the material.

Additionally, many practice tests have a section explaining the answer choices. It can be tempting to read the explanation and think that you now have a good understanding of the concept. However, an explanation likely only covers part of the question's broader context. Even if the explanation makes sense, **go back and investigate** every concept related to the question until you're positive you have a thorough understanding.

As you go along, keep in mind that the practice test is just that: practice. Memorizing these questions and answers will not be very helpful on the actual test because it is unlikely to have any of the same exact questions. If you only know the right answers to the sample questions, you won't be prepared for the real thing. **Study the concepts** until you understand them fully, and then you'll be able to answer any question that shows up on the test.

It's important to wait on the practice tests until you're ready. If you take a test on your first day of study, you may be overwhelmed by the amount of material covered and how much you need to learn. Work up to it gradually.

On test day, you'll need to be prepared for answering questions, managing your time, and using the test-taking strategies you've learned. It's a lot to balance, like a mental marathon that will have a big impact on your future. Like training for a marathon, you'll need to start slowly and work your way up. When test day arrives, you'll be ready.

Start with the strategies you've read in the first two Secret Keys—plan your course and study in the way that works best for you. If you have time, consider using multiple study resources to get different approaches to the same concepts. It can be helpful to see difficult concepts from more than one angle. Then find a good source for practice tests. Many times, the test website will suggest potential study resources or provide sample tests.

Practice Test Strategy

If you're able to find at least three practice tests, we recommend this strategy:

UNTIMED AND OPEN-BOOK PRACTICE

Take the first test with no time constraints and with your notes and study guide handy. Take your time and focus on applying the strategies you've learned.

TIMED AND OPEN-BOOK PRACTICE

Take the second practice test open-book as well, but set a timer and practice pacing yourself to finish in time.

TIMED AND CLOSED-BOOK PRACTICE

Take any other practice tests as if it were test day. Set a timer and put away your study materials. Sit at a table or desk in a quiet room, imagine yourself at the testing center, and answer questions as quickly and accurately as possible.

Keep repeating timed and closed-book tests on a regular basis until you run out of practice tests or it's time for the actual test. Your mind will be ready for the schedule and stress of test day, and you'll be able to focus on recalling the material you've learned.

Secret Key #4 – Pace Yourself

Once you're fully prepared for the material on the test, your biggest challenge on test day will be managing your time. Just knowing that the clock is ticking can make you panic even if you have plenty of time left. Work on pacing yourself so you can build confidence against the time constraints of the exam. Pacing is a difficult skill to master, especially in a high-pressure environment, so **practice is vital**.

Set time expectations for your pace based on how much time is available. For example, if a section has 60 questions and the time limit is 30 minutes, you know you have to average 30 seconds or less per question in order to answer them all. Although 30 seconds is the hard limit, set 25 seconds per question as your goal, so you reserve extra time to spend on harder questions. When you budget extra time for the harder questions, you no longer have any reason to stress when those questions take longer to answer.

Don't let this time expectation distract you from working through the test at a calm, steady pace, but keep it in mind so you don't spend too much time on any one question. Recognize that taking extra time on one question you don't understand may keep you from answering two that you do understand later in the test. If your time limit for a question is up and you're still not sure of the answer, mark it and move on, and come back to it later if the time and the test format allow. If the testing format doesn't allow you to return to earlier questions, just make an educated guess; then put it out of your mind and move on.

On the easier questions, be careful not to rush. It may seem wise to hurry through them so you have more time for the challenging ones, but it's not worth missing one if you know the concept and just didn't take the time to read the question fully. Work efficiently but make sure you understand the question and have looked at all of the answer choices, since more than one may seem right at first.

Even if you're paying attention to the time, you may find yourself a little behind at some point. You should speed up to get back on track, but do so wisely. Don't panic; just take a few seconds less on each question until you're caught up. Don't guess without thinking, but do look through the answer choices and eliminate any you know are wrong. If you can get down to two choices, it is often worthwhile to guess from those. Once you've chosen an answer, move on and don't dwell on any that you skipped or had to hurry through. If a question was taking too long, chances are it was one of the harder ones, so you weren't as likely to get it right anyway.

On the other hand, if you find yourself getting ahead of schedule, it may be beneficial to slow down a little. The more quickly you work, the more likely you are to make a careless mistake that will affect your score. You've budgeted time for each question, so don't be afraid to spend that time. Practice an efficient but careful pace to get the most out of the time you have.

6

Secret Key #5 – Have a Plan for Guessing

When you're taking the test, you may find yourself stuck on a question. Some of the answer choices seem better than others, but you don't see the one answer choice that is obviously correct. What do you do?

The scenario described above is very common, yet most test takers have not effectively prepared for it. Developing and practicing a plan for guessing may be one of the single most effective uses of your time as you get ready for the exam.

In developing your plan for guessing, there are three questions to address:

- When should you start the guessing process?
- How should you narrow down the choices?
- Which answer should you choose?

When to Start the Guessing Process

Unless your plan for guessing is to select C every time (which, despite its merits, is not what we recommend), you need to leave yourself enough time to apply your answer elimination strategies. Since you have a limited amount of time for each question, that means that if you're going to give yourself the best shot at guessing correctly, you have to decide quickly whether or not you will guess.

Of course, the best-case scenario is that you don't have to guess at all, so first, see if you can answer the question based on your knowledge of the subject and basic reasoning skills. Focus on the key words in the question and try to jog your memory of related topics. Give yourself a chance to bring the knowledge to mind, but once you realize that you don't have (or you can't access) the knowledge you need to answer the question, it's time to start the guessing process.

It's almost always better to start the guessing process too early than too late. It only takes a few seconds to remember something and answer the question from knowledge. Carefully eliminating wrong answer choices takes longer. Plus, going through the process of eliminating answer choices can actually help jog your memory.

Summary: Start the guessing process as soon as you decide that you can't answer the question based on your knowledge.

How to Narrow Down the Choices

The next chapter in this book (**Test-Taking Strategies**) includes a wide range of strategies for how to approach questions and how to look for answer choices to eliminate. You will definitely want to read those carefully, practice them, and figure out which ones work best for you. Here though, we're going to address a mindset rather than a particular strategy.

Your chances of guessing an answer correctly depend on how many options you are choosing from.

How many choices you have	How likely you are to guess correctly
5	20%
4	25%
3	33%
2	50%
1	100%

You can see from this chart just how valuable it is to be able to eliminate incorrect answers and make an educated guess, but there are two things that many test takers do that cause them to miss out on the benefits of guessing:

- Accidentally eliminating the correct answer
- Selecting an answer based on an impression

We'll look at the first one here, and the second one in the next section.

To avoid accidentally eliminating the correct answer, we recommend a thought exercise called **the $5 challenge**. In this challenge, you only eliminate an answer choice from contention if you are willing to bet $5 on it being wrong. Why $5? Five dollars is a small but not insignificant amount of money. It's an amount you could afford to lose but wouldn't want to throw away. And while losing $5 once might not hurt too much, doing it twenty times will set you back $100. In the same way, each small decision you make—eliminating a choice here, guessing on a question there—won't by itself impact your score very much, but when you put them all together, they can make a big difference. By holding each answer choice elimination decision to a higher standard, you can reduce the risk of accidentally eliminating the correct answer.

The $5 challenge can also be applied in a positive sense: If you are willing to bet $5 that an answer choice *is* correct, go ahead and mark it as correct.

Summary: Only eliminate an answer choice if you are willing to bet $5 that it is wrong.

Which Answer to Choose

You're taking the test. You've run into a hard question and decided you'll have to guess. You've eliminated all the answer choices you're willing to bet $5 on. Now you have to pick an answer. Why do we even need to talk about this? Why can't you just pick whichever one you feel like when the time comes?

The answer to these questions is that if you don't come into the test with a plan, you'll rely on your impression to select an answer choice, and if you do that, you risk falling into a trap. The test writers know that everyone who takes their test will be guessing on some of the questions, so they intentionally write wrong answer choices to seem plausible. You still have to pick an answer though, and if the wrong answer choices are designed to look right, how can you ever be sure that you're not falling for their trap? The best solution we've found to this dilemma is to take the decision out of your hands entirely. Here is the process we recommend:

Once you've eliminated any choices that you are confident (willing to bet $5) are wrong, select the first remaining choice as your answer.

Whether you choose to select the first remaining choice, the second, or the last, the important thing is that you use some preselected standard. Using this approach guarantees that you will not be enticed into selecting an answer choice that looks right, because you are not basing your decision on how the answer choices look.

This is not meant to make you question your knowledge. Instead, it is to help you recognize the difference between your knowledge and your impressions. There's a huge difference between thinking an answer is right because of what you know, and thinking an answer is right because it looks or sounds like it should be right.

Summary: To ensure that your selection is appropriately random, make a predetermined selection from among all answer choices you have not eliminated.

9

Test-Taking Strategies

This section contains a list of test-taking strategies that you may find helpful as you work through the test. By taking what you know and applying logical thought, you can maximize your chances of answering any question correctly!

It is very important to realize that every question is different and every person is different: no single strategy will work on every question, and no single strategy will work for every person. That's why we've included all of them here, so you can try them out and determine which ones work best for different types of questions and which ones work best for you.

Question Strategies

READ CAREFULLY

Read the question and answer choices carefully. Don't miss the question because you misread the terms. You have plenty of time to read each question thoroughly and make sure you understand what is being asked. Yet a happy medium must be attained, so don't waste too much time. You must read carefully, but efficiently.

CONTEXTUAL CLUES

Look for contextual clues. If the question includes a word you are not familiar with, look at the immediate context for some indication of what the word might mean. Contextual clues can often give you all the information you need to decipher the meaning of an unfamiliar word. Even if you can't determine the meaning, you may be able to narrow down the possibilities enough to make a solid guess at the answer to the question.

PREFIXES

If you're having trouble with a word in the question or answer choices, try dissecting it. Take advantage of every clue that the word might include. Prefixes and suffixes can be a huge help. Usually they allow you to determine a basic meaning. Pre- means before, post- means after, pro - is positive, de- is negative. From prefixes and suffixes, you can get an idea of the general meaning of the word and try to put it into context.

HEDGE WORDS

Watch out for critical hedge words, such as *likely, may, can, sometimes, often, almost, mostly, usually, generally, rarely,* and *sometimes*. Question writers insert these hedge phrases to cover every possibility. Often an answer choice will be wrong simply because it leaves no room for exception. Be on guard for answer choices that have definitive words such as *exactly* and *always*.

SWITCHBACK WORDS

Stay alert for *switchbacks*. These are the words and phrases frequently used to alert you to shifts in thought. The most common switchback words are *but, although,* and *however*. Others include *nevertheless, on the other hand, even though, while, in spite of, despite, regardless of.* Switchback words are important to catch because they can change the direction of the question or an answer choice.

FACE VALUE

When in doubt, use common sense. Accept the situation in the problem at face value. Don't read too much into it. These problems will not require you to make wild assumptions. If you have to go beyond creativity and warp time or space in order to have an answer choice fit the question, then you should move on and consider the other answer choices. These are normal problems rooted in reality. The applicable relationship or explanation may not be readily apparent, but it is there for you to figure out. Use your common sense to interpret anything that isn't clear.

Answer Choice Strategies

ANSWER SELECTION

The most thorough way to pick an answer choice is to identify and eliminate wrong answers until only one is left, then confirm it is the correct answer. Sometimes an answer choice may immediately seem right, but be careful. The test writers will usually put more than one reasonable answer choice on each question, so take a second to read all of them and make sure that the other choices are not equally obvious. As long as you have time left, it is better to read every answer choice than to pick the first one that looks right without checking the others.

ANSWER CHOICE FAMILIES

An answer choice family consists of two (in rare cases, three) answer choices that are very similar in construction and cannot all be true at the same time. If you see two answer choices that are direct opposites or parallels, one of them is usually the correct answer. For instance, if one answer choice says that quantity x increases and another either says that quantity x decreases (opposite) or says that quantity y increases (parallel), then those answer choices would fall into the same family. An answer choice that doesn't match the construction of the answer choice family is more likely to be incorrect. Most questions will not have answer choice families, but when they do appear, you should be prepared to recognize them.

ELIMINATE ANSWERS

Eliminate answer choices as soon as you realize they are wrong, but make sure you consider all possibilities. If you are eliminating answer choices and realize that the last one you are left with is also wrong, don't panic. Start over and consider each choice again. There may be something you missed the first time that you will realize on the second pass.

AVOID FACT TRAPS

Don't be distracted by an answer choice that is factually true but doesn't answer the question. You are looking for the choice that answers the question. Stay focused on what the question is asking for so you don't accidentally pick an answer that is true but incorrect. Always go back to the question and make sure the answer choice you've selected actually answers the question and is not merely a true statement.

EXTREME STATEMENTS

In general, you should avoid answers that put forth extreme actions as standard practice or proclaim controversial ideas as established fact. An answer choice that states the "process should be used in certain situations, if..." is much more likely to be correct than one that states the "process should be discontinued completely." The first is a calm rational statement and doesn't even make a definitive, uncompromising stance, using a hedge word *if* to provide wiggle room, whereas the second choice is a radical idea and far more extreme.

BENCHMARK

As you read through the answer choices and you come across one that seems to answer the question well, mentally select that answer choice. This is not your final answer, but it's the one that will help you evaluate the other answer choices. The one that you selected is your benchmark or standard for judging each of the other answer choices. Every other answer choice must be compared to your benchmark. That choice is correct until proven otherwise by another answer choice beating it. If you find a better answer, then that one becomes your new benchmark. Once you've decided that no other choice answers the question as well as your benchmark, you have your final answer.

PREDICT THE ANSWER

Before you even start looking at the answer choices, it is often best to try to predict the answer. When you come up with the answer on your own, it is easier to avoid distractions and traps because you will know exactly what to look for. The right answer choice is unlikely to be word-for-word what you came up with, but it should be a close match. Even if you are confident that you have the right answer, you should still take the time to read each option before moving on.

General Strategies

TOUGH QUESTIONS

If you are stumped on a problem or it appears too hard or too difficult, don't waste time. Move on! Remember though, if you can quickly check for obviously incorrect answer choices, your chances of guessing correctly are greatly improved. Before you completely give up, at least try to knock out a couple of possible answers. Eliminate what you can and then guess at the remaining answer choices before moving on.

CHECK YOUR WORK

Since you will probably not know every term listed and the answer to every question, it is important that you get credit for the ones that you do know. Don't miss any questions through careless mistakes. If at all possible, try to take a second to look back over your answer selection and make sure you've selected the correct answer choice and haven't made a costly careless mistake (such as marking an answer choice that you didn't mean to mark). This quick double check should more than pay for itself in caught mistakes for the time it costs.

PACE YOURSELF

It's easy to be overwhelmed when you're looking at a page full of questions; your mind is confused and full of random thoughts, and the clock is ticking down faster than you would like. Calm down and maintain the pace that you have set for yourself. Especially as you get down to the last few minutes of the test, don't let the small numbers on the clock make you panic. As long as you are on track by monitoring your pace, you are guaranteed to have time for each question.

DON'T RUSH

It is very easy to make errors when you are in a hurry. Maintaining a fast pace in answering questions is pointless if it makes you miss questions that you would have gotten right otherwise. Test writers like to include distracting information and wrong answers that seem right. Taking a little extra time to avoid careless mistakes can make all the difference in your test score. Find a pace that allows you to be confident in the answers that you select.

KEEP MOVING

Panicking will not help you pass the test, so do your best to stay calm and keep moving. Taking deep breaths and going through the answer elimination steps you practiced can help to break through a stress barrier and keep your pace.

Final Notes

The combination of a solid foundation of content knowledge and the confidence that comes from practicing your plan for applying that knowledge is the key to maximizing your performance on test day. As your foundation of content knowledge is built up and strengthened, you'll find that the strategies included in this chapter become more and more effective in helping you quickly sift through the distractions and traps of the test to isolate the correct answer.

Now it's time to move on to the test content chapters of this book, but be sure to keep your goal in mind. As you read, think about how you will be able to apply this information on the test. If you've already seen sample questions for the test and you have an idea of the question format and style, try to come up with questions of your own that you can answer based on what you're reading. This will give you valuable practice applying your knowledge in the same ways you can expect to on test day.

Good luck and good studying!

Student Development, Learning, and Diversity

Student Development

SIGMUND FREUD'S DEVELOPMENTAL THEORY RELATIVE TO THE ADOLESCENT YEARS

After a latency period wherein school-age children suppress sexual id impulses to focus on developing social relationships and learning academic content, Freud termed his fifth and final stage of psychosexual development the genital stage, which begins with puberty and continues throughout life. Freud considered this stage as a kind of reprise of the phallic stage in early childhood, when children first discovered their genitals. Both stages are periods involving *exploration*. A physician by training and background, Freud accorded primary importance to the physical areas and processes of the body. Each of his stages is organized around an erogenous zone: oral in infancy, around nursing; anal in toddlerhood, around toilet-training; phallic and genital in preschool and teen years respectively, around sexual drives, with a calm latency period in between when such urges are buried in favor of the outward focus on friendships and school. The powerful physical changes and events of *puberty* are Freud's focus for the genital stage. Unlike his follower Erikson, Freud felt the personality was basically formed by adolescence and did not essentially change much thereafter; so this was his final stage, which he believed applied to adults as well.

ERIK ERIKSON'S THEORY OF HUMAN DEVELOPMENT
EARLY CHILDHOOD YEARS

Erikson took major influences from Freud's theory in also viewing major life events, e.g., nursing during infancy; toilet-training during toddlerhood; exploration during preschool years; and school during school years as central to each developmental stage. But his orientation was psychosocial, not psychosexual: rather than Freud's focus on physical erogenous zones and parent-child relationships, Erikson focused on personal self-images and social interactions. In each of Erikson's stages, a nuclear conflict must be resolved. Toddlers (c. two to three years) confronting toilet-training experience autonomy vs. shame and doubt. In learning physical control, successful children develop independence; failing children develop self-doubt and shame. According to Erikson, preschoolers (c. three to five years) encounter the nuclear conflict of initiative vs. guilt. At these ages, they are exploring their environments and need to experiment with exercising personal control over their surroundings. Children who succeed in interacting with and manipulating their environments develop a sense of purpose. Children who fail in this endeavor by exerting excessive power, and/or by receiving disapproval from their parents for their efforts, develop guilt feelings. School-age (c. 6-11 years) children face industry vs. inferiority. Successful coping with new social and academic requirements develops feelings of competence; failure develops feelings of inadequacy.

ADOLESCENCE AND EARLY ADULTHOOD

Unlike his predecessor and strong influence, Sigmund Freud, Erikson believed people continue to develop throughout life. Hence he proposed stages for each life period until death. He identified the nuclear conflict characteristic of every stage as being identity vs. role confusion in adolescence (c. 12-18 years). Teenagers begin developing their individual personal identities. *Social relationships* are the focus of this stage. Teens that are successful in defining their personal roles and identities develop feelings of being *true to themselves*. Teens who fail in this endeavor develop *confusion*

15

about their roles in life and *weak and/or poorly defined self-images*. Young adults (c. 19-40 years) are included in teenage years because Erikson's theory associates the final teen year as part of young adulthood. This is Erikson's stage of intimacy vs. isolation. Once adolescents have defined their personal identities, they progress forming intimate, loving relationships with other young adults. *Relationships* are the focus of this stage. Successful individuals develop *strong relationships*; those failing develop *isolation and loneliness*.

ALBERT BANDURA'S CONTRIBUTIONS TO EDUCATION

Albert Bandura's social learning theory emphasized the importance of social interaction in learning. Bandura accepted principles of behaviorist learning theories like antecedent stimuli, behaviors, and consequent stimuli that punished or rewarded (reinforced) behaviors. However, internal cognitive processes, and social contexts of learning, became more central in Bandura's theory. Also, he believes learning does not necessarily change behavior. Bandura discovered children learned indirectly by watching others—i.e., vicarious or observational learning: seeing others receiving rewards for certain behaviors, they imitated those actions to obtain similar rewards. This discovery contradicted the empiricist claim that learning requires direct experience. Bandura also discovered children witnessing violent actions by living persons (cf. his Bobo doll experiments) or by people they saw in video recordings would then display more aggressive behaviors imitating what they observed. This influenced education and parenting: adults, realizing children's behavior was influenced not just directly by experiencing violence, but also indirectly by observing it, became more concerned about controlling what children observed. Bandura identified attention, retention, reproduction, and motivation as conditions necessary to modeling and observational learning. Bandura's concept of reciprocal determinism states individuals and environments mutually influence each other. His concept of self-efficacy identifies belief in one's individual competence to perform specific tasks and skills.

JEROME BRUNER'S CONTRIBUTIONS TO EDUCATION

Bruner, like Piaget and many others, embraces constructivist philosopher, i.e., by interacting with their environments, children actively construct their learning, knowledge, and realities. His emphasis on discovery learning is based on constructivism. He defined learning as not only remembering existing, culturally imparted or acquired ideas and actions, but moreover inventing or creating these on one's own. Bruner feels "culturally invented technologies" amplify human abilities, rather than providing all knowledge. He influenced education by advising that its goal should be producing autonomous learners. Bruner posited three modes of representation in child cognitive development. 1) Enactive representation: action-based information based on motor responses, retained in muscle memory, emerging in infancy. 2) Iconic representation: visual image-based information, emerging around 1-6 years of age. 3) Symbolic representation: coded or symbolic storage of information, emerging c. 7 years and older. For example, the category "dogs" symbolically represents all dog breeds, types, and individuals. We remember information symbolically in words, numbers, etc. Bruner's concept of the spiral curriculum enabled teaching complex ideas to all ages by initially structuring them simply and increasing difficulty gradually. Bruner (with Wood and Ross) originated the concept *scaffolding*—temporary, gradually withdrawn support matching student needs.

JOHN DEWEY'S CONTRIBUTIONS TO EDUCATION

Psychologist, philosopher, educator, and social activist John Dewey was a prominent member of the Progressive social reform movement, a president of the American Psychological Association, a functional psychology pioneer, a Pragmatist and Instrumentalist philosopher, and the foremost theorist in modern American education. Like Rousseau and Froebel, he believed in experiential "learning by doing." He shifted schools from authoritarian and teacher-centered, rote-learning methods to democratic classrooms, relevant curricula, and participatory activities. He emphasized the social, interactive nature of the learning and educational processes. Dewey believed education not only conferred knowledge, but moreover taught children how to live. His humanist psychology and instrumental philosophy informed his opinions that education should enable children to realize their full potential, and to apply those abilities toward the greater good. He also viewed education as an important force for social reform and change. He believed education should not concentrate exclusively on being either child-centered or curriculum content-centered, but balance the two. Like Bruner, he believed education should prepare autonomous learners—who were also ethical and reflective. He also professionalized the role of teachers as social service providers producing higher character and community intelligence standards, not merely vocational trainers preparing students for work with limited job skills and information.

JEAN PIAGET'S THEORY OF COGNITIVE DEVELOPMENT

Piaget, like Bruner and others, believed in constructivism, i.e., children were not passive learners but actively constructed their own learning, knowledge, and worlds through interacting with their environments. He observed children as being "little scientists" from birth who experimented with and acted upon the environment to learn about it. Piaget formulated four stages of cognitive development. 1) Sensorimotor: infants respond to sensory input with motor responses. 2) Preoperational: wherein young children are *egocentric*, unable to see others' physical or mental perspectives. They think *intuitively*, not logically, unable to focus on more than one physical attribute of an object at a time (*centration*), categorize and classify, or follow structures and sequences of reasoning. They see things *animistically*, by attributing human qualities and behaviors to inanimate objects; and *magically*, by attributing events and others' actions to their own thoughts or words. 3) Concrete operations: school-age children can classify, perform other logical mental operations, and reverse them as long as they have concrete objects or events for reference. 4) Formal operations: preadolescents and adolescents develop the ability to perform abstract mental operations without concrete support, understanding and manipulating abstract concepts in math, philosophy, law, politics, etc. Piaget's theory influenced education, guiding educators not to present content to children who are not cognitively ready or able to understand; and introducing concepts and material appropriately to cognitive levels.

LEV VYGOTSKY'S CONTRIBUTIONS ON TEACHING PRACTICES TODAY

Like theorists after him, e.g., Erikson, Bruner, Bandura, and others, Vygotsky, who lived during the Russian Revolution, stressed the importance of social interaction to learning. He differed from his contemporary Piaget's belief in invariant stages of cognitive development, believing instead that it varied among societies because culture heavily influenced it. Two of the most influential concepts in Vygotsky's theories were the more knowledgeable other (MKO), i.e., a person (or a computer, software program, etc. can be included) with a higher level of skill or understanding—whether peer, older child, or adult—than a given student; and the zone of proximal development (ZPD), which interact with one another. The ZPD is the distance between two levels of cognitive development: (1) the level of actual development, where a student can accomplish something independently; and (2) the level of potential development, where a student can accomplish something with guidance or assistance from an MKO. Vygotsky emphasized ability and potential above knowledge: what one could learn was more important than what one already knew. He also was first to prove that self-talk or inner speech (whose existence others agreed to, but not its cognitive value) was important to activity self-regulation, social competence, and learning.

LAWRENCE KOHLBERG'S THEORY OF MORAL DEVELOPMENT

Kohlberg based his theory on Piaget's two stages of moral development, heteronomous (other-directed) morality and autonomous (self-directed) morality; but Kohlberg extended these to three distinct levels and six stages, with each level encompassing two stages. Similarly to Erikson's belief regarding psychosocial development, Kohlberg believed moral development continued throughout life. Kohlberg's level one is preconventional morality. In stage one, obedience and punishment, young children (and some adults) view rules as absolute and fixed; obedience averts punishment. In stage two, individualism and exchange, children judge actions by whether they meet one's own interests or needs. They can understand and appreciate *reciprocity,* but only if it also is in one's best interests. At level two, conventional morality, stage three involves interpersonal relationships, nicknamed *"good boy-good girl."* Conforming to meet social roles and expectations, concern for how choices affect relationships, and being "nice" predominate. Stage four, maintaining social order, focuses on respecting authority, doing one's duty, following rules, maintaining law and order, and considering overall society. Level three is postconventional morality. In stage five, social contract and individual rights, people still find laws and rules important, but only with individual members' agreement. By stage six, universal ethical principles, individuals apply internalized justice principles, regardless whether they conflict with rules and laws.

Bloom's Taxonomy

Bloom organized learning into a hierarchy of six cognitive levels, from simplest to most challenging. Remembering involves retaining, recalling, retrieving, recognizing, reproducing, or repeating names, facts, lists, and other pieces of information. Understanding requires also being able to find, identify, select, describe, explain, discuss, review, restate, and/or translate information, rather than only remembering it. Applying requires learners to interpret information they understand; to use it appropriately, e.g., for solving problems; to illustrate, demonstrate, or dramatize it; write about it, etc. Analyzing means that learners must be able not only to remember, understand, and apply information, but moreover to break it down into component parts; assign information to different categories; make comparisons and contrasts between and among pieces or sets of information; use information to make calculations; differentiate and discriminate among different information; examine information; question its truth, accuracy, or credibility; experiment with it; test its veracity; and criticize information. Evaluating demands the learner assess and appraise information, make estimates and/or predictions based on it, rate it, judge it, and defend it. Creating, the highest level, involves proposing, developing, planning, designing, formulating, preparing, collecting, composing, organizing, and managing information, including both original ideas and/or original uses of existing information.

Physical and Cognitive Characteristics of Typically Developing Children
Early Childhood

Physically, children gain c. 2.5 inches and 5-7 pounds, decreasing yearly. Preschoolers become taller and slimmer, losing baby fat. Preschooler heads are less oversized for bodies than top-heavier toddlers', but still somewhat large. *Cognitively*, continuing brain maturation plus wider life experiences enable significant progress in attention, planning, and language. Reasoning develops from 4-7 years, but is not logical. By 5 years, gross motor skills gain automaticity, and fine motor skills improve significantly.

Middle and Late Childhood

Physically, growth is slow and consistent—2-3 inches and 5-7 pounds annually. Heads and waists become smaller proportionately to height. Bones and muscle tissue strengthen. Motor skills gain coordination and smoothness. By 10-12 years, fine motor coordination and manipulative skills approximate adults'. *Cognitively*, brain circuitry continues developing, especially in the prefrontal cortex, improving cognitive control, attention, and reasoning. In Piaget's concrete operations stage, children can reason logically and reverse mental operations, but need physical objects, events, or examples for reference.

ADOLESCENCE

Physically, uberty combines physical and sexual maturation with hormonal changes. *Cognitively*, structural changes improve information-processing, reasoning, decision-making, and self-control. However, though the emotion-related amygdala matures earlier, the prefrontal cortex controlling emotions only matures by 18-25 years. Adolescents reach Piaget's formal operations, understanding abstract concepts and performing and manipulating entirely mental operations.

LINGUISTIC, AFFECTIVE, AND MORAL CHARACTERISTICS OF CHILDREN WITH TYPICAL DEVELOPMENT

EARLY CHILDHOOD

linguistic : greater sensitivity to spoken phonological features; linguistic rule systems understanding; learning and applying syntactic rules to speech; dramatic vocabulary development; changing speech "registers" and styles based on situation, improving conversational skills.

Affective: by 4-5 years, self-awareness; self-conscious emotions like guilt and pride; understanding of and ability to discuss both personal and others' emotions, causes and results, increase.

Moral: most are at Kohlberg's level one of preconventional reasoning with external punishments and rewards until c. 9 years.

MIDDLE AND LATE CHILDHOOD

Linguistic: understanding the alphabetic principle; categorizing; whereas younger children respond sentence-sequentially, e.g., prompted "dog" and saying "barks"; or "eat" and "lunch"; older children respond with like parts of speech, saying "cat" or "horse" to "dog," and "drink" to "eat." From age 6-11, vocabulary grows from c. 14,000-40,000 words. Complex grammar comprehension develops, and metalinguistic awareness, knowing, and thinking about language.

Affective: more varied coping strategies. Self-regulation and self-efficacy influence achievement.

Moral: many are at Kohlberg's level two conventional reasoning, stage 3, "good boy-good girl", adopting parental morality.

ADOLESCENCE

Linguistic: skills advance, including complex spoken and written sentences; writing stories following story grammar rules; consistently accurate inferences from text; understanding figurative language, idioms, and metaphors.

Moral: Kohlberg's postconventional reasoning is possible—recognizing alternatives, social contracts, and developing universal moral standards transcending laws.

DEVELOPMENTAL MILESTONES FOR ADOLESCENTS

Physically, most adolescents will have completed puberty by the time they are around 15-17 years old. While girls are more likely to be mature physically by these ages, boys may still be in the process of physical maturation: girls are typically about two years ahead of boys in physical growth spurts and sexual maturity. It is common for adolescents to be concerned about their bodies, e.g., their weight, size, or shape. Adults need to be vigilant for eating disorders during later adolescence, particularly in girls. Cognitively, older teenagers may begin to learn more clearly defined work habits, especially if they begin to work after or before school, on weekends, and/or during the summers. They typically become more concerned about their future plans for attending post-secondary school, getting jobs, and what kinds of work they will want to do. They develop the ability to provide reasons for the choices they make more competently, including being able to explain their moral decisions regarding what is right and wrong. Adults should encourage adolescents' adequate sleep, exercising, and nutritious diets; and be available to provide support and advice while creating opportunities for and encouraging teens to use their judgment, problem-solving, and conflict resolution skills.

Emotionally and socially, teenagers around 15-17 experience decreased conflict with parents, and display more independence from them. Socially, they spend more time with friends, less with parents. They demonstrate more interest in dating and relationships, developing emotional capacities for sharing and caring more deeply and more intimacy. While it should not be ignored, it is also typical for teenagers to feel considerable depression or sadness. These emotions can contribute to reduced school performance, unprotected sex, and substance use or abuse. Morally, older teens can think abstractly according to Piaget and hence are capable of the highest moral development levels according to Kohlberg, understanding the concept of the social contract and even developing universal moral principles of human rights beyond legalities. Adults can show affection; spend time in mutually enjoyed activities with teenagers; encourage teen volunteerism and extracurricular interests and pursuits; ask about their feelings, including suicidal ideations; observe any behavior changes; respect teen opinions; show interest in teen activities; compliment and celebrate efforts and achievements; encourage responsible decisions, including regarding Internet and social media use; help teens plan ahead for difficult situations, e.g., involving peer pressure and/or others' risk behaviors; discuss responsibilities, expectations, and respectful behavior in workplaces and public; and respect teen privacy needs.

WAYS IN WHICH DIFFERENT TYPES OF STUDENT DEVELOPMENT CAN RESPECTIVELY INTERACT

When a student's cognitive development is ahead of his/her physical development, the child is likely to become frustrated when s/he can conceive of many things mentally, but cannot execute them physically. This is especially of younger children still having more physical development to achieve. Conversely, when a student's physical development is ahead of his/her cognitive development, young children are apt inadvertently to damage property and/or harm peers, younger children, or pets. Linguistic development affects social development in that more advanced language levels often facilitate social communication—but not always: some children show advanced language skills development, yet lack commensurate social skills. In another way, some less linguistically advanced students are skilled at using nonverbal communication skills to support social interactions. Some young students also have superior emotional intelligence (EQ) without necessarily having equally high academic or linguistic skills. More advanced affective development in elementary-age children can influence their moral development: the more children are able to share, take others' perspectives, empathize, and engage in prosocial behaviors, the more able they are to understand and internalize less rigid, more mutual, and socially-oriented morality.

Linguistic development interacts with cognitive development: psychologists find very high positive correlations between vocabulary and intelligence test scores. Teachers can enhance adolescent linguistic mediation skills with exercises regarding literal vs. metaphorical word meanings, and enhance pragmatics (using language to meet needs) through question-asking skills instruction. Teens whose cognitive development precedes their physical development excel academically but not athletically may be stereotyped by peers as "nerds," and those with superior physical skills but lacking equal academic success as "jocks." Teens whose physical development far precedes their cognitive development may inadvertently harm others, particularly when rapidly gaining adult strength. Similarly, adolescent affective development influences cognitive development because the amygdala matures sooner, generating intense teen emotions; yet the prefrontal cortex, which will eventually control those emotions, does not mature until young adulthood. Affective maturity influences moral levels in that the more emotionally mature the student, the more able s/he is to relate to others' needs, use prosocial behaviors, and understand universal human rights. Teen social interactions are increasingly influenced by emotional intelligence (EQ) development. Both affective and social developments interact with moral development when teens must make difficult ethical decisions involving others in social contexts.

TEACHER CONSIDERATIONS FOR STUDENTS IN EARLY AND LATER ADOLESCENCE

Middle school teachers who find some 6th-graders acting out in class or not completing work may attribute these instances to behavior problems, but experienced teachers with developmental perspectives point out that they may actually be adjustment problems: transitions between schools can be difficult for students; teachers may not realize the extent of variation among schools. Distinguishing adjustment or developmental difficulties from more severe problems is easier for teachers who have worked with students of every age. Whereas elementary-age students have concrete operations, including reversibility, adolescents have formal operations, including application of abstract concepts to specific phenomena. For example, an 8-year-old understood objects that looked smaller underwater did not shrink because, with reversibility, s/he could see they were the same size when removed; but did not understand why they looked smaller underwater. By the student's teens, s/he understands water is denser than air, light waves travel at differing speeds through media of different density, and applies this to understand why objects look smaller underwater. Teachers can use deductive reasoning with teens that younger students could not follow. Hypothetico-deductive reasoning or "if-then" propositions enable adolescents to speculate about possibilities, e.g., going to college, moral dilemmas about justifying killing, etc.

IMPACTS OF COMMUNITY, RACIAL, AND CULTURAL DIFFERENCES

With American demographics rapidly changing, schools reflect societal racism. Racial and cultural differences cannot be overlooked anymore. It is not only necessary, but moreover healthy for minorities to express their racial and cultural identities. Teachers, administrators, school staff, parents—all school community members—must be involved in designing learning experiences founded on understanding and respect for racial and cultural diversity. While educational experts believe this requires the whole society to unite for success, they concede that as this has not occurred, the educational system must still strive for resolution of racial and cultural conflicts through collective efforts. While schools are desegregated, surrounding cities and suburbs are not. Neighborhoods, the foundations of American society, are subject to racial and economic limitations. Because children learn from each other, their education is strongly affected by community factors of housing costs, incomes, lending policies, and racial and institutional discrimination. While some Latino parents believe bilingual education can overcome discrimination and black parents believe desegregation promotes equality, some Latino parents see desegregation as impeding their objectives by dissipating Latin influence and destroying bilingual programs. Experts call for compromise, noting that both must coexist by law.

STAGES IN ADOLESCENT DEVELOPMENT FROM THE PERSPECTIVE OF DEVELOPMENTAL PSYCHOLOGY

Despite age variances and overlaps, early adolescents develop new self-images based on physiological changes and apply emergent logical cognitive and rational judgment skills. Mid-adolescents endeavor to separate from parents; their cognitive and emotional abilities expand. They become adventurous, experimenting with various ideas while exploring their relationships to self, the opposite sex, and groups; and struggling to differentiate or reconcile their own values vs. those of parents and authority figures. They develop responsibility and self-reliance, assume greater control of educational and vocational opportunities and activities, and seek to establish their place in and contribute to society. Late adolescent identity and social role stabilizes; they gain integration and consistency in psychology and worldview. Balance among fantasy, reality, and aspirations; shifts from immature self-interest toward caring for and giving to others; and establishment and pursuit of realistic life goals are characteristics. Teachers must determine overall class functioning levels for planning lessons. For instance, lessons should help adolescents advance cognitively from Piaget's concrete operations to formal operations stage. To resolve Erikson's conflict of industry vs. inferiority, younger adolescents must experience school success; to resolve identity vs. role confusion, older adolescents must form satisfying future action plans. Hands-on activities like those Piaget offered can further these goals.

ASSIGNMENTS FOR DEVELOPING GOAL-SETTING, PEER INTERACTION, AND DECISION-MAKING SKILLS

GRADES 6-8

Identify resources (e.g., research sources) furthering goal progress. Analyze influences of supports and obstacles in completing goal action steps, and better ways of overcoming barriers and using supports. Differentiate long- and short-term goals. Apply goal-setting skills to academic success development. Set a positive social interaction goal. Teachers: use interest or incentive inventories, planning sheets, discuss goal-setting steps, and lead self-regulation and self-monitoring games.

GRADES 8-10

Set a goal in a sport, hobby, musical instrument, or interest to accomplish in a month or two. Plan goal timeframes and action steps. Monitor progress and adjust plans as necessary. Evaluate goal achievement levels, and identify contributing or detracting factors. Analyze what you learned and would do differently.

GRADES 9-11

Identify who helped you achieve a goal and how. Analyze why you could or could not overcome goal obstacles, an unexpected opportunity's goal achievement impact, why schedule conflicts could require changing goal timeframes, how substance use could impede and academic achievement contribute to long-term goal achievement.

GRADES 10-12

Set long-term academic or career goals with action steps and completion dates. Anticipate obstacles and make contingency plans. Analyze how current health behavior decisions might affect long-term educational or career goals. Evaluate summer job goal feasibility based on your ability to execute action steps timely. Self-evaluate goal achievement. Create a behavioral contract to enhance a coping strategy and document progress in a journal.

EARLY ADOLESCENT COGNITIVE DEVELOPMENT

Individual differences in early adolescent cognitive development vary widely. Young teens develop metacognition, independent thought, high curiosity, and broad interests, though they typically do not maintain most. They prefer learning peer interactions, active experiences over passive ones, and learning about subjects useful and interesting to them. These teens develop abstract thought, analyze and synthesize information, formulate and test hypotheses, think reflectively, tackle complex ideas, understand metaphorical nuances and traditional wisdom's meanings, consider ideological issues, argue positions, question authority, and appreciate sophisticated humor. As Piaget stated, they make sense of the world building on their background knowledge and individual experiences. Young adolescents are more interested in authentic and real-life learning than traditional academic content. They frequently observe adult behavior keenly and are inquisitive about adults. Their abilities to anticipate needs, develop personal goals, and consider the future improve. Teachers must offer widely varied educational materials and approaches, from structured to challenging for concrete to abstract learners; plan curriculum around real-life concepts; provide experimentation and other authentic activities; enable peer and adult discourse; hands-on experience and direct environmental interaction; acknowledge changing interests by ensuring exploration opportunities; supplying forums for exploring reasons for home, school, and societal rules; and teach by example as role models.

ADOLESCENT MORAL DEVELOPMENT

The ability to make principled choices increases with moral development. Young adolescents, developing abstract thinking, typically become idealistic, highly valuing fairness in human interaction. They start reconciling their understanding of others caring about them with their own adolescent egocentrism as they advance into Kohlberg's moral development stage of interpersonal conformity. They graduate from self-centeredness to more consideration for others' feelings and rights. They ask impossible, sweeping questions, and do not tolerate trivial adult answers. They typically embrace parental values while developing personal values. They cease seeing complex ethical or moral issues in black-and-white, realizing shades of gray but unready to address these—putting them at risk for unsound ethical or moral decisions. Teachers must acknowledge and utilize the connection between teen cognitive and moral development by planning lessons cultivating critical thought, higher-order thinking skills, and higher moral reasoning levels. For example, writing assignments articulating their feelings and thoughts; opportunities for examining behavior options and consequences; experiences requiring contemplating ethical or moral dilemmas and potential responses—helping students solve problems, develop values, and set their own behavioral standards. Teachers can provide scenarios whereby students explore concepts of justice, equity, and fairness. Schools should also offer curricula and programs addressing racism, sexism, discrimination, and similar social issues.

ADOLESCENT EMOTIONAL AND PSYCHOLOGICAL DEVELOPMENT

Seeking unique personal identities and independence characterize adolescent emotional and psychological development. While searching for adult identities, teens try to balance peer approval with adult acceptance, experiencing conflict from competing family and peer allegiances. Self-discovery and identity quests can increase vulnerable feelings as sensitivity to self-other differences grows. Young adolescence is typified by unpredictability and intensity. Teens tend to display restless, moody, inconsistent, or erratic behavior, including alternating inferiority and superiority and swings between anxiety and bravado. Self-esteem is fragile or low at these ages. Teens are notoriously self-conscious, and hypersensitive to criticism of their exaggerated perceived flaws. Emotional situations can provoke childish behaviors, unilateral arguments, and naïve opinions. Emotional volatility places teens at risk for poor decisions. As David Elkind noted, adolescents think their experiences are unique in the "personal fable." Teachers and schools can support identity formation with curricular and instructional exploration opportunities, organizational structures, advisory programs, and educational practices supporting positive adult and peer relationships, group cohesion, and caring atmospheres. Other positive outcomes include building student self-esteem, explaining its importance to development; explaining friendship's importance and the normalcy of changing allegiances; avoiding sarcasm, humiliation, or harsh criticism; providing self-expression and self-assessment opportunities, including reading, role-play, and drama; and helping teens realize their problems are not unique.

CLASSROOM INSTRUCTION THAT TEACHERS CAN DIFFERENTIATE AMONG STUDENTS

Based on each student's learning profile, interests, readiness, and learning levels, teachers can differentiate classroom instruction. Four elements for differentiating instruction are: (1) content to learn; (2) the process students use to master content; (3) products students will produce, requiring practice, application, and extension and elaboration of what they learn in a unit; and (4) learning environment, i.e., how the classroom functions and how students experience it. Some examples of differentiating processes include: (1) set up interest centers where students can explore subcategories of class subjects they find most interesting. (2) Assign tiered activities with different levels of complexity, challenge, or support for acquiring the same skills and understanding. (3) Provide hands-on supports, like manipulatives, for students needing these. (4) Combine work commonly assigned to the entire class with individualized work for specific students into lists of tasks, making personal agendas to complete during designated and/or spare time. (5) Differentiate durations students take to finish tasks, allowing advanced students to examine topics in-depth and enable added support for struggling students.

ELEMENTS OF CLASSROOM INSTRUCTION THAT TEACHERS CAN DIFFERENTIATE AMONG STUDENTS

To address the needs of individual students in a class, teachers can differentiate things like (1) content; (2) processes and activities whereby students learn content; (3) products students create by applying and demonstrating what they learned; and (4) learning environment, i.e., how students perceive the classroom and how it functions. Some examples of differentiating products for elementary school students include: (1) design rubrics matching and extending various student skill levels. (2) Offer choices to students in how to demonstrate learning, like between writing a letter, creating a labeled art mural, or producing a puppet show. (3) Invite students to design their own product assignments, providing they include necessary components. (4) Give students options to work on projects in small groups or individually. Some examples of differentiating an elementary school learning environment include: (1) furnish materials reflecting diverse home and cultural backgrounds. (2) Establish clear guidelines matching individual student needs for independent work. (3) Ensure the classroom contains both areas for collaboration and areas for undistracted quiet work. (4) Help students realize some classmates need to sit quietly, while others must move about. (5) Develop routines enabling students to get help when teachers are temporarily busy with others.

DECISION-MAKING AND GOAL-SETTING SKILLS

Young people are able to develop some independence and recognize they have some control over their lives by learning to set goals. First, they must decide what they want to accomplish. This decision-making helps motivate children to achieve things, not for external rewards or to please other people, but for their own satisfaction. This helps them develop internal locus of control and intrinsic motivation. One step adults can help with is first defining what a goal is. They might use the analogy of a hockey or soccer goal. Explain that winning a goal is the end product of much hard work; setting a goal is describing what you want to get done or the place you want to get to, and that involves planning for something you want to understand or do better. Another step for adults to help children determine their priorities is by listening more than talking. Observing some strengths and needs is acceptable, but encourage children to talk about themselves. For example, observe a child has learned something, and ask what s/he next wants to do with this skill. Ask if a child is worried about anything in school that will be difficult.

Teach students how to talk about goals to understand and set them. For example, they must define what they want to accomplish, by when, and which related skills they already know. Children of any age may conceive unrealistic goals. For example, a child who has not learned how to ice skate may decide s/he wants to place ice hockey. Rather than squelching aspirations by telling the child this will be impossible or too difficult, help the child refine the goal into smaller associated goals as steps to the ultimate goal. For example, suggest setting the preliminary goal of learning ice skating. This generalizes to all goals: they are not accomplished all in one attempt, but rather involve series of many steps. Assist children with task analysis, breaking a goal down into its smaller component steps or skills. They can make each skill or step into a smaller or shorter-term goal toward the main goal. Help students make visual reminders, e.g., a worksheet with a drawing of a ladder, to list steps toward a goal on the rungs; a goal board with a drawing of a soccer goal, etc. Also help students track and mark their progress, and celebrate success.

IMPACTS OF STUDENT SUBSTANCE USE AND ABUSE ON DEVELOPMENT AND LEARNING

Not only are the physical and neurological development of younger children incomplete, even adolescents have yet to undergo full brain development. Therefore, using alcohol and other drugs can cause damage to their central nervous systems and other body systems and organs. Damage can be temporary or permanent, reversible or irreversible. In addition to interfering with attention in school, substance use can interfere with myelination, whereby brain and nerve cells develop coating sheaths, both protecting them and facilitating impulse and signal transmission. This process continues into young adulthood. The heart, lungs, liver, kidneys, other organs and systems are still developing and can be damaged, sometimes irreparably, at early ages. Substance use also undermines motivation to learn and achieve. Under the influence, students attend to the effects they experience, not acquiring new information or getting anything done. When use becomes abuse, addiction causes focus only on getting more of the needed substance to relieve withdrawal symptoms and reproduce the original high—which latter is impossible and leads to ingesting increasing amounts. Students neglect hygiene and schoolwork, attendance and grades fall, and dropouts become more common. Substance use and abuse triggers or exacerbates anxiety, depression, paranoia, schizophrenia, bipolar disorder, and other mental disorders.

CONDITIONS LEADING TO GANG INVOLVEMENT

The organizational structures and activities of gangs are extremely complex social phenomena. In low socioeconomic urban neighborhoods, gangs often develop in part to protect members against violence from adult criminals and other gangs. This positive motivation and protective benefit are still accompanied by undesirable effects. Gang involvement is more likely during adolescence, when students search to form personal identities. Many economically disadvantaged urban youth lack adult supervision, mentoring, and role models. Gang membership fills needs for group affiliation, belonging, identity, rules, and behavioral direction (even if behaviors are undesirable). Youth struggling to reconcile newly discovered abstractions and complexities find security in adversarial relationships among gangs, defining "us vs. them" mentalities that are less equivocal or contradictory. These enmities also provide concrete foes for youth feeling helpless to control or combat larger, seemingly unassailable foes of social ills like poverty, illiteracy, crime, discrimination, lack of opportunity, etc. Even in affluent communities, gangs may form to fulfill the same needs for social acceptance, allegiance, group identity, rules, etc.—sometimes particularly with inadequate parental or adult involvement, communication, and role modeling. Youth with unformed or unstable identities, vulnerable to peer pressure, are at higher risk for committing criminal acts as gang members. This can curtail their education, work, freedom, and life.

PEER-RELATED ISSUES

Before adolescence, very young children first developing autonomy find it very important to become their own persons and do things independently. These early assertions of self are reflected in the very individual, sometimes bizarre way young children may dress or eat when allowed to select their own clothing, unusual dietary choices, etc. However, social acceptance and peer pressure are extremely powerful forces. By the time they are in school, children begin showing concern for belonging to groups and fitting into social contexts. Student responses to social pressures reach greatest prominence during adolescence. Although adolescent quests for personal identities and defining social roles seem to recapitulate early childhood's assertion of autonomy in some respects, teenagers are additionally both hypersensitive to peers' perceptions and opinions and highly concerned with social acceptance. Teens struggling with identity issues can also feel threatened about defining their individuality, which informs their impending adult identities—which signal accompanying adult responsibilities. Conforming to group norms assuages adolescent self-consciousness and hypersensitivity to criticism by preventing teens from standing out; and reassures them that, as group members, they are not facing adulthood and its responsibilities alone.

Middle and high school teachers find many students very concerned with wearing certain clothes, eating and drinking certain foods or drinks, listening to certain music, and doing many things simply because "everybody" is doing them. "Everybody" can be everyone in a class, a school, a certain grade or age group, a circle of friends, etc. Adolescents develop exaggerated self-consciousness and hypersensitivity, leading to preoccupation with others' opinions and fear of standing out, seeming different, and not fitting into a group. As teens are also working to define their individual identities, teachers can appeal to adolescent investment in this process by reinforcing their independent choices, individual decisions, and affirming their uniqueness as persons. They can support teens in resisting peer pressure, whereby adolescents take advantage of others' social vulnerability by attempting to control them to conform by asking them what is right for them, not others; and expressing and demonstrating their approval and pride in students' asserting and being themselves. Teachers can also exploit peer-related issues by assigning cooperative learning projects; encouraging and rewarding academic club participation; and emphasizing other learning experiences involving positive social interactions, whereby group identification and interdependence promote collective and individual learning.

CONTEMPORARY MODEL OF THE WHOLE CHILD APPROACH

The Association for Supervision and Curriculum Development (ASCD) and US Centers for Disease Control and Prevention (CDC) have collaborated to produce the Whole School, Whole Community, Whole Child (WSCC) model to coordinate public health, school health, and educational processes, policies, and practices to improve health and learning, which are interrelated. They say a whole child approach to learning, teaching, and community involvement means each child deserves to be safe, healthy, supported, engaged, and challenged. Related to this model, ASCD's Whole Child Initiative aims to help educators, policymakers, families, and community members realize a vision of educating the whole child through collaborative, sustainable action. ASCD's School Improvement Tool is a totally online needs assessment that educators in schools and districts worldwide can use to determine what practices to implement or improve to realize the whole-child education vision. The tool enables educators to survey, numerically score, and color-code schools regarding key criteria, e.g., all students enter school healthy, and learn about and practice healthy lifestyles; learn in physically and emotionally safe environments; are actively engaged in learning, connected to school and community, and supported by caring, qualified adults; have access to personalized learning; are challenged academically, prepared for college or employment success; and school whole-child approaches are sustainable.

TYPICAL CHALLENGES ENCOUNTERED BY MIDDLE AND HIGH SCHOOL STUDENTS

Students entering puberty are experiencing rapid physiological and psychological changes. For some, the magnitude and speed of these changes present major adjustment challenges. For example, a formerly small boy suddenly grows a foot within one school year. Understanding limb pain and becoming winded easily are normal with growth spurts will help; he may also need help adjusting to his change in appearance. Though increased height and muscle mass are gratifying and get girls' attention, he must modify his self-image accordingly. A girl practicing gymnastics since childhood, formerly compliant with coaches' rigorous demands, begins rebelling at these now while developing her individual young adult identity. She resents pressures for weight control because she cannot stop her body from growing larger and developing new curves. Educators can help her decide if she wants to continue, possibly with different coaches, in less competitive capacities or reduced hours. Another girl practicing ballet since childhood, responding to external and internal pressures, over-exercises, severely restricts her diet, and purges for weight control, developing anorexia and bulimia. In addition to referral to counseling, educators can encourage her to talk, give her permission not to be perfect, avoid pressure, offer choices, and provide things and activities she can control other than her body.

HELPING STUDENTS ADDRESS EDUCATIONAL AND CAREER ISSUES

Most adolescents are aware of which things they find interesting, but may need some assistance in relating these interests to higher education and career paths. For example, several students share a love of animals. However, one of them excels in and enjoys all math subjects, biology, and chemistry. Another absolutely hates math and science, but loves bathing, drying, combing, brushing pets and making them look beautiful, and has a talent for handling animals gently. A third student is extremely nurturing, always rescuing lost and hurt animals and nursing them back to health. A fourth student loves animals but admires wildlife more than pets; is concerned about endangered species and extinction, already volunteering for conservation efforts; and wants to improve habitats for captive animals. The first student may consider a career as a veterinarian, the second as a professional pet groomer, the third as a veterinary technician or in an animal rescue organization, and the fourth as a wildlife biologist and/or zoo curator. Some students need higher education to qualify for careers they want, others to explore further or discover career preferences, and others for additional life experience and social maturity.

Learning Processes

FACILITATING YOUNG CHILDREN'S LEARNING THROUGH PLAY ACTIVITIES

Adults often observe young children talking about what to play. They should assist this planning by discussing with children who they will be, what will happen, etc.; and encourage children to plan together. If play breaks down, e.g., children wrangle over a toy or object, adults can intervene, pretending to knock on a door, asking if this is a good time to visit—redirecting their attention from distractions, refocusing and extending play time. To engage children in establishing safe environments for play, adults can do more than simply providing them with age-appropriate play materials by involving children in actively developing play rules to help them avoid sustaining or causing injuries and keep them safer. Young children have strong capacities for imitation, imagination, and creativity. Adults should encourage the latter, replacing the former. When children imitate violent or foolish behaviors they have observed, adults can refocus their play on other skills, problem solutions, and roles for accomplishing equal results than derivative actions with narrower scope. Storytelling and painting for younger children, and writing for older elementary-age children, are more controllable ways to work through issues impeding creativity and imagination to access and exercise them.

PROCESSES WHEREBY ADOLESCENT STUDENTS ACQUIRE AND INTEGRATE NEW KNOWLEDGE

Younger children have had less time to generate a limited repertoire of schemata about the world and either fit new experiences into these or create new ones. However, older students, having had more time and life experiences, have accumulated more schemata and made more modifications in them to construct more extensive, detailed, and sophisticated knowledge. The first learning process they engage in when encountering new information or experiences is activating their existing knowledge, examining what they already know and believe. When new information or skills are congruent with prior knowledge and extend or supplement without significantly redefining it, older students integrate these into their present belief and value systems. This second process represents assimilation, i.e., acquiring additional knowledge without disequilibrium. When new information and experiences challenge adolescents' fundamental understandings, beliefs, or values, this creates cognitive dissonance, hence disequilibrium. Students then accept or reject the new input, reconstructing or repositioning existing beliefs if needed and resolving dissonance. This third process represents accommodation, i.e., acquiring new knowledge through encountering and resolving disequilibrium, and restoring a new equilibrium informed by new positions or beliefs. Teachers can facilitate ELL access to meaningful learning by relating new concepts taught in English to student L1s, activating their prior or existing knowledge. When teachers pair unfamiliar with familiar language and experience, this facilitates concept understanding and acquisition.

SOURCES OF ACADEMIC DIFFICULTY FOR ELL STUDENTS

Some school difficulties for ELL students are directly attributable to teaching and learning environment deficits. These include lack of student access to effective ESL or bilingual instruction, mismatches between middle-class-oriented instruction and low socioeconomic student backgrounds, cultural and linguistic differences that create communication gaps between learners and teachers, etc. Other ELL students may additionally have specific learning disabilities, which require specialized instructional methods to enable successful learning. Experts believe many educators lack expertise to differentiate limited English-language proficiency from true learning disabilities as sources of school failure, evidenced by overrepresentation of ELL students in special education classes. Additional problems include shortages of both assessment instruments and trained assessors that are appropriate and linguistically and culturally relevant, and in special educators trained in concurrently addressing linguistically related as well as disability-related student needs. Factors necessary to ELL success include recognizing the importance of student L1s, collaborative community and school relationships, shared educator knowledge bases of effective instructional methods for ELLs, effective teaching, and academically rich programs that integrate instruction in basic and higher-order cognitive skills in both L1s and English.

DEVELOPMENTALLY APPROPRIATE PRACTICES FOR KINDERGARTEN ENVIRONMENTS

According to early childhood education experts, developmentally appropriate practice (DAP) must ensure that classrooms, instructional techniques, and assessment methods for young children consider three main aspects: age, individual growth patterns, and cultural influences. Educators can try various strategies, observing which are effective for different situations and learning goals: acknowledge children's actions and words by commenting, giving positive attention, or sometimes simply observing nearby. Encourage effort and perseverance, not only products and accomplishments. Make feedback specific, e.g., "That didn't reach the basket; try throwing it harder." Model—show, not just tell, approaches to problems and interpersonal behaviors—e.g., saying you must think about why something didn't work or admitting you missed part of a child's message, requesting repetition. Demonstrate correct physical procedures. Add challenge slightly beyond current skills, e.g., once children count objects after subtracting some, hide subtracted ones, requiring strategies other than counting. Decrease challenge as needed, e.g., guide children to touch objects while counting. Ask questions stimulating thought, e.g., "If you couldn't talk, how would you tell classmates what to do?" Give children hints or cues furthering progress, e.g., supply a word rhyming with a child's name, or ask the child for additional words. Directly provide verbal labels, names, facts, and other information. Accompany demonstrations and modeling with clear verbal directions for behaviors and actions.

TEACHER EXPECTATIONS, TEACHER BEHAVIORS WITH STUDENTS, AND STUDENT PERFORMANCE

In an experiment, Harvard psychologist Robert Rosenthal (1964) told teachers a standardized IQ test was a "special" test predicting dramatic IQ growth, identifying randomly selected students as about to make significant intellectual gains. In the following two years, teacher expectations became self-fulfilling prophecies: those students' IQs actually did increase. Rosenthal's additional research identified myriad, nearly imperceptible ways teacher expectations influence interactions with students. They consistently smile, nod at, and touch; give more approval; offer more specific feedback; and allow more time for answering questions to students they expect to succeed. Exemplary teachers strive to motivate all of their students to achieve more than they thought they could through high expectations. Dean of University of Virginia's Curry School of Education and researcher Robert Pianta (c. 2012) compared two approaches to changing teacher expectations: talking to convince teachers via information that their beliefs are incorrect, vs. intensive training in new teacher behaviors. The latter shifted teacher beliefs more than the former. For example, a teacher believing boys are disruptive quashes a boy's loud, effusive response, emotionally disengaging and frustrating the student. Contrastingly, a teacher without that belief encourages the student to continue, but while sitting quietly. Different beliefs prompt different interpretations of the same behavior.

INTERACTING WITH STUDENTS WHO DISPLAY PROBLEMATIC BEHAVIOR

Experts observe we must change our own behavior to change others' behavior. Educational researchers have found teacher expectations and resulting behaviors subtly yet powerfully influence student behavior. There are several suggestions for teacher behaviors to influence student behaviors. For instance, observe how every student engages, interacts, and what s/he likes doing to comprehend their capabilities. Listen to students, try to understand their goals and motivations, and note their perceptions of classmates, yourself, and assignments you give. Engage with students: ask about and listen to their individual interests without offering opinions or advice. Experiment with different responses to challenging behaviors. Instead of your first impulse, stop and consider the behavior's motivation or function, which could be to connect with you. If or when time permits, interact with students in nonacademic games or activities of their choice; observe student strengths and interests. Assign projects wherein students use preferred media to express, individually and in groups, their extracurricular interests. Consider school through students' eyes. Reflect on your own worst and best teachers, supervisors, and bosses. List five words describing how you felt when interacting with them, and what they did or said specifically to evoke those feelings. List how your students might describe you. Consider parallels between your beliefs and their responses, and how your expectations shape their perceptions of you.

ROBERT MARZANO'S STRATEGIES FOR IMPROVING TEACHING QUALITY AND STUDENT ACHIEVEMENT

According to expert Robert Marzano, instructional strategies for effective teaching and learning include: (1) identifying similarities and differences. Students more easily understand, and frequently solve, complex problems through analyzing them more simply by breaking concepts into similar and different characteristics. Teachers may identify these directly and then guide student inquiry and discussion, or have students identify them independently. Research finds the former helps identify specific items, while the latter promotes broader understanding and variation. Venn diagrams and charts are useful visual graphics for showing similarities and dissimilarities. Teachers should also engage student classifications, comparisons, analogies, and metaphors. (2) Summarizing and note-taking. Students comprehend better through analyzing subjects, revealing essential content, and restating it in their own words. Studies find students must be aware of the information's basic structure and delete, retain, and replace some components. Teachers should give students summarizing rules; prepare notes; use consistent note formats, allowing student refinements as needed; have students question, clarify, and predict coming occurrences in texts; and provide time to review and revise notes, often the best test study guides. (3) Reinforcing effort, giving recognition. Connect effort and achievement through success stories and student log-keeping and analysis. Personalize or individualize symbolic, not tangible rewards.

Marzano's strategies include: (1) homework and practice. Students extend learning beyond classrooms. Studies find homework amounts should vary by grade levels, parents should be minimally involved, students should adapt skills as they learn them, and the primary indices of practice effectiveness are speed and accuracy. Teachers should explain homework purposes to students and parents; try to give students feedback on every assignment; vary feedback delivery to maximize effectiveness; inform students whether homework is practice or to prepare for coming units; establish homework policies, advising students to maintain consistent settings, time limits, and schedules; assign timed quiz homework, having students report speed and accuracy; allocate practice time, focusing on difficult concepts. (2) Visual or nonlinguistic representations: studies show knowledge is stored in linguistic and visual forms, and students achieve more using both. Visual representation both stimulates and increases brain activity. Represent information with physical models and movements, relationships with symbolic images and words. (3) Cooperative learning: applied consistently and systematically—not overused—with small groups, cooperative activities enhance learning. Group students by multiple criteria, e.g., common interests or experiences; vary objectives and group sizes; and design projects around core components of individual and group accountability, face-to-face interaction, group processing, appropriate social skills, and positive interdependence.

(1) Objectives and feedback: give student learning direction through setting goals—not overly specific, readily compatible with students' personal goals. Setting each unit's core goal, inviting student personalization identifying areas where they want to know more, helps students consider their own interests and engage actively in goal-setting processes. Define specific student goals and grades they will receive for achieving them through writing contracts. Feedback should be corrective (comparing student achievement to specific knowledge levels as with rubrics), specific, and timely. Invite students to lead feedback sessions. (2) Hypothesis formulation and testing: studies show deductive reasoning—from general principles to specific predictions—most effective. Students must explain hypotheses and conclusions, whether deductive or inductive (from specific observations to generalizations). Ask students to predict what might occur if some aspect of government, transportation, or some other familiar system changed. Have students build things using limited resources, generating inquiries and hypotheses about what might or might not work. (3) Help students apply pre-existing knowledge for additional learning using questions, cues, and advance organizers. Studies find these must focus on important content, be highly analytical, and presented before lessons or activities. Pausing briefly after questions increases students' answer depth. Vary advance organizer styles—graphic images, skimming text, telling stories, etc.—for pre-"learning" exposure.

LEARNING ACTIVITIES THAT PROMOTE BOTH CRITICAL THINKING SKILLS AND OWNERSHIP OF LEARNING

In *Democracy and Education* (1916), John Dewey wrote that true student involvement is stimulated by activities that "give pupils something to do, not something to learn; and the doing is of such a nature as to demand thinking, or the intentional noting of connections; learning naturally results." Thus the same learning activities that promote higher-order thinking, including critical thinking and organizational and time-management skills, also promote student ownership of learning. While interests in community issues fluctuate, students regularly find school-based issues important. Issues—curricular, extracurricular, or leadership-related—must also be relevant, reflecting student identities, interests, and passions; and student roles meaningful, enabling their design, implementation, and evaluative participation for improving student learning and schools. Schools can involve students as planners in designing new buildings, developing classroom behavior guidelines, selecting textbooks, researching careers and planning coursework accordingly, participating in principal or administrator hiring, etc. Students as teachers learn about all curriculum subjects in exchange for instructing teachers how to use technology, enhancing ownership and meaningful involvement. Students as professional development partners collect and analyze data and participate in team development as learning community members. Students as decision-makers in student government influence school climate, policy, and curriculum.

AGE-APPROPRIATE STUDY SKILLS

Research finds when students must analyze information to identify its most important aspects and then express it in their own terms, they need to know how the information is basically organized, and be able to remove, replace, and preserve elements of it. Thereby they understand it better. These learning processes are included in note-taking and summarizing. Teachers can provide students with rules for summarizing; prepare their own notes for students; and adhere to regular note-taking formats, including necessary student refinements. When teachers prepare their lecture or lesson notes in outline form, students can more easily take notes in outline form. Having students question text, clarify as needed, and make predictions improves their summarizing skills. Allotting time and encouraging students to review and revise their notes frequently enables them to study for tests at their highest potential. Advance organizers help students activate and build on their prior knowledge to learn further. Teachers should introduce analytical advance organizers concentrating on essential subject matter before learning experiences and vary their style, e.g., skim text, tell stories, produce graphic images, etc.

STEPS STUDENTS NEED TO DO IN SCHOOL AND LIBRARIES IN ORDER TO WRITE RESEARCH PAPERS

(1) Topic: appeal to student curiosity; possible yet somewhat challenging for student skill and learning levels; support grade-level standards so library research matches classwork. Triangulate data, confirming topics in three kinds of available, readable sources; cross-check encyclopedias to broaden or narrow as needed. (2) Subtopics: informed by what students want to know; provide blueprints or outlines for examining topics. Brainstorm for general subtopics, e.g., physical characteristics, habitats, diets, enemies, offspring of specific animal species. "Pre-search" specific subtopics in topic-specific book tables of contents and encyclopedia subheadings. Research time management depends on controlling subtopic number (minimum three) and difficulty. (3) Sources: three kinds minimum, print or non-print; text, images, ideas. Consider student age, ability, topic for primary and secondary sources. Require MLA, APA, Turabian, or other accepted styles to prevent plagiarism and cite sources or use Creative Commons. Teach fair use and copyright regulations. Source evaluation offers lifelong skills. (4) Read, think, select: model, discuss, practice critical reading strategies—scanning, skimming, visual clues, chunking; asking what is important; identifying information supporting subtopics. (5) Note-taking: using subtopics as titles, pre-sort notes; beginners copy facts, phrases, and keywords, citing sources; experienced researchers summarize or paraphrase. (6) Sort notes by subtopic, then into paragraphs. Advanced is logical plan-based, e.g., concepts, timeline, etc. Rereading all notes per section, rearranging into logical order consolidates new information, cementing learning. Number notes consecutively. Write from notes, inserting previous knowledge.

ROLES PLAYED BY TEACHERS AND STUDENTS IN DIFFERENT INSTRUCTIONAL MODELS

In traditional teacher-centered instructional models, the teacher plays the most active role, delivering instruction through lectures and lessons; assigning homework; and creating, administering and grading tests while the students play more passive roles of attending to, absorbing, retaining, and repeating information. In more progressive student-centered instructional models, if the model espouses inquiry and discovery learning, for example, students play more active roles as teachers encourage and guide them to ask their own questions, form their own hypotheses, investigate and test these, and draw their own conclusions. When teachers differentiate instruction for students with diverse needs, teachers may play varying roles of part-time individual tutor; part-time whole-class instructor; and, when teachers include small-group cooperative learning, part-time group facilitator and guide. Teachers providing one-on-one intensive training to students with profound disabilities play highly directive, active roles. At the other end of the spectrum, when students conduct independent projects, teachers may serve only as consultants or occasional advisors until they grade the projects. While some students need explicit instruction, research also finds that while rote memorization works with factual information, active student participation and teaching learning or thinking *skills*, not just information, produces more original thinkers and lifelong learners.

COMMUNITY, HOME, AND SCHOOL FACTORS WITH REGARD TO TEACHING AND LEARNING

<u>Community</u>: socioeconomic factors affect learning. For example, students living in more affluent communities have more educational resources and supports like after-school activities, learning and tutoring centers, and educational product stores. Affluent neighborhoods are also populated with more highly educated residents: students are expected to pursue post-secondary educations. In low-income neighborhoods, economic survival often takes precedence over education, or high school diplomas are primarily for obtaining after-graduation employment. <u>Home</u>: parents with higher incomes can access more educational resources. Frequently more educated, they regard education more highly, have higher educational expectations and goals for children, serve as their role models, and either directly or indirectly educate them. Doctors, lawyers, educators, etc. are more likely have children pursuing similar educations and careers. Conversely, some children with less-educated parents have been motivated to become first in their families to attend college. <u>School</u>: urban schools where riots occur make school unsafe. Students cannot concentrate, so they stop attending. Less dramatic but equally important is classroom environment. Consider true stories of a speech language pathologist (SLP) required to conduct therapy between library shelf "stacks," and a teacher's aide instructing ELL students in school hallways. Such uncomfortable, distracting, and/or noisy settings interfere with teaching and learning.

CHARACTERISTICS SHARED BY EFFECTIVE LEARNING GROUPS

Experts find all kinds of effective learning groups share certain common characteristics. For example, their teachers are always involved actively as guides, coaches, questioners, evaluators, and resource people in student group learning processes. Groups are given work to do that is meaningful to students and challenges them. Teachers ensure students clearly understand learning objectives and schedules, and teachers monitor these. Cooperating is more important than competing. All students in each group are actively involved; groups are heterogeneous. Learning group processes enable students to feel comfortable with asking questions and discussing topics and issues. Students in learning groups experience the sense that they are able to achieve more by learning with each other than they could by learning individually. Although learning groups demand adequate social skills and interpersonal interactions, grouping is not primarily for social purposes. Group time is not considered "free time" for either students or teachers. With effective learning groups, teachers can evaluate individual student members, whole groups, or a combination of both. Teachers are able to assess group work through multiple instruments, e.g., presentations, interviews, portfolios, rubrics, quizzes, etc.

INCORPORATING DIFFERENT LEARNING MODALITIES TO OPTIMIZE INDIVIDUAL STUDENT LEARNING

Students need not have sensory or cognitive processing disabilities to learn better through one sensory modality than another. All students have learning styles. Teachers can optimize classroom learning by including multiple and alternative modalities in lessons. For example, some students are auditory learners: they have greater sensitivity, attention, comprehension, and retention for what they hear than what they see or touch. Teachers can provide audiobooks and earphones along with books during reading times. This strategy also benefits students who do have visual impairments. Other students are visual learners: they attend, understand, and remember what they see better than what they hear or touch. Pairing visuals with sounds enhances their learning and other experiences. For example, Walt Disney's classic film *Fantasia* provides visually rich animated sequences accompanying classical music by Tchaikovsky, Grieg, Mussorgsky, etc. Students with haptic learning styles respond to tactile stimuli. Teachers can give younger students materials with varied textures to accompany story reading, assigning older students projects to interpret literature, science lessons, etc. by constructing collages, models, or displays with different textures. Students with kinesthetic styles learn through physical movement. Teachers can let them dance to music and apply exercise and sports movements to physics, mathematical, and other principles, etc.

BENEFITS OF LEARNING THEORY TO EDUCATION

Behaviorism, or learning theory, has given educators a wealth of tools because it is practical, not only theoretical; applies to all organisms including humans, regardless of cognitive or intellectual level; gives clear procedures and steps to follow; deals only with observable, measurable behaviors, eliminating much ambiguity; follows logical sequences; can change behaviors much faster than other methods; and has undergone much research, yielding specific information about reinforcement schedules and corresponding response rates, effective and ineffective techniques, etc. For example, for students with cognitive or intellectual disabilities (ID) who have difficulty understanding or remembering complex tasks with multiple steps, task analysis derives from behaviorism in its principle of breaking tasks down into smaller, more manageable steps, teaching them separately until mastered, and then connecting them one more at a time. Students with autistic spectrum disorders (ASD) as well as IDs can have horrible trouble making transitions between activities. Behaviorist shaping, via reinforcing successive approximations toward an ultimate target behavior; and chaining, similar to the step-connecting portion of task analysis; are both highly valuable. Students with communication deficits might scream in class to get teacher attention; differential reinforcement of another behavior (DRO) or differential reinforcement of an incompatible behavior (DRI), e.g., raising a hand, waving, touching the teacher's arm, or operating a signal button or switch teaches more acceptable replacement behaviors.

Student Diversity

STUDENT DIVERSITY

Many people think of visible racial differences—African-American, Caucasian, Asian, Asian Indian, Hispanic, Native American, Pacific Islander, etc.—when they think of diversity. However, diversity also includes socioeconomic, from the highest wealthy tiers to the impoverished and everything in between; homelessness; living in transitional housing; all manners of disabilities, both obvious and "hidden"; intellectual and creative giftedness; urban, suburban, exurban, and rural living; different home cultures; learning English as a new language; illiterate families, parents with advanced degrees, and everything in between; younger and older ages than classmates; and many more. General principles include: treat students as individuals with unique, complex identities; ask open-ended questions, inviting reports of experiences and observations. Do not ask students to speak for their minority group. Pronounce every student's name correctly. Be aware of influences on student responses by making eye contact with everybody. Extend wait time to include more reflective and less assertive students. Ask questions challenging dominant students by drawing out quieter students in small groups; talk with and encourage students outside class. Vary teaching methods to address various learning styles and expand student strategy repertoires. Establish egalitarian norms and rules, promoting respect. Be cognizant of potential student performance anxiety in competitive settings, but not overprotective. Empathetically and tactfully give clear, straightforward standards, assessment criteria, and early feedback.

Native English speakers, including teachers, may take for granted the many idiomatic expressions we use, e.g., "between a rock and a hard place," "once in a blue moon," etc. But because they do not convey literal meanings, these sayings confuse students whose first language is not English, causing them to miss important concepts. Teachers should avoid using idioms. If they do, they should translate and/or explain them. All students benefit from linguistic redundancy, e.g., seeing print or writing while hearing speech; ELLs especially benefit. Teachers reinforce information by presenting it in multiple forms. They should also examine whether the examples they give assume or favor certain experiences or backgrounds, e.g., hobbies or activities preferred by one gender; examples based on regional, cultural, historical, or political knowledge unfamiliar to students from other countries, regions, or cultures. Teachers should provide diverse examples. They can learn some of these from their students. Teachers should not assume students who do not speak up do not know class material: Asian and other cultures find silence respectful and frown on attracting attention, while some students have learned responses to aversive consequences for participating. Teachers should also examine classroom humor to ensure jokes do not disparage any groups or differences, which occurs surprisingly often.

COGNITIVE DISABILITIES

(1) Intellectual disability (ID): students function intellectually two standard deviations or more lower than average age peers. Adaptive functioning may be equal, higher, or lower than intellectual functioning depending on strengths, background experience, and training. Students often learn the same ways as others, but at slower rates. Developmental milestones occur at later ages; learning accomplishments take longer periods to acquire. Emotional and social maturity often correspond to mental age, but also frequently advance beyond it with experience. Students have difficulty understanding abstract concepts, interpreting things literally and concretely. (2) Autism spectrum disorders (ASD): considered an emotional as well as cognitive disability, the spectrum ranges from profound to negligible impairment in activities of daily living and behavior. Intelligence ranges from profound ID to gifted. ASDs often impair social understanding and interaction, e.g., observing, interpreting, and producing nonverbal signals indicating emotions, attitudes, etc. Students have difficulty recognizing sarcasm, figurative language, humor; starting conversations; and conversational give-and-take. Behavioral characteristics include repetitive actions, restricted interests, rigid routines or schedules, focusing on one activity for long times, and difficulty transitioning among activities. (3) Specific learning disabilities: students are not intellectually impaired, but have deficits processing linguistic and/or numeric information. Typically their school achievement is far behind their intellectual ability.

AUDITORY DISABILITIES

(1) One auditory disability not involving the hearing mechanism is central auditory processing disorder, a neurological deficit in interpreting the structure and meanings of speech sounds. Other

auditory disabilities involve hearing loss. (2) Totally deaf students cannot hear any sound, often not even with hearing aids. (3) Hard of hearing students have hearing loss but some residual hearing. Hearing loss can be sensorineural, i.e., the cochlea, cochlear hair cells, and acoustic or auditory nerves do not function; or conductive, i.e., something in the outer or middle ear prevents conduction of sound waves, e.g., outer-ear wax buildup, middle-ear pus, fluid from otitis media infection, fused or immobilized middle-ear ossicles from otosclerosis, etc. Sensorineural hearing loss is irreversible, but cochlear implants enable hearing for some. Conductive hearing loss is most often treatable with surgery, medication, hearing aids, etc. Slight hearing loss, i.e., inability to hear whispering, is measured at 25-40 dB; mild hearing loss, i.e., understanding conversation with normal loudness up to 3-5 feet, 41-54 dB; moderate hearing loss, i.e., only understanding loud speech nearby, 55-69 dB; severe hearing loss, i.e., hearing only loud voices a foot away, 70-89 dB; profound hearing loss, i.e., feeling vibrations but not hearing tones, 90 dB or more. Noise-induced hearing loss is only at middle frequency (c. 4000 Hz).

VISUAL IMPAIRMENTS

The definition of 20/20 vision is reading at 20 feet from a Snellen eye chart what one normally should see. Comparably, 20/200 vision is reading at 20 feet what one should see at 200 feet. Legal blindness is defined as 20/200 after correction in the better eye. Low vision is described as anywhere from 20/200 to 20/70 after correction in the better eye and a visual field of 30 degrees or less. A visual field of 20 degrees or less is tunnel vision. Travel vision ranges from 5/200 to 10/200. Motion perception is 3/200 to 5/200, typically for moving objects. Seeing bright light from 3 feet away but not movement, i.e., below 3/200 vision, is light perception. Not seeing strong light directly in the eyes is total blindness. Students may be born blind or become blind adventitiously. Some children are born with congenital cataracts, causing opacity clouding the lenses and blindness unless surgically removed with a replacement lens implanted. Students with diabetes can develop diabetic retinopathy, i.e., vascular changes causing retinal hemorrhaging and blindness. Some students inherit glaucoma, wherein inner-eye fluid buildup creates pressure which causes visual impairment and blindness when untreated. Genetically, students may inherit total or red-green color-blindness; lack of pigment in albinism causes photosensitivity and vision problems. Accidents or injuries include retinopathy of prematurity from insufficiently regulated incubator oxygen, eyeball punctures, and retinal dislocation or detachment.

MOTOR OR PHYSICAL DISABILITIES

Physical or motor disabilities impair mobility and may also affect coordination, balance, strength, and/or flexibility. Some students are missing one or more limbs, congenitally or through accident, injury, or amputation. They may use prostheses and/or wheelchairs, walkers, canes, crutches or other mobility aids. Students with cerebral palsy have neurological deficits in control and coordination of muscular movements. Impairments range from a slight limp to being in a wheelchair or bed-bound. Cerebral palsy (CP) patients often have dyspraxia or apraxia, i.e., impaired development of their motor coordination. This can affect any body parts, e.g., speech muscles, hand grasp, fine motor skills, walking, etc. with varying degrees of severity. CP also causes spasticity, i.e., excessive muscle tension or rigidity; athetosis, i.e., excessive involuntary body movements; or both combined. Students born with spina bifida may have foot, ankle, or lower-limb weakness to below-waist paralysis, depending on the spinal level of incomplete neural tube closure. Students with severe type 1 diabetes may require amputations when the disease impairs blood circulation, especially in their lower extremities. In addition to assistive and adaptive devices and prostheses, treatments include physical therapy for large muscles, occupational therapy for small muscles, recreational therapy for adapted activities, etc.

SPEECH OR LANGUAGE DISORDERS

Speech or language disorders may involve speech only, language only, or both. Speech-only disorders include articulation disorders, the most common of which makes children distort, substitute, or omit certain speech sounds—typically consonants—at ages above typical norms for correct pronunciation. Typical remediation is speech therapy, which can include exercising articulatory muscles, audio feedback, targeting correct articulatory positions, tools (tongue depressors and bite plates), etc. Voice disorders include hypernasality, often secondary to cleft palate; hoarseness secondary to vocal polyps, nodules, or dysarthria (a neurological muscular control disorder); too-high, too-low, or unstable pitch; volume control problems, etc. Treatment depends on causes: nodules and polyps are surgically removed, clefts are repaired, and therapeutic techniques address other problems. Another speech disorder is stuttering, or rate and rhythm disorders. A variety of therapies exists, such as breathing methods, delayed auditory feedback, etc. Some stutterers actually outgrow the condition regardless of therapy. Some become "fluent stutterers." Some benefit greatly from some therapies, some little or none. Language disorders include delayed language development, secondary to intellectual disability or environmental deprivation; aphasia, secondary to neurological damage or deficits, e.g., traumatic brain injury or cerebral palsy, impairing expressive and/or receptive language processing; and language-related learning disabilities, like dyslexia (reading) or dysgraphia (writing). Language disorder therapies include stimulation and practice.

IMPACTS SENSORY IMPAIRMENTS HAVE ON LEARNING

Students with visual impairments miss a lot of input in our highly visually-oriented society. Orientation and mobility specialists can help them navigate school and other public environments more independently. Blind students may have canes or service dogs to aid mobility; teachers must plan for these and classmate interactions with them. In classrooms, blind and visually impaired students benefit from magnifiers, large-print texts, seating close to the board and teacher, audiobooks, and text-to-speech computer software for adapting texts; speech-to-text software for dictating written compositions; Braille materials or OptaCons for reading; and modified lighting, brighter and/or with less glare depending on the type and degree of impairment. Teachers can also provide materials with bright, solid colors and bold black outlines. Students with hearing impairments are safer in environments that accompany sound-based fire alarms with strobe lights. Teachers and classmates must remember to face or touch them to get their attention; speak face-to-face with students who read lips; include American Sign Language (ASL) interpreters in conversations or lessons for students who have them; and accompany spoken instruction and discussion with supplementary visual information. Speech-to-text software enables deaf and hearing-impaired students to read spoken language. Educators must also respect and teach classmates the importance and strength of deaf culture for students identifying with it.

BEHAVIORAL DISORDERS

Attention deficit hyperactivity disorder (ADHD) is familiar to many: student attention spans are deficiently short; students are too easily distracted; self-regulation deficits cause impulsive behaviors; students display excessive physical activity and have difficulty sitting still, focusing attention, and persisting in the same activity for extended durations. Medication like Ritalin, Cylert, other stimulants—even caffeine—enable better focusing, but must be accompanied by behavioral therapy. Some students are identified with oppositional defiant disorder (ODD), symptomatized by irritability, aggression, hostility, negativity, and defiance. They frequently lose their tempers, argue with adults, purposely irritate others, blame others for their behaviors and mistakes, express or demonstrate anger and resentment, and act vindictively and spitefully. Roughly half of preschoolers with ODD outgrow it by age 8, a few develop ADHD instead, and some develop comorbid disorders (anxiety, depression). Some develop conduct disorder (CD) in a few years. ODD students tend to have better school performance but worse social skills than CD patients. CD is the severest childhood psychiatric disorder, involving physical aggression to people and animals, bullying, cruelty, property destruction, lying, theft, and serious rule or legal violations. Nearly 20 percent of teens with ODD or CD have antisocial personality disorder (APD)—an extension of CD—in adulthood. Multisystem therapy is most effective; many improve, but few completely recover.

Different disorders can cause similar classroom behaviors. For example, students with intellectual disabilities (ID), autism spectrum disorders (ASD), communication disorders, attention deficit hyperactivity disorder (ADHD), and others can all display disruptive behaviors. The reasons may differ, but the net results are the same. Some inappropriate behaviors are caused by lack of maturity or understanding, as with IDs. Students with ASDs, communication disorders, or ADHD may explode out of frustration over not having their needs met. Students with communication deficits may scream, hit, or throw things in lieu of having the language or speech skills to express what they feel, need, or want. ADHD students unable to sit still or concentrate often disrupt classes with out-of-seat behavior, excessive movements, vocal interruptions, etc. ASD students can have "meltdowns" or tantrums at sensory overload, having to switch activities, etc. Students with IDs or emotional or behavioral disorders often have immature or deficient self-regulation abilities. Attention-seeking behaviors are frequently inadvertently reinforced by the attention of adults trying to address them. While it requires planning and consistent, systematic implementation, behavior modification techniques can successfully resolve many behavioral dilemmas by teaching more acceptable replacement behaviors for communicating, meeting needs, making adjustments, and establishing and reinforcing self-control and social interaction skills.

LEARNING STYLE, GENDER, CULTURE, SOCIOECONOMIC STATUS, AND PRIOR KNOWLEDGE AND EXPERIENCE

Learning style: student A is nonplused by verbal teacher explanation of a new physics concept, but lights up immediately when shown a drawing of it (visual learning style). Student B does not understand the drawing, but "gets" it exactly when guided by the teacher to act it out physically (kinesthetic learning style). Gender: boys are physically aggressive; girls engage in relational aggression (hurting feelings, undermining self-esteem and reputations). Boys respond positively when educators redirect their aggression to athletic competition; girls when educators redirect their energy to performing services helping others. Culture: students from Asian, Latin, and Native American cultures prefer cooperative over competitive activities; helping others and being part of the group is more important to them than standing out individually. They volunteer to speak in class less not for lack of preparation but to show respect. Socioeconomic status: students in poverty miss school from lacking proper clothing and shoes. Malnutrition impairs ability to concentrate, remember, and perform. Affluent parents can afford private tutoring if their children struggle with academic subjects; poor ones cannot. Prior knowledge and experience: students with marginal literacy cannot write stories but excel at oral storytelling, a strong and familiar tradition in their cultures and families.

MOTIVATION, SELF-CONFIDENCE, SELF-ESTEEM, COGNITIVE DEVELOPMENT, MATURITY, AND LANGUAGE

Motivation: the best-designed and implemented instruction will fail if students are not first motivated. Research finds internal locus of control, wherein students attribute their success or failure to causes within themselves (ability, effort, interest, or ambition, for instance), more motivating for achievement than external locus of control, wherein students attribute their success or failure to outside causes (unfair tests, poor teachers, distracting classmates, classroom conditions). Teachers engage student interest by selecting subjects students want to know about, and offering choices of learning activities and specific subtopics to investigate. Self-confidence: students lacking overall self-confidence hesitate to try anything, anticipating failure. They need encouragement and approval of themselves as persons, plus ample reinforcement of every initial small success. Others only lack self-confidence for specific tasks or subjects; Bandura calls this self-efficacy. Providing alternative learning methods and enabling successful experiences improve self-efficacy. Self-esteem: largely determines self-confidence. Teachers can raise self-esteem by showing and communicating that they value and care about students, entrusting them with responsibilities, and recognizing their accomplishments. Cognitive development: students cognitively ahead of or behind classmates need differentiated instruction appropriate to their cognitive levels for engagement and achievement. Maturity: teachers must consider whether emotional or social maturity differs from physical and/or cognitive maturity and interact appropriately. Language: many teachers mistake ELL deficits for learning disabilities, causing overrepresentation in special education.

AMERICANS WITH DISABILITIES ACT (ADA)

Signed into law in 1990, the ADA granted the same civil rights protections based on disabilities as previously accorded by the 1964 Civil Rights Act based on race, color, religion, gender, or national origin. The ADA was thus modeled on the Civil Rights Act, and also on the 1973 Rehabilitation Act requiring federally funded programs and activities to provide equal access to persons having disabilities. The terms of the ADA include public buildings, facilities, programs, and activities, which include all public school buildings, facilities, programs, and activities. Hence this law makes it illegal for public schools to prevent students with disabilities from accessing them because of architectural and other barriers. Titles II and III of the ADA include enforceable standards for accessible design and construction of buildings and facilities, barrier removal, alterations, and accessibility. Predating the Individuals with Disabilities Education Act (IDEA), which would more extensively address the rights of children with disabilities to education, the ADA also requires equal opportunities, participation, and benefits from public facilities for individuals with disabilities, "in the most integrated setting appropriate to the needs of the individual." This foreshadowed the IDEA's later emphasis on inclusion. The ADA prohibits discrimination based on disability.

INDIVIDUALS WITH DISABILITIES EDUCATION ACT (IDEA)

Passed in 1975 and reauthorized a number of times since, IDEA guarantees the right of children with disabilities to a free, appropriate, public education (FAPE) in the least restrictive environment (LRE) possible that meets their educational needs. The right to education of school-aged children is covered in IDEA Part B; Part C, added subsequently, addresses the right to early intervention and early childhood education of babies and toddlers with disabilities. The LRE clause has dual purposes: (1) to prevent segregation of children with disabilities to special schools or classes, and (2) to be interpreted differently according to the needs of every individual student. An important provision of IDEA is that every student to receive special education and related services for an identified, eligible disability must have an Individual Education Plan (IEP). An IEP team including students, teachers, parents, special educators, therapists, and others involved develops the student's IEP, identifying goals the student needs and is able to achieve; related, specific learning objectives; timeframes; and numerical criteria for determining success. The IEP includes any assistive and adaptive devices and equipment and other supports the student requires to achieve identified educational goals.

SECTION 504 OF THE REHABILITATION ACT OF 1973

Section 504 protects the rights of people with disabilities in activities and programs receiving federal funds by prohibiting discrimination against them based on disability. When the US Department of Education (ED) provides financial assistance to public school districts and other local or state education agencies, activities, or programs, it enforces Section 504. ED also has an Office for Civil Rights (OCR), headquartered in Washington, D.C. with 12 enforcement offices, to ensure civil rights laws including Section 504 are followed. Section 504 requires school districts to provide "free, appropriate public education" (FAPE) to each of their qualifying students with disabilities. This law defines an appropriate education as designed to meet disabled students' individual educational needs as well as ensuring that non-disabled students' needs are met; provided together with non-disabled students as much as meets the needs of the student with disabilities; having established evaluation and placement procedures to prevent inappropriate placement or misclassification, and periodic reevaluations; affording due process for parents to receive mandated notices, review their children's records, and challenge identification, evaluation, and placement choices.

ELEMENTARY AND SECONDARY EDUCATION ACT'S (ESEA)

The Every Student Succeeds Act (ESSA), replacing the ESEA and NCLB acts, demands fair, rigorous accountability for all school performance levels; meeting diverse learner needs; and more equitable provision of fair opportunities for student success; to ensure opportunity and equity for every student. The reauthorization of ESEA into ESSA requires its programs to offer a wide range of supports and resources enabling students to graduate, attend college, and establish careers. ESSA includes programs for meeting the special educational needs of ELL students, students with disabilities, homeless students, Native American students, migrant workers' children, and delinquent and neglected students. It states the federal government's responsibility for giving assistance to rural school districts, districts sustaining impacts of federal activities and properties, and other high-need areas and regions. The 2010 ESEA reauthorization also proposed to increase support for inclusion and better outcomes for students with disabilities as a supplement to funding for the Individuals with Disabilities Education Act (IDEA). This support includes more appropriate, accurate assessment measures of students with disabilities; better teacher and administrator preparation for meeting diverse learner needs; and better locally and state-determined curricula, incorporating universal design principles, implemented by more districts and schools.

The ESEA's 2010 reauthorization continues formula grants to states and school districts for ELL programs, allowing a variety of program types and ELL teacher professional development. The 2010 reauthorization requires new state criteria for consistent eligibility determination, placement, and program or service duration based on valid, reliable state ELP assessments; and system implementation for evaluating ELL program effectiveness and garnering data on ELL subgroup achievement for driving better district program improvement decisions and effective program selection. This reauthorization also proposed new, competitive grants to states, districts, and nonprofits for innovative program development; best-practice knowledge base building; ELL instructional practice improvement; and funding research, leadership, and partnerships for effective teacher development. Another provision requires states to adopt and implement statewide ELP standards by grade, aligned with state academic content standards for college and career readiness. Strengthening formula grants for meeting migrant student educational needs included updating the funding formula for timelier, accurate data incorporation; and facilitating and reinforcing interstate endeavors for supporting migrant student transitions into local communities and schools. Funds for homeless students were changed from Title I allocation shares to allocations based on student numbers. The administration proposed to remove service obstacles, clarify statutory ambiguities causing service delays, and require grantees to report academic outcomes.

CHARACTERISTICS OF ELL STUDENTS AS A POPULATION

The ELL student population is widely heterogeneous. Some families speak no English at home, only English, or several languages. They may identify only with American culture, strongly with several cultures, or deeply with one non-American culture. They have been stigmatized for not speaking English, speaking English, or how they speak English. They live in communities sharing common culture, without other ELLs, or have lived in America for generations. They struggle or excel in school—some in specific subjects. They may feel competent or disaffected in school. ELL immigration status, birthplace, socioeconomic status, academic knowledge, language proficiency levels, and expectations of school all vary. ELL student prevalence has extended from a few to all US states. This diversity within and among ELLs requires multiple responses for meeting educational needs. Disabilities are not more prevalent among ELLs: research shows assessments not distinguishing ELL status from disability cause misdiagnoses. Educators should not assume ELL students learn English easily or readily. Also, English oral fluency does not equal mastery: systematic academic assessments are necessary. Differing L1s, previous education, socioeconomic and immigration status mean not all ELLs learn English the same way. Accommodations benefit not only ELLs, but others. Vocabulary is not the sole focus of ELL instruction: structures and meanings are equally important, even with limited ELP.

INSTRUCTING ELL STUDENTS EFFECTIVELY

Teachers should give ELLs challenging, meaningful curriculum content, text choices, and authentic reading and writing activities. Placement by academic achievement, not ELP, with high-quality instruction in challenging classes enables greater learning and performance. Technology supports ELL motivation, writing and editing skills development, and class blog and website collaboration. Teacher awareness of ELLs' previous literacy experiences, backgrounds, and L2 learning benefits and challenges enables more effective instruction. ELLs are challenged to understand implicit cultural norms and knowledge; learn to translate and code-switch; develop metalinguistic awareness; negotiate differences between school literacy practices and home or community; and address the social, cultural, and political dimensions of linguistic status issues. Studies show ELL reading comprehension, writer identity development, and peer collaboration are developed through extracurricular composition. Teachers can use these methods to promote ELL investment in school learning, decrease home-school distance, and help students view their home languages and cultures not as obstacles or discards, but educational resources and contributors. Teachers should teach K-12 ELLs academic literacy basics and help them connect school content to their own knowledge.

CLASSROOMS WHERE ALL STUDENTS PARTICIPATE AND HAVE THEIR EDUCATIONAL NEEDS MET

Establish a classroom climate where students feel safe, secure, and engaged in learning rather than unchallenged or threatened. Discuss how students want the classroom to work and how to maintain the best climate. Promote cooperation, involvement, and a stimulating, inviting, productive, learner-friendly environment with functional, appealing arrangements and displays through a classroom plan, including students in decision-making processes. Organize the classroom to allow movement, stations for long-term involvement and learning, and easy technology and information access. Engage students in the processes of developing, comprehending, and maintaining procedures and routines, with a limited number of positively stated, specific, clear rules; practice and reinforce these throughout the school year. Assign and manage meaningful assignments with purposes, in real-life settings with audiences. Prepare for teaching: active student involvement in planning, preparing, implementing, and assessing learning units reduces behavior and discipline issues. Consider having students create and submit actual proposals to organizations, corporations, or city councils needing new ideas. Consistently communicate and reinforce class procedures and routines. Discuss behavior in class. Discuss adding, removing, or changing procedures. Have students enforce rules. Students' having a voice enables superior classroom functioning. Consistently celebrate success. Evaluate and reflect daily or weekly throughout the year.

INCLUSIVE PRACTICES IN REGULAR EDUCATION CLASSROOMS WITH SPECIAL EDUCATION STUDENTS

According to expert Peter Westwood (2003), research into effective instruction finds that effective teachers keep the focus on academics; give students maximal opportunities for learning; demonstrate good classroom management; use work-oriented, business-like styles; express enthusiasm; communicate high expectations to students of what they can achieve; apply strategies for keeping students motivated, on-task, and productive; introduce new material step-by-step; use explicit and direct instruction techniques; structure all content; give clear explanations and instructions; closely monitor student activities; demonstrate appropriate strategies for approaching tasks; utilize varied resources; adjust instruction to individual student needs; reteach as needed; give students frequent feedback; and spend considerable amounts of time doing whole-class, interactive teaching. In classes including special education students, teachers include: descriptive praise and encouragement, ample guided practice, fast-paced lessons, high engagement and participation levels of all students, careful curriculum content sequencing and control, positive peer assistance and interactions, many practice and application opportunities, modeling of effective school task completion methods, interactive group teaching, and teaching students how best to attempt new learning tasks.

CREATING SUPPORTIVE, POSITIVE CLASSROOM ENVIRONMENTS FOR STUDENT DIVERSITY

(1) Teachers can intentionally teach responsible behaviors. To afford a multidimensional approach for every student, particularly those requiring more intensive intervention, teachers can collaborate with parents, school psychologists, and counselors. General behaviors to teach include communication skills, social skills, character development, anger management, self-control skills, conflict resolution, decision-making skills, taking responsibility for one's actions, and developing emotional intelligence (EQ). (2) Teachers can establish classroom harmony through creating warm, supportive atmospheres wherein every student feels s/he is an important class member. Class meetings, class-building and team-building activities engender senses of a learning community and class ownership. Experts use the acronym "VIABLE": students develop self-respect and respect for authority figures when they feel they are *valued* by teachers and classmates, *included* in classroom activities, *accepted* in their classrooms and schools, have senses of *belonging* to cooperative learning groups, and adults who *listen* to and *encourage* them. (3) Teachers can empower students and promote their sense of class ownership by involving them actively in disciplinary processes. Instead of being part of the problem, students become part of the solution. Activities include arranging study and homework buddies; peer tutors, mediators, and counselors; peer recognition; assigning classroom responsibilities; and student-led conferences.

Invite or involve parents to meet student needs together. The "crucial Cs of parental support" are parent-teacher Communication, Connection, and Collaboration. Invite other teachers and staff—administrators; school psychologists, counselors, social workers, nurses; speech language pathologists (SLPs), occupational therapists (OTs), physical education (PE) teachers, special education teachers, music teachers; ELL or bilingual teachers, etc.—to collaborate in solving learning and discipline problems. Encourage and praise students' positive steps, efforts, strengths, progress, and improvement, not just finished products. Encouragement helps students self-validate and reflect on their own responses to their strengths and accomplishments. Effective praise is informative and appreciative, not evaluative or controlling. Build senses of accomplishment and capability in all students, and particularly in those lacking the following: focus on improvement, not perfection; turn mistakes into learning opportunities; let students struggle and succeed within ability levels; build upon student strengths; analyze past successes, then focus on the present; acknowledge task difficulty; use task analysis; teach positive self-talk; celebrate all students' successes and achievements. Develop positive teacher-student relationships to receive and give respect. Listen to students. Communicate positive expectations. Involve students in class decision-making: use a suggestion box; provide "voice and choice." Show enthusiasm for teaching and learning. Show interest in student interests. Keep communication open. Accept and value diversity and individual differences. Model positive, helpful, and kind behaviors.

Motivation

MOTIVATION THEORY

Self-determination: student propensity for initiating activities independently, as opposed to only doing what teachers tell them to do. Achievement motivation research finds student motivation to learn and perform is stronger based on internalized motives, e.g., interest in subject matter, self-efficacy, desire to know things, desire to succeed, career ambitions, etc. By comparison, externalized motives, e.g., to gain rewards from teachers, schools, or parents; to avoid punishment; to impress teachers, classmates, friends, parents, etc. are not as effective. Attribution: how and where we assign cause. Students with more internal locus of control attribute their success or failure to personal abilities and actions; students with more external locus of control attribute successes or failures to people, actions, events, or situations outside themselves. Cognitive dissonance: discomfort with contradictory information; we adjust our schemas (mental representations) to reflect new information, form new schemas, or reject the information to restore congruence and resolve the discomfort. Classical conditioning: associating an unrelated stimulus with one that elicits a certain reflexive reaction can condition it to evoke the same reaction. Pavlov repeatedly paired bell-ringing with meat powder to make a dog salivate; eventually bell-ringing alone evoked salivation. Operant conditioning: manipulating antecedents and consequences shapes behavior; positive reinforcement strengthens probability of repeating behavior; punishment weakens it. Negative reinforcement removes a reinforcer or reward, decreasing behavior repetition.

PROMOTING STUDENT MOTIVATION

Teachers delivering instruction with enthusiasm and energy are role models: demonstrating their motivation and passion motivates students. Teachers showing why they are interested in subject content personalize it for students. Getting to know students, belief in student ability, strong interest in their learning, and personal interest in student backgrounds and concerns inspire personal student loyalty. Many students want to know the application, utility, or real-life relevance of content before further engagement. To do this, use many examples and explain how it prepares them for future opportunities. Design activities directly engaging students in material, offering mastery opportunities: discovery learning requiring reasoning through problems to discover underlying principles independently satisfies students. Positive social pressure makes cooperative learning activities effective. Design assignments with challenges appropriate to student abilities and experiences. Set realistic performance goals; help students set and achieve reasonable goals. Tests and grades should show mastery, not shortcomings. Allow all students opportunities to achieve the highest grades and standards; avoid grading on curves. Make criticism constructive, feedback nonjudgmental. Criticize specific performances, not performers. Seek means of stimulating advancement; emphasize improvement opportunities. Avoid classifying students as leaders or followers. Give students as much choice and control over their learning, assessment, and performance as possible.

INTRINSIC MOTIVATION

Students intrinsically motivated to learn are attracted to and fascinated by subjects, recognize their relevance to real life, feel a sense of accomplishment from mastering them, and feel called to them. Their reasons for learning are typically because the content interests them, they find it improves their thinking skills, and/or they find school success rewarding. Advantages include that intrinsic motivation sustains itself and has more longevity than external rewards; teacher efforts to build internal motivation typically involve efforts to further student learning as well, typically focusing not on rewards or punishments but on subject matter. Disadvantages include more specialized preparation, taking longer to produce behavior change, and requiring teachers utilize a variety of approaches in different students. Getting to know individual students and what interests them, connecting student interests to subject content, and strong teacher interest in subject content (and demonstration thereof) support developing intrinsic motivation in students.

According to one model, students offered opportunities to engage in learning activities first decide whether an activity is interesting to them or not. They engage in activities that interest them. If not immediately finding interest in an activity, they then evaluate it according to two criteria: whether or to what extent it is stimulating, i.e., it attracts their curiosity, affords a challenge, and/or appeals to their sense of fantasy; and whether or to what degree it affords them personal control—i.e., it is not too difficult for them to accomplish, and allows them some measure of free choice in the specific topics, learning styles, methods, procedures, materials, and forms of assessment they can use to acquire knowledge and demonstrate understanding. If students perceive an activity as both stimulating and controllable, they consider it potentially interesting or valuable and engage in it. If either or both conditions become inadequate, students disengage unless influenced by some extrinsic motivation. Students are more likely to repeat engagement in activities they find repeatedly stimulating and controllable, and discard those repeatedly not satisfying these criteria. Research finds the more constructive teacher criticism is and the more freely and often teachers praise student efforts, the more encouraged and self-motivated students become.

INCLUDING STUDENTS IN INSTRUCTIONAL DECISIONS

All human beings want some control over their circumstances and activities. This is especially important to K-12 students: as minors, they have less legal and practical power and control over their lives than adults. Students perceiving teachers as having all the control over their instruction are more likely to respond only to external rewards and punishments and less likely to develop internal motivation to learn and achieve academically. When teachers include students in instructional decisions, students feel ownership of the content and their learning. For example, teachers can ask students which aspects and topics within curriculum subjects interest them and let students choose topics they are interested in for papers and projects. They can give students choices among working independently, in pairs, or in small groups for some learning activities. Teachers can offer students options for how to weigh different assignments and assessments to determine their grades. Including papers, projects, tests, presentations, and other varied ways of assessing students allows them more control over how they demonstrate their learning. Participation and control in their instruction increases student motivation for acquiring and demonstrating knowledge.

INTERNAL VS. EXTERNAL MOTIVATION

External motivations include teacher and parent expectations of students; rewards students can earn by demonstrating learning; and grades, which determine passing, promotion, retention, graduation, future opportunities, college admissions, scholarships, etc. Applying external motivators typically requires little preparation or effort, frequently does not require much teacher knowledge about individual students and their interests, and produces more immediate behavior changes. However, designating appropriate rewards and punishments becomes challenging when students become habituated, requiring escalation over time. External rewards frequently distract students from learning subject matter. They are not durable: students lose motivation once rewards and punishments are discontinued. Additionally, multiple experiments (e.g., Lepper, Deci) show external rewards can decrease internal motivation: students of all ages continued to engage in activities without rewards as they found them inherently interesting, whereas those given rewards for engaging in them discontinued engagement when rewards ceased; extrinsic rewards apparently reduced intrinsic interest. Internal motivations, including student interest in subject matter and learning and desire for knowledge and success, require more teacher time and effort and take longer to change behavior, but are durable, not dependent on rewards or punishments. Additional factors affecting student motivation include how stimulating activities are and how much control students have over them.

Contrasting with internal motives that students have for learning and succeeding academically, grades are external motivators. While they provide an index of how a student performed in classroom activities and assessments—which can vary in accuracy—grades by themselves do not give students intrinsic reasons to learn or achieve. Students displaying extrinsic motivation might say they need certain letter or number grades to pass courses and accomplish graduation from high school, to the next grade, receive rewards promised by teachers or parents, or avoid punishment. This differs from students saying that certain grades prove they know, understand, or have mastered subjects. Though some view formative assessment grades as feedback, these often do not inform adjusting performance. In an expert's (Wiggins, 2012) analogy, suppose a student's goal in PE is to run a five-minute mile, already having achieved 5:09. Suppose at the end of the first lap of a mile race, her coach yelled, "B-plus on that lap!" This does not support progress toward the goal. But the coach's yelling individual lap times, feedback, and advice: "You're on pace for 5:15," "You're not swinging your arms," "You need two seconds off the next lap to finish under 5:10—pick it up," provides specific information and advice for progress toward the goal.

SHOWING STUDENTS THE APPEAL OF INSTRUCTIONAL CONTENT

Teachers can encourage student interest in subject content by showing its appeal. To show novelty, comment how you have not seen anything quite like a certain topic or activity. To show utility, describe a topic as including valuable ideas you will use later in the course and being a topic they will use over and over in both school and life. To show applicability, point out how relevant certain subject matter is to the course and everyday life. To show anticipation, prompt students to ask themselves while reading what next logical step the text foreshadows. To show surprise, remark that the class has used some subject matter in many different ways, and then whet their interest, saying, "If you think you've seen them all, just wait until our next activity." To show challenge, suggest students will find the upcoming material very interesting and invite them to rise to a challenge. To show feedback, predict that when students try an assigned activity, they will discover whether they really understood the previous lesson or not. To show closure, announce that many students have asked about a topic or phenomenon, telling them they will now finally find out more and why.

Foundations of Literacy

WORD IDENTIFICATION STRATEGIES

Fifty percent of words read (including by adults) comprise 100 high-frequency words, including *the, and, to, you, he, it,* and *said.* Beginning readers seldom recognize words immediately. They need to develop this—not only to increase instant-recognition vocabulary, but also because many high-frequency words are irregular phonically (e.g., *to, said*). <u>Reading copious amounts of fairly easy text</u>

best develops instant high-frequency word recognition. <u>Context clues</u> include: (1) <u>semantic or meaning clues</u>, e.g., expecting a story about cats to include words like *purr, whiskers,* and *tail.* More specific sentence context clues include considering possibilities like *scratch, play,* and *jump* for the sentence "My cat likes to____." (2) <u>Syntactic clues</u> help determine parts of speech through word order, e.g., the missing word in the preceding example is a verb, dictated by syntax. (3) <u>Picture clues</u> inform word meaning through illustrations, e.g., a picture of a cat jumping would help complete the sentence in the above example. Context clues work best combined with word-part, word-sound, or phonics clues. <u>Word structure clues</u> enable more experienced readers' recognizing common letter clusters in words, including affixes and inflectional endings. <u>Analogy clues</u> help readers identify simple syllables and words through phonemic awareness of word-initial sounds and rhymes, e.g., students familiar with *will* and /f/ can identify *fill.*

PRE-READING COMPREHENSION STRATEGIES

<u>Word splash</u>: clarifies purpose for reading, motivates reading, engages students in writing, and offers fun. Dictate to students, so they must try to spell, 7-10 familiar and unfamiliar key words from text; have them write seven-line minimum short stories using all words and share with partners. Have several students read stories aloud. Compare to text during reading. <u>Key words</u>: like word splash, except instead of stories, students write informational paragraphs explaining selected key words. <u>Prewriting questions</u>: have students survey text, writing questions it will likely answer, to seek answers during reading. <u>Story</u>: teachers select 10-15 key concepts, words, or phrases from several chapters of text, listing them in sequence of appearance in chapters—enough to form impressions, but not to pre-construct whole text episodes. <u>Pictures</u>: have students view illustrations, sidebars, and/or text boxes in texts to predict subject matter. <u>Think-pair-share</u>: in a cooperative learning activity, students write their thoughts on an open-ended question or topic, share with partners, combine both partners' input into one concise statement, and share it with the class. This also applies both during and after reading. <u>KWL Charts</u>: students write what they *know, want* to know, and *learned.* Also use this during and after reading.

READING COMPREHENSION STRATEGIES

<u>Making connections</u>: *text-to-self (T-S)* connections are of text to personal reader experience. *Text-to-text (T-T)* connections are between currently and previously read texts. *Text-to-world (T-W)* connections are between text and real-world events. <u>Questioning</u>: questions facilitate text clarification and deeper understanding. Question-answer relationships (QAR) include four question types divided into two sections: (1) *in the book*, including *right there* or *think and search*; and (2) *in my head*, including *author and you* or *on your own.* Teachers can model codes according to student needs for various question types and/or even collaborate with students to create codes. <u>Visualizing</u>: when students form mental images of text, they create three-dimensional movies from books; engage with text in memorable, personalized ways; and adjust their images throughout reading. <u>Inferring</u>: students make inferences when they "read between the lines" of text—making educated guesses based on pictures, context clues, and other evidence; predicting coming text events; drawing conclusions; and determining unfamiliar word meanings. <u>Determining importance</u>: differentiating fiction from nonfiction and important from unimportant information are informed by knowing purposes for reading. <u>Synthesizing</u>: as students accumulate more information, their thinking evolves. New information triggers new schema formation, schema re-evaluation, or schema modification; students put together information from multiple sources and/or information components.

<u>Do now</u>: give students a quick, thought-provoking question or statement, requiring responses three to five minutes in length, focusing them on that day's targeted concept to introduce new concepts and units, review learned concepts, or record thoughts for later discussion and reflection. Also use

before and after reading. <u>Response sheets</u>: help students connect text to existing knowledge and later become relevant study guides. Students write key statements on left, personal responses on right. <u>Post-it notes</u>: give students Post-it notes, amounts based on text length. Have them write questions to ask in class, ideas and thoughts, and summaries regarding text while reading. Notes can later be moved from books to folders for study guides. <u>Text rendering</u>: establishes student-text interaction. Students mark texts or attached Post-it notes using codes, highlight words, and make marginal notes. Have students read aloud and restate main ideas, share connections and reflect: assess reading success, thinking diversity, and potential clarification issues. <u>Re-reading</u>: have students target specific, key concept-defining, illustrating, or supporting text—also giving them practice in locating information quickly using headings, titles, italicized or boldfaced words, etc. <u>Chunking</u>: break text into paragraphs, meaningful chunks containing some whole ideas, making long texts more manageable. This technique is also usable before and after reading. <u>Literature circles</u>: small-group, student-centered, teacher-facilitated, regular reading discussions. Students choose topics; everyone takes notes. Model repeatedly before independent student use; team or co-teaching helps. Assign and rotate discussion director, connecter, and summarizer roles.

<u>Expert jigsaw</u>: break large text into intact content chunks; assign students to read various sections, a few reading the same ones. "Expert groups" reading the same chunk discuss main ideas and important points. Then group one member of each "expert group" together and have each explain content from their chunk to the rest. Have each group share all information with class aloud, record comments on the board, clarify any misconceptions, and add any omitted information. <u>Reflection</u>: give a guiding question or prompt to help connect new learning to existing knowledge; have students write a few lines in notebooks or journals about what they just read. <u>Whip</u>: for ensuring every student participates, gathering data, enabling student sharing of varying responses to an open-ended question, reviewing a concept quickly, and identifying errors and misconceptions for clarification. Corrective and critical comments from anyone are prohibited, encouraging sharing. Weak readers also experience models of text-based thinking and varying perspectives. Go around the room, having each student answer aloud a text-based question. <u>I-search</u>: in a user-friendly inquiry research project, students choose topics according to an open-ended, broad question; list topic questions; research various sources; write papers describing topic selection reasons and processes, search processes, topic discoveries, and conclusions.

READING ENRICHMENT INTERVENTIONS FOR BOTH ADVANCED AND STRUGGLING READERS

Some researchers (Reis et al, 2004) observed the literature shows reading comprehension and school achievement correlate; major factors influencing at-risk students' lower literacy and achievement include socioeconomic status, classroom environment, and teacher training. Little research addresses diverse student reading needs in all grades; students need self-determination, choice, and copious text in varied print types and genres. Teachers must meet diverse student needs, from those with learning disabilities to gifted and advanced readers, etc. Even advanced texts or resources available in classrooms are not used: advanced or gifted readers typically receive identical materials and instruction to grade-level and below-grade-level readers. Testing the effects of intervention using their Schoolwide Enrichment Model Reading (SEM-R) on oral reading fluency, comprehension, and attitudes toward reading, researchers found this student-centered, enriched program including 25-35 minutes daily of extended, structured, independent silent reading self-selected, challenging books with supported, individualized instruction increased oral reading fluency. Compared with basal readers, comprehension and attitudes were unaffected, making much grouped instruction unnecessary. Compression or streamlining eliminated repetition for advanced readers; teachers coached struggling readers more as independent reading times increased. Though many reform models recommend direct instruction for struggling readers, enjoyable and enriched independent reading of self-selected texts improved fluency for culturally diverse urban students and advanced readers alike.

STRATEGIES FOR DIFFERENTIATING INSTRUCTION RELATED TO READING COMPREHENSION AND LEARNING

Tiered assignments and products are varied in abstractness or concreteness, complexity, step numbers, learning modalities, and independence by student readiness level, e.g., students with moderate topic understanding write articles; those with advanced understanding prepare debates. Compacting eliminates instruction and practice of content for students who have mastered it. Teachers assess student knowledge levels and mastery needs; plan student learning activities, excusing students from mastered skills or materials; plan enriched, accelerated reading; study; timelines; and student choice for time freed by eliminated content. Independent study focuses on student interests. Teachers and students co-plan reading and projects based on curriculum content and student needs. Teachers provide structure, guidance, timelines, clear success criteria; students document processes in journals or process logs. Interest groups enable student topic choice. Complexity and independence levels can be differentiated. As enrichment, students can read and study topics beyond general curriculum. Flexible grouping exposes students to collaboration with widely varying peers, avoiding labels (e.g., struggling or advanced readers). Multiple question levels promote problem-solving skills, student challenge and accountability, benefiting all students. Learning contracts enables congruency with student learning styles, planning skills, independent work, and eliminates unnecessary practice. Teachers can use choice boards, organizers offering varied reading-based activities, requiring students choose products focusing on different skills and learning styles.

PREDICTION, PRIOR KNOWLEDGE, THINK-ALOUDS, AND ANALYZING TEXT STRUCTURE

Prediction: have students read a portion of narrative text, stop, and predict what they think will happen next. Model for inexperienced or hesitant students, ask their opinions, and invite similar and different predictions. Read further, comparing teacher and student predictions with text. Discuss whether plot developments seem logical, whether they prefer text or their own predictions, why they found events expected or unexpected, etc. Prior knowledge: have students think about experiences in their own lives similar to text characters' experiences in fictional or nonfictional narratives; and background information they already knew about topics in informational or expository texts. Guide discussion: ask students without similar literal experiences when they had similar feelings or thoughts to text characters, which common elements evoked these, if any; and/or how or why their experiences or responses differed from characters'. Comprehension monitoring: have students mark, highlight, or make notes while reading to identify main ideas, note their agreement or disagreement, and identify questioned or confusing parts for class discussion; assign shorter, more manageable passages and supervise in-class reading; periodically interrupt student reading, asking questions about main ideas, clarifying misunderstandings, explaining unclear portions. Think-alouds: model the thought process for students, demonstrating logical connections and sequential steps for deriving text meaning. Have students practice. Analyzing text structure helps students understand plot and character development, using evidence to support arguments, etc.

GRAPHIC REPRESENTATIONS, MENTAL IMAGERY, QUESTIONING, INFERENCES, AND SUMMARIZING

Graphic representations: some students with more visual, not verbal learning styles understand material better by seeing images than reading words. Provide illustrations, diagrams, etc., illuminating concepts and narratives. Venn diagrams visualize similarities and differences, common and overlapping areas, and relationships; cause-and-effect diagrams illustrate chains of novelistic or historical events, etc. Mental imagery: read a passage aloud; model describing mental pictures imagining what the author describes. Have students read other passages aloud and describe their own mental imagery. Tell students to pretend they are making movies of books. Explain how imagery makes reading three-dimensional. Questioning: use think-alouds to model asking questions about text to clarify meaning; discover new information; wonder about author purposes, content, and format; interrupt reading long enough to form mental images; wonder about text-related topics of personal interest, etc. Identify question types (*in the book*: *right there, think and search*; *in my head*: *author and you, on your own*) and have students follow suit. Inferences: get students to "read between the lines" by demonstrating using textual evidence for informed guessing, predicting, ascertaining unknown word meanings, and drawing conclusions; have them practice. Summarizing: read a passage aloud; model summarizing main points, events, and ideas. Have students practice summarizing different text, providing feedback regarding including unnecessary details, omitting important information, etc.

RELATIONSHIP AND INTERRELATIONSHIP BETWEEN LISTENING, SPEAKING, READING, AND WRITING

Children learn to understand the spoken language they hear receptively sooner than they develop the ability to speak language expressively. In a similar fashion, they learn to understand language they read receptively ahead of learning to use written language expressively. Moreover, they learn to listen and speak before they learn to read and write. Although listening and speaking are concurrent learning processes, as are reading and writing, receptive understanding still precedes outward expression somewhat. This naturally allows students to understand input they receive first, enabling them to produce comprehensible output thereafter. Barring specific learning or other disabilities, children demonstrating good listening comprehension and oral language skills are more likely to acquire better reading and writing skills. Phonemic awareness helps children understand spoken language, while phonics helps them relate spoken to written language. Hence listening skills support not only speech skills, but also reading development; reading skills support writing development. In school, students must listen and speak to teachers and classmates about content subjects; read content subject material; and write to answer tests, compose prose essays, papers, stories, dramas, poems, etc. about content subject topics. Without literacy skills, they cannot learn or perform academically or adequately in life.

INTEGRATING STUDENT LISTENING, READING, WRITING, AND SPEAKING SKILLS

Unlike historical approaches that taught academic subjects separately, today's instructional standards advocate integrating oral and print literacy into all content subjects across the curriculum. This is not only because of the vital importance of literacy for all students, employees, and citizens, but moreover because all content subjects involve literacy in some way or other. Even mathematics includes solving word problems, plus explaining math concepts, processes, and procedures verbally. As an example, suppose a teacher designs a social studies unit on a certain Native American tribe that historically lived in the school's location. The teacher might introduce the unit with a lesson or lecture about this tribe: students use listening skills in attending, comprehending, note-taking; and speaking skills answering teacher lesson or lecture review questions. The teacher assigns textbook reading on the tribe's history, including timelines; agricultural, scientific, cultural, and spiritual contributions; interactions with settlers, etc. Students then employ reading, listening, and speaking skills in classroom discussions. The teacher assigns each student to read an additional book outside the text with more in-depth information on this tribe, using reading skills. Relating tribal influences to contemporary culture, some write reports, practicing writing skills; others give presentations, practicing speaking skills.

WRITING FOR AUTHENTIC PURPOSES

Students write for authentic purposes when they write material for real-life reasons, addressing it to real audiences. Authentic writing is the most similar to the writing we experience in real life. To use authentic purposes and writing as an instructional strategy, teachers can do several things. First, they can support students by providing them with print-rich environments. Young children, even those not reading yet, should be surrounded by attractive, appealing books combining pictures and simple text, which they can access independently. For older students unmotivated to read, teachers should offer texts on topics personally interesting them; select texts with plenty of good illustrations, show movies adapted from novels, take turns reading together, start class or group discussions of reading, etc. Teachers should also expose students to varied writing genres and formats, and let them choose among these for reading. Giving students opportunities to interact with others in response to reading also prepares them for authentic writing. To enable authentic writing, teachers must help students realize that writing is a recursive process, not just a linear task finished in the first attempt.

SUMMARIZING TEXT AND SYNTHESIZING INFORMATION

The greatest challenge in summarizing is judging what to include or omit. First make sure students understand the full text content, including main ideas and details. Have them closely observe topic sentences and key words repeated throughout the text. Then have them cross out unneeded information in texts or copies, and underline points they find most important—including words and phrases. Have students then follow the original text's organization and tone, while maintaining objective viewpoints, to write a summary of the text in their own words, avoiding opinions and documenting and punctuating quotations correctly. Inform students their summaries should be 15-20 percent of the original text length. Have them compare their summaries to original texts for accuracy. Give students examples of well-written and poorly-written summaries; many are available online. Through synthesis, students incorporate new information into their existing knowledge bases and extend literal text meanings to include inferences. Help students synthesize through questions, e.g., how can this information be shown visually? How would an artist illustrate these details? Which parts of the text can you use for new ideas or products? Which graphic organizer would you use to present this information? How can you use these facts in a dramatic presentation, reader's theater script, or persuasive letter?

DEVELOPING LESSONS IN CONTENT-AREA WRITING

Effective content-area writing entails not repeating facts but inquiry, discovery, and synthesis. Multiple-choice and short-answer tests more efficiently show facts students know about subjects; writing requires and enables students to assemble what they learned and apply it to new contexts. Establish content objectives before planning or assigning writing activities. Develop ideas for different writing formats to explore learning objectives: assignments offering only a choice of a report or essay, giving main topics and page length or word count with minimal instructions and no details, frequently fail by not letting students explore the available range of writing formats and not providing any assistance. Include fiction, drama, journalism, TV, movie media, etc. in assignments as well. For example, with a unit on the solar system, instead of a report on the solar system's origins and planet locations, assignments could be short stories about interplanetary travel, narrated in first person; video newspaper stories about life on each planet; TV special programs on the solar system, including types of information and camera footage to use; essays about space travel possibilities during the student's lifetime; reports on rocketry's progress since World War II; letters to NASA about future interplanetary travel plans; or students' own ideas, with teacher guidance.

INSTRUCTING STUDENTS TO WRITE IN CONTENT AREAS

Ensure that course content is central to the writing process: what the writing communicates takes precedence; how it communicates this is incidental. Ensure that students know the content material before they write: student writing allows their understanding of content to shine. Design writing activities that involve students' synthesizing and organizing their knowledge rather than simply regurgitating information. Give students real or imagined audiences so they feel they are writing for somebody other than their teacher. Assign writing activities that enable students to take on the roles of learners and researchers. Teach the writing process: help students develop a strong grasp of content by devoting plenty of time to prewriting planning and organization. Do not wait until students turn in papers: provide support and assistance while they write, helping them solve problems as they develop. Offer peer revision activities, including support via revision guidelines and checklists. Teach revision before copyediting: have students clarify their work's substance and content first. Proceed to copyediting the usage, mechanics, spelling, etc. only during final writing phases. Publicize student writing through publication, oral readings, demonstrations, shows, etc., so teachers are not their only reader audiences.

FORMAL AND INFORMAL ASSESSMENTS

Formal: woodcock-Johnson Reading Mastery; Stanford Achievement and Diagnostic Reading Tests; state achievement tests; Test of Reading Comprehension (TORC); Gray Oral Reading Tests-Diagnostic (GORT-D). Informal: content-area literacy assessments; teacher observations; Qualitative Reading Inventory III; informal literacy inventories; diagnostic interviews, reading preparation, silent reading, oral reading, retelling; miscue analysis; Burns/Roe Informal Reading Inventory; cloze procedures; student attitude or interest surveys; demographic data; report card grades; promotion and retention data; attendance, disciplinary records. Formal and informal assessments are required, particularly for ELLs, when assessment and learning are inseparable. Observational literacy checklists include using text structure and context clues, selecting graphic organizers, and rereading for clarification. Brief anecdotal records note observations, e.g., student vocabulary comprehension difficulty, good response to concept definition maps and other graphic organizers, etc. Reading portfolios indicate student reading times, book choices and quantities, reading goals, insights and questions, informing instructional strategies. Informal reading inventories inform word identification, retelling, and comprehension skills for reading levels, general strengths and needs. Formal literacy tests should be valid, reliable, give standard scores, and identify student literacy skills and needs. In-depth data analysis is crucial. Disaggregating data is necessary to meet diverse student needs and learning styles. Content-area teachers must integrate literacy strategies into lesson plans, monitoring student progress. Experts advise progress-monitoring teams, meeting regularly.

Responsive Learning Environments

The Learning Environment

RELATIONSHIP BETWEEN ACADEMIC INSTRUCTION AND CLASSROOM MANAGEMENT

When educators teach and encourage students to take responsibility for their own behaviors rather than taking total responsibility for guiding student behaviors, teachers and students approach and understand content differently. Moreover, when instruction is more demanding (e.g., students address novel problems and/or create products), teachers must make more complex management decisions. This relationship between instructional activity levels and management complexity supports research evidence of the inseparable, complex interrelationship of instructional curriculum and classroom management. Teachers must help students learn to meet concurrent academic demands for comprehending and manipulating content, and social demands for interacting with others to demonstrate that content knowledge effectively. This broader view of classroom management has redirected research from controlling behavior to creating and sustaining learning environments—including furniture arrangements, classroom decorations, developing and communicating rules and routines, and interacting with students. Research shows teachers implementing systematic classroom management approaches when school years begin have students demonstrating higher task engagement and academic achievement. Researchers also identify strategies eliciting low misbehavior and high involvement as communicating awareness of student behavior, overlapping activities, smooth transitions, instructional momentum, and whole-class-focused attention alerting.

UNDERSTANDING STUDENT GROUP DYNAMICS AND MANAGING THEIR BEHAVIOR

Be aware of individual students' group roles, e.g., leader, instigator, conscience, intimidator, enforcer, procurer, or negotiator; develop friendly relationships with the first three, and keep the first two on-task. Know group-required behaviors, conversation topics and interests, and what maintains a group's cooperation and unity. Place a daily "do-now" activity on the board or students' desks to start upon arrival before lessons, preparing students for lessons and continuing ongoing group or team tasks and activities. Greet and converse with students, always respectfully. Pleasantly remind and encourage desired behaviors before classes begin. Engage group leaders in task preparations (equipment setup, writing assignments on boards or overheads, reading assignment directions, handing out worksheets): others follow. Include cooperative learning groups, and allow collaborative team answers. Recognize and reward good behavior. Never embarrass students in front of classmates, which provokes individual and group rebellion. Determine behavior reasons and functions, e.g., boredom, overly easy or difficult assignments, confronting or embarrassing students, favoritism, group leader behavior contagion, pre-existing issues, distracters, etc. Prevent escalation using low-impact interventions: interest in student work, encouragement, good-natured humor, physical proximity, touch, interrupting oneself mid-sentence and using the "teacher glare," reminding classes and groups of times they did well, and changing lesson presentation to become more interesting than any distraction(s).

PRODUCTIVE CLASSROOM ENVIRONMENTS FOR STUDENTS AT DIFFERENT DEVELOPMENTAL LEVELS

Teachers must take into account the developmental levels of their students to establish positive classroom environments for them. For example, teachers should not expect young children to begin preschool having already learned to share with other children. Teachers can model sharing and cooperation for them, and encourage and reward their imitating teacher examples as well as

51

spontaneous prosocial behaviors, which researchers have observed in young children. Teachers can also observe whether young students engage in unoccupied behavior; independent or solitary play; onlooker behavior; parallel, associative, or cooperative play; and influencing factors, e.g., how well children know each other, offer matching activities, and introduce experiences at the next higher level. Teachers can offer peer collaboration opportunities to older elementary and middle school students by assigning study buddies, partners for peer tutoring, working together, or think-pair-share and similar activities. Small groups can also be formed for planning, organizing, and implementing team or group learning projects, although teachers must remember that students have typically not developed social interaction skills to the extent of high school students, and so must guide them accordingly. In high school, teachers can extend productive learning environments beyond classrooms to surrounding communities, engaging students' abstract cognitive skills to promote respect, social conscience, and action through service projects.

RESPECTING DIVERSITY AND PROMOTING THE ACTIVE ENGAGEMENT OF ALL STUDENTS

Honor student experiences: create safe spaces, enrich curriculum using student experiences, and give students opportunities to learn from each other's perspectives and experiences. View different identity groups from asset-based orientations, let students define their own identities, and avoid or challenge stereotypes. Select texts reflecting demographics of and relevant to specific classes, and assign discussions or reflective writing about reading. Share personal anecdotes inviting student sharing. Student-centered classroom setups should include multicultural decorations or imagery reflecting our society's diversity and student backgrounds. Arrange furniture and materials to support comfort, ownership, dialogue, and collaboration. Structure classrooms for maximal student voice and participation. Involve students in setting norms and expectations, considering gender, language, and cultural and communication differences. Give students daily classroom jobs accommodating different learning styles, innovative student approaches, and real-life responsibility and work skills. Use gender-neutral categories and practices and let students choose group identifications. Build shared inquiry and dialogue through respect, trust, voice, humility, and active listening skills. Revisit participation norms: include and value small-group participation, written and artistic responses, and active listening as well as verbal communication. To create safe climates, actively teach emotional-social skills, work to create positive relationships, build community, prevent or intervene with bullying, focus explicitly on understanding and appreciating differences, practice and teach meaningful conflict resolution, and teach students to challenge exclusion and bias.

INSTRUCTIONAL STRATEGY FOR COMMUNICATING HIGH EXPECTATIONS

Experts (Marzano, 2010) advise: (1) as early as possible, identify students for whom you have lower expectations. Once formed, negative expectations are hard to admit and change. (2) Identify student similarities. Though teachers resist admitting they automatically form expectations based on student appearance, speech style, or ethnicity, research finds early expectations based on such characteristics. Expectation patterns do not indicate bigotry or racism when people actively work to keep biases from controlling their thoughts and behaviors. (3) Identify your differential behaviors toward low-expectancy students, which are far more important than your expectations. Students observe and make inferences based on teacher behaviors. Affectively, teachers make less eye and physical contact, smile less, and lightly or playfully converse less with low-expectancy students. Academically, they ask them less challenging questions, call on them less frequently, explore their answers in less depth, and reward less rigorous responses from them. (4) Consciously treat high-expectancy and low-expectancy students the same way. Affectively this is relatively easy, but academically more challenging: students habituated to low teacher expectations may experience discomfort when teachers challenge them more. However, ultimately this enables students to ask clarifying questions and risk communicating new ideas.

RESPONDING TO ALL STUDENT CULTURAL, LINGUISTIC, AND FAMILIAL BACKGROUNDS AND NEEDS

Students learn more when challenged by high teacher expectations, including open-ended questions and assignments requiring critical thinking skills. Explicitly teaching skills for studying, working with teachers, and completing college applications to students whose parents never attended college fills "cultural capital" gaps, preparing underrepresented students for college. Give students adult responsibilities for collaboratively contributing to planning, coaching, financial activities, etc. Diversity becomes a resource; students learn varied skills. Teacher knowledge and caring about individual students promotes their participation. Understanding student home cultures aids educator understanding of student behavior inside and outside classrooms. Encouraging active parental participation greatly supports student academic success through mutually understanding parent, classroom, and school expectations of teachers and students; helping parents converse to prepare children for classroom communication; helping parents pursue GED or ESL programs; and referring parents to community resources for arts, sports, science programs, and homework help. Eliciting and validating student background experiences, e.g., using semantic webbing to inform lesson planning and increase student engagement. Selecting curriculum for cultural relevance—student ethnic groups' contributions to US history and culture—enhances student self-esteem, makes lesson topics meaningful, and enables authentic, interactive language, literacy, and thinking skills. Culturally compatible social learning organization and communication expectations and norms make teaching and learning more effective.

DEVELOPING STUDENT ORAL AND WRITTEN COMMUNICATION SKILLS

<u>Oral</u>: the inside-outside circle – students, facing each other in two concentric circles, pair up; take turns speaking and listening; and rotate partners. Choral response – teacher asks a question, gives a signal, allows wait-time, says "Everyone..." and initiates signal, and the students respond in unison. Think-pair-share – students rehearse responses with partners, getting corrective feedback or elaboration help before whole-class sharing. Dialogic reading – teachers read books with individual students or small groups using "CROWD" prompts: sentence *completion*; asking questions requiring student text *recall*; *open-ended* questions about book pictures; *w-questions* (who, what, when, etc.) about pictures; and *distancing* book pictures and words to students' own life experiences. PEER prompts: *prompting* students to talk about text, *evaluating* responses, *expanding* responses, and *repeating* prompts at higher levels. <u>Written</u>: written responses, same answers – teachers ask questions; students write answers on whiteboards; teachers allow wait-time, say "Everyone..." and students hold up written responses. Written responses, varying answers – like same answers, but students check answers with partners, revise as needed; teachers call on individual students. Think-pair-share activities also enable students to get peer feedback about written responses before sharing them with the whole class.

COMMUNICATING EXPECTATIONS TO STUDENTS

By always behaving fairly and consistently in class, teachers model integrity for students, who understand better what is expected of them by witnessing the teacher meeting his/her own high expectations. Reinforce expectations daily, and repeat continually—sometimes through gentle reminders, other times interrupting instruction to discuss expectations as indicated—to change student attitudes. Support and inform student success through parent-teacher collaboration by communicating to parents your expectations of both students and parents. Prepare "achievement contracts" outlining mutual expectations students sign when the school year begins. Give students time to find answers themselves, only giving hints or ideas, not supplying correct answers immediately. Periodically, have students write about how they think they are doing and suggestions for improving the class. Always speak to students positively, emphasizing their ability to learn your instruction. Let students view you as a real person; get to know them. This attitude motivates some students to work harder to please teachers. However, avoid the trap of being students' friend; maintain authority as their teacher. Tell students exactly what you expect, making activity and assignment standards perfectly clear. Ensure every student knows s/he can earn high grades by working hard enough. Let students revise poorly-graded work, promoting mastery learning.

GOOD STUDENT-TEACHER INTERACTIONS AND RELATIONSHIPS

Good student-teacher interactions and relationships enhance classroom atmosphere. Research has generated a significant body of literature showing that the quality of teacher-student relationships influences student academic achievement and behavior. Teachers showing students respect and guiding them to respect each other encourage active learners. Learning more about students, interacting and communicating with them, and providing appropriate feedback establish relationships promoting effective teaching and learning. When students have opportunities to communicate with one another, they share responsibility for learning, discuss diverse viewpoints, and shape class direction. Classes with predominant lecture formats are frequently well-organized; teachers typically know content well and clearly present material, but student-student interaction opportunities are lacking. More student-focused classes present small-group, paired, and whole-class discussion opportunities. Tasks having multiple potential solutions or answers can shift lesson direction, generate deeper thought processes, and enhance discussion quality. Small-group discussions particularly enable enough chances to listen, consider others' ideas, and all students to have a voice. Gallery walks, professional communication projects, classroom data explorations, structured academic controversy discussions, open-ended teacher questions, cooperative learning methods, structured jigsaw activities and other discussion exercises, conceptual multiple-choice questions about lesson themes combined with peer instruction, and in-class think-pair-share assignments are all ways to improve classroom interactions.

TEACHER ENTHUSIASM

Numerous studies identify teacher enthusiasm as a behavior which prominently affects student learning. Research also shows that a combination of teacher enthusiasm and constructive feedback enables students to learn more. Investigators find more enthusiastic teachers spend more time on presentation and positive performance feedback. Enthusiastic teacher behaviors include the following: variation in vocal tone, pitch, volume, and pace is important. Teachers with monotonous, droning voices inspire student boredom. Teachers reflect their excitement with teaching and learning through their eyes by making eye contact with students; using their eyes expressively, e.g., raising eyebrows, opening eyes wide, etc.; and using their eyes as well as their ears to listen to students. Judicious teacher use of body language, gestures, and other nonverbal communications also communicate enthusiasm. Effective teachers clap hands, give high-fives, make OK signs, thumbs-up, etc. Sweeping arm motions, energetic body swinging, hand gestures, and facial expressions showing pleasure or displeasure, amusement, disappointment, and approval express enthusiasm. Moving around the classroom not only enables teachers to monitor students, but also makes them less predictable and boring. Nonverbal behaviors also reinforce verbally encouraging students.

INSTRUCTIONAL SKILLS AND PRACTICES THAT FOSTER INNOVATION

One expert (Hiam, 2011) identifies "five I's" as components of innovation curriculum: imagination, inquiry, invention, implementation, and initiative. Initiative is the foundation enabling the four others. Although daydreaming is discouraged in classrooms, teachers must learn creative expression skills to encourage student <u>imagination</u>. Master teacher collaboration with invention and creativity experts on curriculum design is one recommended solution. To fuel imagination, educators must connect seemingly unrelated topics, skill-sets, and ideas. Most inventions are innovative combinations of multiple domains. Writing across the curriculum, combining arts and sciences, etc., stimulates imagination. To encourage <u>inquiry</u>, students—not teachers—must ask most of the questions. Students must question, explore, and research curiously to innovate. Teachers can incorporate student question-asking exercises following activities into established curricula. Educators must challenge students to <u>invent</u> new and better ways to solve problems and apply learning to real life more often—weekly, not once or twice throughout school or only through science fairs. <u>Implementation</u> must also be increased: students get insufficient practice putting ideas into action, learning from mistakes, refining plans, and persevering. <u>Initiative</u> is more common in non-hierarchical and individualistic societies. Teachers need preparation for mentoring and coaching students in initiative-based learning; schools must support teachers' guiding students by supplying resources and valuing decentralized activities. Challenge, encouragement, and support develop self-efficacy and agency, promoting invention.

ASPECTS OF HOW INFORMATION AND COMMUNICATION TECHNOLOGY (ICT) SUPPORTS STUDENT LEARNING

Education is socially oriented and greater teacher-student personal contact is associated with quality education; ICT is compatible with and supportive of student-centered learning environments. ICT can have a transformational role in teaching and learning. Student-centered learning incorporates experiential and hands-on learning, self-directed student learning, and flexible learning activities. Students must not simply remember information to understand and apply it; they must question, grapple with ideas, discover things on their own, and construct knowledge, with teachers not being information presenters but facilitators—which also enhance their attention, interest, and motivation. Contrasting with teacher-directed learning, student-centered learning is more congruent with constructivist learning. Researchers conclude that to make complex information their own, students must individually discover and transform it. As facilitators, teachers provide opportunities for students to discover ideas, apply them, and consciously utilize their own learning strategies. Thus curriculum design is shifting from emphasizing informational content to competencies and how information will be used. Teachers use ICT in lesson planning and presentation; students use ICT for exploration, practice, and preparing assignments and presentations; administrators and teachers use ICT to complete administrative tasks more efficiently. Technology-facilitated, student-centered approaches facilitate multimedia presentation, enhancing learning; and encourage student responsibility for learning.

ASSISTIVE COMMUNICATION TECHNOLOGY

Some students have speech and language disorders; some with autism spectrum disorders, cognitive, or other disorders may have limited communication skills or be completely nonverbal. Because academic success depends on communication, assistive communication technology can help students overcome learning obstacles. Visual representation systems are effective for students having difficulty with auditory receptive and verbal expressive, but greater visual processing abilities. augmentative and alternative communication (AAC) systems and devices are assistive technologies facilitating communication. They range from low-technology to high-technology. Low-tech systems and devices are typically easy to use and inexpensive, including dry-erase boards, albums, folders, binders, and other ways of storing and transmitting images. Mid-tech systems and devices include simple, battery-operated or electronic voice output communication aids (VOCAs); overhead projectors; and tape recorders. High-tech systems and devices are more complex and expensive, including computers; software programs, e.g., speech-to-text and text-to-speech software; adaptive keyboards and other hardware; and more complex VOCAs. Special education student Individualized Education Programs (IEPs) must include any kinds of assistive technology required for them to achieve learning objectives and succeed in school. AAC systems and devices enable interactive student-teacher communication, effectively giving voices to students appearing to lack them.

INCLUSIVE CLASSROOM ENVIRONMENTS THAT PROMOTE EQUITY AND RESPECT FOR STUDENTS

When teachers initiate open dialogues, they engage students in a democratic process and provide opportunities for group decision-making requiring compromise, not competition. Teachers can rearrange classrooms to facilitate group decision-making and student interaction, e.g., sitting in circles, moving all desks to one side, reversing the room's front and back, and letting students learn from their decisions to democratize classroom spaces. They can assign group projects, which should be multidimensional, equally emphasizing textual, graphic, creative, presentation, and other components to address different skills and learning styles. Group projects also require member interdependency for successful completion, and vary in group composition. Rather than the typical forms of talking and writing for classroom sharing, wherein the loudest or fastest student gains the floor, teachers can vary protocols, e.g., visual art; paired and/or small-group sharing; allowing more time for reflecting, organizing their thoughts, and writing; and activities enabling thinkers, talkers, writers, and visual artists to share ideas. During class discussions, creating conflict regarding topics gives students more realistic experiences of complex issues. When students take various views of issues, not for competition or winning but for consensus, it affords experiences that demonstrate the complicated, messy nature of real-life democratic processes.

ORGANIZATION OF CLASSROOM DESKS

The classic rows and columns model of student desk placement facilitates a teacher-centered learning environment. All students are facing the teacher who, because of the orientation of student desks, is the fulcrum of every discussion. Eye-contact between dialoguing students in rows and columns of desks may be impractical or impossible. Students can be easily distracted and hard to monitor. Alternatively, teachers might choose to use a U-shaped configuration in which every student has a "front-row" seat. U-configurations are conducive to lively discussion; any student can maintain eye contact with any other student. However, U-configurations may not allow a teacher to reach every student's position. A third option might be pods of three or four. Although pods are not good for lectures and whole class discussions, they are particularly useful for student-centered pedagogy incorporating group projects or collaborative problem solving. Pods will most efficiently allow students to be in close proximity to their neighbors while also allowing a teacher more efficient access to every student and the opportunity to coach them through difficulties when they arise.

FLIPPED CLASSROOMS

A "flipped" classroom is a pedagogical model in which the traditional uses of time inside and outside of the classroom are reversed. Traditional time inside the classroom is devoted to teacher-centered (i.e., passive) activities like lecture. In a "flipped" classroom passive learning exercises are reserved for outside of the classroom. Either the teacher will record audio or video segments for students to consume at home or the teacher will make use of pre-existing content (e.g., Mometrix Academy or Khan Academy). Traditionally time outside of the classroom is devoted to more student-centered (i.e., active) experiences such as problem solving. Because traditional homework is generally individual, problems are often less challenging and less instructive. In a "flipped" classroom, problem solving and other traditional homework is done inside the classroom allowing students to collaborate on more challenging problems with additional assistance from the teacher.

In the student-centered "flipped" classroom model, student learning effectiveness is increased because both halves of the reversal facilitate deeper understanding. Students have more time to digest material at home and can pause or replay lectures as often as they like. In the classroom students can solve more challenging and instructive problems through the assistance of classmates and their instructor.

Classroom Management

COOPERATIVE GAMES FOR PRESCHOOLERS

Musical chairs, duck-duck-goose, and similar traditional games exclude children from the fun by emphasizing competition; cooperative games teach preschoolers to listen, follow directions, develop movement and problem-solving skills, and collaborate. "Help": balancing paper napkins on heads, children move about, freezing if napkins fall; touch to unfreeze classmates. "Robots": pairs take turns as robot and commander. Commanders direct robot movements to negotiate obstacles, reaching preset goals. "Balloon keep-up": outdoors or in gyms, children collaborate to keep balloons aloft. "Cooperative musical chairs," or "islands": when music stops, children share, not compete for, remaining chairs or islands. "Roll it": children sitting in a circle, feet touching, roll a ball to others, keeping it steadily moving; as children master rolling, add more balls. The goal is to keep control rolling as many balls as possible. "Cooperative duck-duck-goose": children walk in place in a circle; "it" chooses a goose, who walks, runs, or skips around the circle, chooses another goose, giving everybody a chance. "Cows and ducks" (also known as "frogs and dogs," "cats and snakes," or "chickens and goats"): whisper animal names in children's ears; each moos, quacks, etc., traveling; children making the same sounds group and move together like their animals. "Find it": call a color to moving children; first one finding something that color touches it; second holds the first's hand, etc., until all connect.

KINDERGARTEN SCHEDULES BALANCING ACTIVE VS. RESTFUL ACTIVITIES

Kindergarteners apparently have boundless energy, yet fatigue quickly; short attention spans demand change. Teachers therefore must alternate active movement with restful activities to prevent both exhaustion and boredom. Kindergarteners thrive through independently and cooperatively working with small peer groups, conversing, choosing activities, and practicing and applying skills they are learning. Organizing and managing learning environments via learning centers matches kindergartener identities and ways of learning, developing "learning to learn" skills of autonomy, initiative, persistence, creativity, resourcefulness, risk-taking, reasoning, and problem-solving. For example, children decide to create their own board game: they collect materials from learning centers; make a game board, markers, dice, rule book, timer, and (using a computer graphics program) design and print play money; use classroom word walls, charts, or ask the teacher and peers for help writing numbers and words; play their finished game repeatedly, and teach others how. This includes student choice; multiple learning domains; all curriculum areas; teacher guidance; and physical, cognitive, language, emotional, and social development. Skills play develops: literacy is learned through print concepts, reading, writing, linguistic communication, and purposeful writing; mathematics is learned through shapes, number concepts, language, predicting, measuring money, and time; science through exploring materials' physical properties and recycling materials; social studies through collaboratively developing, following rules, geographic thinking and mapping, and money use; arts through drawing and creating; and technology through basic computer use and software navigation.

ESTABLISHING AND MANAGING PRODUCTIVE CLASSROOM LEARNING ENVIRONMENTS

For students to take risks, engage effectively in challenging activities, and collaborate, teachers must make classrooms emotionally safe. Establish a rule for students and yourself, e.g., "We do not laugh at others, tell them to shut up, put them down, or insult them." For all students to participate, teachers must make classrooms intellectually safe. Habituate them to starting work whenever you say, "Please begin," starting with easier tasks, ensuring they know more challenging tasks will follow. Make tasks complex and rich, giving diverse students opportunities to excel and assist peers. Accomplished teachers establish active-learning environments—students thinking, speaking on-task, and working collaboratively near 100 percent of the time—and not only closely observe and measure the quantity (number or proportion of students, amount or proportion of time) of on-task behavior, but also the quality (strength, depth) of student attention and engagement. Newer teachers can start developing lessons and skills for creating ongoing active-learning environments by analyzing which activities really engage their students. Make participation inclusive every day by identifying some questions every student can answer simply; have them raise an index finger when ready; when all do, have them whisper answers or signal, e.g., thumbs-up, thumbs-down, or thumbs-sideways.

FACILITATING STUDENT CONFLICT RESOLUTION

Researchers (Crawford and Bodine, 2001) from the National Center for Conflict Resolution Education report most major conflicts escalating into violence begin as more minor incidents, e.g., unprovoked contact, using others' belongings without permission, etc. Few interactions are initially predatory, yet conflicts rapidly escalate. Most conflicts happen between or among acquaintances, either at school or in the home. Violent behaviors commonly share a retribution goal. Violent acts reflect not lack of values, but value systems accepting violence. Based on these findings, experts (Concordia Online Education, 2013) offer four instructional strategies for effective classroom conflict resolution. (1) Role-playing requires viewing behaviors from others' perspectives, teaches empathy, can add humor to resolving conflicts, and enable examining conflicts more objectively for insights about sources. (2) Have students track conflicts they partake in or witness over time, recording observations in journals (keeping identities anonymous), and discuss student reactions pros and cons. (3) Teach good listening behaviors: eye contact, not interrupting, asking questions, avoiding giving suggestions or advice, nodding and smiling as positive reinforcement, and restating messages in one's own words. (4) Have involved students write about conflicts, providing cooling-off or time-out periods and requiring reflection, including how they felt and retrospectively better alternatives. For example, listing three things they would do differently; model and teach using conflicts as learning opportunities.

STUDENT BEHAVIOR MANAGEMENT APPROACHES

To curtail misbehavior by exercising authority while eliciting minimal emotional distress, and additionally model reasonable, respectful use of authority, a "simple authority statement" promptly and authoritatively expresses disapproval as objectively as possible. If it is either unnecessary or unwise to confront students directly, teachers can redirect student energy to other behaviors, e.g., learning activities. This stops or interrupts misbehavior without provoking student hostility. For example, younger students or those with attention deficit hyperactivity disorder (ADHD) may not be intentionally misbehaving, but lack impulse control; redirection can restore on-task behavior without damaging a student's self-esteem or self-image. Reminding students calmly of assigned tasks enhances their understanding of target behaviors without communicating unpleasant emotions or judgments. Telling students what they should do "next time" gives students behavioral correction, but avoids discouraging them by focusing on the future instead of what they did wrong this time. Teachers can prevent responding inappropriately in haste by responding with silence to misbehaviors not significantly disrupting class. Silence also enables teachers to make mental notes and consider later which actions (if any) apply, and gives students opportunities for solving their own problems.

HELPING STUDENTS DEVELOP AND EXERCISE ACCOUNTABILITY, RESPONSIBILITY, AND SELF-REGULATION

Any time students display careless or unacceptable behaviors, responding with a "check yourself" message advises students to check what they just did, implicitly communicating that by checking, they will realize what they must do to correct their behavior. This reminds students to practice responsible self-management. When students, especially younger ones assigned individual classwork, become restless and off-task, settle them down and increase their concentration powers through a "clock focus" strategy: on the teacher's prearranged cue, students stand and watch the clock's second hand complete full one-minute rotations, choose how many to watch, and then sit down and resume working once the last rotation is complete. This provides scaffolding for students to develop better behavioral self-awareness, self-management, and self-control. Clock-watching, standing, and teacher cues can be gradually eliminated toward independent on-task self-regulation. Placing a student near the teacher in a "visitor's chair," with returning to regular seating allowed whenever the student feels ready to self-manage responsibly, avoids expressing disapproval. When upsetting emotions arise, model honest communication and interpersonal skills without provoking guilt or defensiveness through "I" statements about personal feelings and needs; avoid "you" accusations or comments.

CLASSROOM TRANSITIONS BETWEEN ACTIVITIES AND LESSONS

During transitions, students frequently become distracted, restless, and misbehave because the lessons and activities before and after, and the transitions themselves, are not standardized. Hence teachers must build bridges for students for efficient transitions. Bridges must be totally consistent, using the exact same prompts, cues, and steps in exactly the same way every time, so students can rely on them. This makes activities and events both before and after transitions immaterial because students always know what teachers expect of them. Teachers can design a uniform transition by chaining several mini-routines, which they must model, teach, and practice. (1) Signal for class attention. (2) Once all students are attending and making eye contact, start directions with "In a moment… (e.g., we're going to start another lesson)" to maintain student attention. (3) Give precisely detailed directions, including prearranging cues, e.g., "When I say 'go,' you will put away your materials, clean off your desks, and quietly meet me in the learning center." (4) Ask if anybody does not know what to do. Once everybody understands, use the prearranged cue (e.g., "go") to impel students toward learning objectives. (5) Observe student activity and confirm they are following directions. Avoid interrupting transitional activity. To address noncompliance, have students repeat the sequence.

CLASSROOM ROUTINES AND PROCEDURES

Effective teachers devote school's first few weeks not to teaching content, but to establishing classroom routines and procedures: research finds lacking these causes most behavior problems. Routines and procedures decrease instruction interruptions, increasing smooth class flow. Experts advise handing out copies of routines and procedures to every student on the first day, retaining extra copies for new students arriving later. Do not expect compliance after merely handing out and going over them once. Teach key procedures once or twice daily over several days. Explain reasons for each routine and procedure, model each for students, give students non-examples of compliance, and have one or more students model each. Go over less important routines and procedures, monitor, and reinforce as needed. Consistency is critical: teaching, monitoring, and reinforcing routines and procedures, and firmly establishing these over the first three weeks of school offers enormous benefits; do not give up after a few days. Routines and procedures include entering and exiting; starting work; attendance; lunch counts; announcements; lateness; absence; makeup classwork and tests; out-of-seat; teacher attention signal; assignments; pencil-sharpening;

59

collecting supplies; carrying, handling, or using equipment; forming groups; group, learning center, and independent work; lining up; restrooms; water or snacks; other school locations; submitting homework and papers; exchanging papers; getting help; asking questions; finishing classwork early; classroom visitors; fire drills, codes, and alerts; sudden illness or injury; checking out materials; end-of-day cleanup; organizing materials; changing classes; homework; dismissal.

THEORETICALLY BASED CLASSROOM BEHAVIOR MANAGEMENT AND MONITORING TECHNIQUES

Based on behaviorism, functional behavior analysis identifies functions, reasons, and purposes of behaviors, enabling identifying and teaching preferable replacement behaviors meeting the same needs and functions. For example, pay attention to students who raise their hands, but not to students who call out answers. Behavior contracts specify precisely what students agree to do, and for what reward. For example, a first-grader becomes bored with teacher read-aloud story time after three minutes, wandering around the room. An initial two-week contract specifies s/he stay seated and attend for five minutes in return for quietly playing with a toy nearby for the remaining time. Future contracts gradually increase attending durations. Contracts teach students verbal obligation, responsibility, self-control, self-monitoring, negotiation, and compromise. Applying the behaviorist principle that positive reinforcement is more powerful than punishment, and the social learning theory principle of vicarious or observational learning, the "catch them being good" technique involves identifying disruptive and non-disruptive behavior instances. At class beginnings, use a randomized beeper or recording; ignoring disruptive student behaviors (whenever possible) and praising nearby students displaying appropriate behavior. (Use time-outs for severe disruptions.) Instead of a teacher singling out or scolding a student and thereby reinforcing disruptive behaviors, students imitate praised classmates for similar rewards. This teaches students they receive no attention of any kind for disruptive behavior, but favorable attention for appropriate behavior.

ESTABLISHING DEVELOPMENTALLY APPROPRIATE BEHAVIORAL EXPECTATIONS OF STUDENTS

Teachers may observe some developmentally unrealistic parental expectations for their children, e.g., expecting them to "do as I say, not as I do" when their own behaviors are not positive models; expecting children to predict how present behaviors will influence future outcomes. While teachers should involve students in behavior changes, teachers cannot expect students to implement changes autonomously. Teachers should consider developmental, not chronological ages of students with cognitive delays or disabilities regarding appropriate expectations. School-aged children and adolescents generally share these cognitive characteristics: they are present-oriented, i.e., they focus on the here and now; usually cannot consider future consequences, which do not seem real to them; have difficulty anticipating consequences of their behaviors beforehand; can understand basic cause-and-effect relationships, provided these are sequenced closely together; have still-developing concepts of time, and difficulty with planning skills. Not standing out as different but fitting in—particularly for adolescents—is a major concern. Expect students to help track goals, not create and track them without reminders; and learn about and select among various choices, not independently make positive choices without concrete rewards and positive parental and adult models.

PROMOTING ETHICAL ACADEMIC WORK HABITS

Rather than threatening students with punishment for cheating, teachers can better promote ethical work habits by serving as positive role models; explaining and initiating class discussions about honesty and responsibility, how these are compromised by using others' work without giving credit, etc.; and praising and otherwise rewarding individual student work as examples of ethical academic practices. Research finds that, just as with academic expectations, having behavioral expectations high enough to challenge students, but realistic enough that they can achieve them with effort, is more effective than lowering expectations—including for mainstreamed students with disabilities. Rather than doing all the work for students in monitoring their behavior, teachers can engage students in monitoring processes and procedures, gradually teaching them the skills and responsibilities needed to self-monitor and self-regulate their behaviors. Teaching monitoring skills also supports teaching students about conflict management and resolution skills. Teaching students active listening skills reduces miscommunications, misunderstandings, and thus conflicts. Having them role-play opposing positions teaches empathy, objectivity, and insight; and advances conflict resolution, as does having them reflect and write about actual conflicts and potential alternative responses.

Communication

WAYS IN WHICH INDIVIDUAL STUDENT DIFFERENCES INFLUENCE CLASSROOM COMMUNICATION

Younger students need concrete terms, examples, and materials; older students can handle increasing abstraction. Teachers should give students of all ages concepts and vocabulary slightly above their current levels for challenge and growth. Both student and teacher communication can be influenced by gender, e.g., volunteering, calling out, or waiting to be called on regardless of knowledge and preparation. Teachers may perceive or treat identical student responses differently according to student gender and/or race, e.g., as assertive vs. aggressive or enthusiastic vs. disruptive. ELL and LEP students may know content, but lack English to express it, or feel uncomfortable with their ELP levels. Numerous studies show when teachers communicate high learning expectations for all students, including ELLs and students with disabilities, they perform better. Emotionally engaging anecdotes, examples, and connecting topics to student prior knowledge, experience, interests, value, and utility stimulate student curiosity and interest. To clarify class goals and purposes, focus on major points, letting students find additional information in other activities. Repeat key concepts and ideas, compare and contrast, summarize, use analogies and metaphors to aid student comprehension and emphasize importance. Structure classes logically: present problems, then develop solutions; frame topics as stories; chronologically recount processes and events; show interconnected ideas' relationship to overarching themes; share outlines; explicitly transition between topics using mini-summaries, connections, or verbal signals.

ENSURING ENGAGEMENT AND UNDERSTANDING OF ALL STUDENTS

Verbally, vary vocal speeds and tones to keep speech interesting to students. Vocal projection facilitates student hearing and also demonstrates teachers' confidence in what they say. Pausing strategically gets student attention, emphasizes transitions in topics, and gives students time to process information. Give ELLs and students with hearing, cognitive, learning, and other disabilities more wait time to allow for translating and processing teacher questions and formulating and translating their answers. Nonverbally, stand up straight and maintain eye contact to project confidence. Smiling communicates valuing what you say. While avoiding distracting apparel and excessive gestures, use movement to express enthusiasm, excitement, and energy. To help explain, illustrate, or clarify complex ideas, use media—not to distract from but to enhance instructional communication. Use chalkboards, dry-erase boards and overheads to demonstrate reasoning behind derivations, illustrate processes, and teach dynamically. Use slide presentations to organize varied visual, audio, and animated content, summarize ideas, and emphasize key points. Animations and videos offer sense of scale and illustrate dynamic processes. Audio can illustrate sounds associated with physical processes and introduce new, historical, or remote voices into classrooms.

Artifacts can incorporate real-life elements, and print or electronic handouts give students detailed images and information. Redundant and multimodal presentations benefit ELL, exceptional, and all students.

CLASSROOM QUESTION TYPES TO ACCESS DIFFERENT LEVELS OF BLOOM'S TAXONOMY

Levels, question types: knowledge and comprehension: what are the main points? What happened when...? Why did...? Application: can you think of other words meaning the same thing? Can you use this word in a different context? Can you think of another example of this? Does the same idea apply to...? Analysis: what effect does this achieve? Why do you think the author chose to do this? Does this fit into a pattern? What is suggested by...? How...? Why do you agree or disagree with this? Evaluation: which of these are most effective? What do you think of this? Do you think this works well? What are the strongest and weakest aspects of this? Synthesis: can you create your own version of this? How can you change the audience, features, etc. of this text? Where else can you see examples of this? Student activities, levels: analysis: debate a topic. Create text-based questions. Draw concept maps exploring connections. Mind-map aspects of a topic or text. Synthesis: study pastiche and parody. Analyze authors and writing styles closely; adopt styles. Experiment with genres, audiences, and text type features. Evaluation: devise reader expectation criteria for various text types. Apply assessment criteria to own and others' work.

ACTIVE LISTENING STRATEGIES

Effective, active listening strategies accomplish multiple goals: teachers show students they care about them, demonstrate attention to their concerns, make them feel understood, establish and develop student-teacher relationships, give students emotional connections with school, model effective listening strategies for students to learn and use, and motivate student learning. Research shows student learning motivation requires feeling connected. In active listening, the listener uses verbal and nonverbal signals, asks questions to clarify, and restates main points for the speaker to confirm or correct. Restating in one's own words can also involve interpreting the speaker's message. For example, a student says, "I don't like this school as much as my other school. People aren't nice." The teacher responds, "You're unhappy here?" The student answers, "Yes. I haven't made any friends. Nobody includes me in anything." The teacher responds, "You feel left out here?" The student confirms, "Yes, I wish I knew more people." Questions, restating, and interpreting clarify factual and emotional message content. When speakers refine listener interpretations, they feel heard, gain insights into their own feelings, and may experience catharsis. Listeners enhance their skills in focusing on speakers and considering implied meanings.

NONVERBAL COMMUNICATION

Open postures communicate receptivity; crossed arms and legs or similar averted body positions communicate the opposite. Ways of walking, sitting, standing, holding one's head, and subtle movements all convey attitudes and feelings. Gestures supplement speech, often unconsciously. Because different cultures assign different meanings to the same gestures, awareness is important to prevent misunderstanding or misinterpretation. Vocal tones and inflections express confidence, affection, anger, and sarcasm; and can even indicate understanding, agreement, and many more. Listeners also attend to speaker loudness, speed, and timing. Eye contact demonstrates interest in our culture; in some other cultures, it is perceived as confrontational and avoiding it shows respect. We communicate affection, attraction, or hostility as well as interest through eye contact; gauge others' responses; and maintain conversational flow. Facial expressions universally show happiness, sadness, anger, fear, surprise, disgust, and other emotions. Personal and social physical space or distance vary by individual, relationship, situation, and culture and can communicate intimacy, dominance, or aggression. Nonverbal communication informs verbal communication by repeating verbal messages; contradicting them; substituting for them; complementing or adding to them, e.g., patting on the back while verbally praising; accenting them; or emphasizing them, e.g., pounding the table, desk, lectern, dais, or pulpit with spoken points.

Questioning Techniques

QUESTIONING STUDENTS

Questions cognitively lower on Bloom's taxonomy—for knowledge and comprehension—are better when imparting or retaining factual knowledge. Open-ended, higher-cognitive questions—for application, analysis, evaluation, and synthesis—should be more than half of those used in higher grades, but elementary-grade students need smaller proportions of these too. Research finds combining higher and lower questions more effective than using either one exclusively. Studies show older students' on-task behavior, response length, number of relevant contributions and questions, peer interactions, complete sentences, and speculative thinking correlate positively with using greater than or equal to 50 percent higher-level questions. Teachers may still need to include explicit instruction, not just many more questions, for complex concepts. Pre-reading questions are effective with older, higher-ability, and interested students, but not with poor readers and younger students, who focus only on material for answering them. Slightly increasing wait-time promotes achievement. Studies find teachers paradoxically allow less wait time for students perceived as poor or slow learners than those perceived more capable. Teachers encourage participation by inviting student responses non-critically, addressing incorrect answers with redirection, and partial answers with probing—both explicit to student answers. Vague feedback, e.g., "Wrong, try again" is ineffective for achievement. Active listening restates student responses, helping clarify student understanding and meaning and encouraging participation.

Teachers ask students questions for varied purposes, e.g., actively involving students in lessons, regardless of questions' cognitive levels. "When did this author live?" "In what period is this work set?" Even low-level knowledge questions involve students as they consider and/or respond. "Why do you think the author did...?" require cognitively higher responses. Teachers might ask "Have you ever...?" or "Do you know anybody who...?" This relates textual events and experiences to students' own lives. Connecting new material to prior knowledge increases motivation and interest. Questions can evaluate preparation and check on assignment completion: in classes with many students not typically hesitant to speak, if nobody answers basic questions about assigned reading, they likely did not do it. Students completing math assignments successfully can likely answer specific questions about the operations they used or solutions they got, while those not doing or understanding it cannot. Questions develop critical thinking skills when requiring students to apply concepts and analyze them, separate inference from fact, evaluate or judge ideas and products, and synthesize components to construct new meaning. Questions help teachers review prior lessons to assess, increase, or refresh student comprehension and retention. They cultivate insights by making students think about topics, assess goal achievement, and stimulate independent learning.

Managerial questions facilitate classroom operations. Rhetorical questions reinforce or emphasize statements and ideas. Closed questions check retention and focus thinking. Open questions promote student discussion and interaction. Probing questions, based on student responses, require students to go beyond first answers. Clarifying: "What do you mean? Can you elaborate?" Increasing critical awareness: "What are you assuming? What are your reasons? What would an opponent say?" Refocusing: "Then what are the implications for...? Can you relate that to...? Let's analyze your answer." Prompting: "What's the square root of 94?" (Student: "I don't know.") "What's the square root of 100?" (Student: "10.") "Of 81?" (Student: "Nine.") "Then what do we know about the square root of 94?" (Student: "It's between nine and 10.") Redirecting to another student: "Do you agree? Can you elaborate on his/her answer?" Factual questions elicit simple

63

information, e.g., "Who wrote this? Who is the main character?" Or they elicit event sequences: "What are the steps for a bill to become law?" "How is hydrochloric acid produced?" "How did Robinson Crusoe react to discovering footprints?" <u>Divergent</u> questions have no right or wrong answer, eliciting exploration of possibilities and both concrete and abstract thinking. For example: "If the Spanish Armada had defeated England in 1588, how would it have changed history?"

Rather than remembering answers, students must figure out answers by higher-order questions, which require generalizing in meaningful patterns relative to facts. <u>Evaluation</u>: requires valuation, judgment, or choice via comparing things and ideas with established standards. Assuming equal resources, would you rate General Ulysses S. Grant or Robert E. Lee more skillful? Why? Which of these two books do you think contributed more to understanding this era? Why? <u>Inference</u>: requires deductive or inductive reasoning. Deductive: if gas temperature remains constant but altitude is increased 4000 feet, what happens to gas pressure? Why? Inductive: considering these world leaders' shared qualities, what can we conclude about required leadership qualities? Why? <u>Comparison</u>: requires discerning similarities, differences, contradictions, and non-relations – How are Social Darwinism and late-19th-century Supreme Court rulings related? How are Pericles' Funeral Oration and Lincoln's Gettysburg Address similar or different? Are clams and mussels the same? <u>Application</u>: requires transferring concepts and principles to different contexts – How did Germany's Weimar Republic demonstrate Gresham's Law? <u>Problem-solving</u>: requires using acquired knowledge, seeing relationships, relating parts to whole – Imagine you grew up thinking dogs were bad, but none bit you; how would you react now? Would the dog's characteristics matter? Explain the idea of prejudice using this example.

SUPPORTING STUDENTS IN ARTICULATING IDEAS

One strategy teachers use to support clear student expression is prompting. Verbal prompting: when a student does not know the answer to the teacher's initial question, the teacher asks additional questions to which the student does know the answers, leading the student to discover more about the answer to the original question. For example, a teacher asks a student a square root s/he does not know; the teacher asks the student two more square roots, one higher and the other lower; the student realizes the unknown answer is between the other two. Nonverbal prompting: nodding or making affirmative sounds and gestures indicating agreement to encourage continuing, pointing at objects or information to give hints, hand-over-hand guidance with manipulatives, etc. Restatement: repeating a student's message in the teacher's own words, either affirming the message or allowing the student to deny or correct the restatement or clarify the message. Student: "This assignment took me all night!" Teacher: "It was too hard?" Reflective listening statements mirror student messages, not just restating them but moreover interpreting implicit meanings. Student: "I will never get this right!" Teacher: "You feel frustrated?" Wait-time enables student processing: understanding questions, recalling information, formulating responses. Research finds three minutes optimal for factual or low-cognitive, and longer for high-cognitive questions.

METHODS THAT PROMOTE HIGHER THINKING LEVELS

(1) After assigned reading or video viewing, ask students what they would have done in a fictional character or nonfictional individual's situation. After students complete projects or assignments, have them write (a.) what they could have done differently, (b.) how, (c.) what they will do differently or additionally next time, and (d.) what they learned during the process of the project or assignment. These both require students to reflect on their experiences and articulate insights and thoughts. (2) In class discussion, have students identify a book or movie's main assumption(s). Ask how they know these are true. Have them research for proof or disproof, teaching the habit of questioning and investigating rather than simply accepting others' assumptions. (3) Have students compare similarities and contrast differences between or among books, movies, experiments,

natural phenomena, etc., guiding them to find relationships. Have them make cause-and-effect graphics identifying relationships among events or actions in history, fiction, or drama. Ask how fictional characters and historical or current figures influence(d) one another; how chemicals interact, causing reactions; why, etc. (4) Ask students to explain how information relates to current study topics. For examining validity, see (2) above; also have students test claims directly when feasible. (5) Review information identified in lessons and classwork, ask what students conclude based on it, and have them explain the logic leading to conclusions. (6) Assign applying newly-learned skills in other classes, field trips, homes, communities, and workplaces.

SETTING THE STAGE FOR EFFECTIVE CLASSROOM DISCUSSIONS

For teachers to get all students engaged in discussing a topic, they need to make it appealing. One way is connecting topics to existing student experience and knowledge, making them more personally relevant. Ask if they have encountered similar situations or felt similarly in other situations: find some commonality between the topic and every student's life experience. Teachers also need to show respect for all student opinions. Experts note teachers' natural inclinations to evaluate, approve or disapprove, and judge student contributions, increasing student fears against expressing thoughts. To create climates welcoming participation, teachers must suspend judgment; instead of responding with "Right," "Wrong," or "That wasn't what I was thinking about," etc., they can respond, "Tell me more about that," "Thank you for sharing your ideas with us," etc. Asking students to elaborate without judging makes them feel safe to progress in their thinking and share it. This teacher acceptance establishing safety also supports student risk-taking. In safe, non-threatening, non-judgmental atmospheres, teacher acceptance encourages students to express potentially controversial or minority views. Making all students feel safe and invited to participate facilitates collaboration: teachers model respecting others' ideas; students with non-judgmental teachers are less likely to fear classmates' judgment.

Assessment, Instruction, and Disciplinary Literacy

Curricular and Instructional Planning

CURRICULUM SCOPE AND SEQUENCE

In curriculum design, curriculum scope is the breadth and depth in which it covers content in each subject; clearly identified learning objectives reflecting local, state, and national standards; or how coherent curriculum is made through instructing basic concepts across several years of content coverage. Scope includes both how much material teachers must cover on any specified topic, and how much teachers should expect students to accomplish resulting from instruction. Sequence is the order in which scope is taught. If educators fail to structure curriculum scope and sequence deliberately, they risk having students miss significant learning when instruction is delivered without adequate planning. As examples, elementary school teachers might use a curriculum organizer table or chart where they enter titles and descriptions of each learning unit by time period, and the subject focus of each unit (e.g., arranged horizontally in columns). In the first column, before the series of units per time period, they can label cells vertically to enter main ideas, i.e., core student understandings; key concepts and questions to focus learning; teacher focus, i.e., unit goals like language development, group work, a culminating activity, etc.; fundamental content; subject foci, e.g., literacy, math, and respective programs, tasks, texts, and resources to use.

Whereas scope represents breadth and depth of content coverage and learning objectives, sequence represents presenting material in logical order. Sequencing reflects the philosophy that students should be instructed starting with concrete concepts, becoming progressively more abstract throughout successive grade levels. After establishing scope, educators must determine when to teach it. This is important when certain learning is often dependent on previous other knowledge, e.g., understanding certain science or geography concepts requires certain numeracy skills. Even when some learning experiences are not reliant on mastering prerequisite knowledge, curricula may be sequenced instead according to increasing complexity, e.g., in science subjects; logical progression, e.g., from the local environment to the global environment in social studies; or psychological valence, e.g., from immediate to more distant interests in vocational education. Teachers must carefully sequence instruction, both within and across key learning areas (KLAs). For example, "reading effectively" would precede "writing effectively" in a curriculum sequence represented by a curriculum map showing English Language Arts (ELAs) taught by KLA because receptive language like listening and reading develops before expressive language like speaking and writing. Critical text interpretation follows reading and writing. Similarly, understanding and applying numbers precedes selecting and utilizing measures.

The scope of a curriculum refers to all of the content it will include within a specified length of time. The curriculum sequence refers to at which points during the time range specific parts of the scope of learning will occur. In other words, educators must decide which content should be taught during certain grade levels, or to certain classes or student groups. Teachers must also determine sequencing within work units, courses, and school years. Hence scope and sequence support maximal student learning, as well as providing continual opportunities for students to learn. By coordinating the scope of curriculum content and the sequence of curriculum instruction, educators give order to their delivery of curricular content. For teaching and learning to be effective, the important parts of all subjects must be included in scope, and must be delivered in the right order for students to benefit. By mapping curriculum scope, teachers can ensure they integrate the state and district learning standards guiding their curriculum. By mapping sequence, they can ensure they address curricular principles as well as matching knowledge prerequisites, increasing complexity, logical progression, psychological preferences, or other factors influencing temporal order.

Curriculum scope and sequence work together to furnish instruction with an organized structure which enables students to receive the maximum numbers of opportunities to learn and to take advantage of these to learn the most that they can. For educators to overlook important parts of subject content instruction is entirely too easy without the organizing structure of curriculum scope and sequence. It is also much more difficult to deliver instruction depending on previous learning, and avoid repeating material over grade levels, without planning sequence in advance. Most states develop scope and sequence directly from state-level standards. Some school districts design curriculum frameworks, which provide the scope of content and sequence in which to teach it. It is also popular for state education departments and district curriculum departments to divide learning sequences into developmental strands or bands. A common method of organizing a curriculum scope is to divide it into key learning areas (KLAs) or integrated themes used as curriculum organizers. Depending on their size, structure, and sector, different schools approach curriculum scope and sequence development through different processes. Some states define scope and sequence in certain subjects, but leave this to individual districts in others.

STANDARDS-BASED LEARNING

In standards-based education, all grade levels and subjects have clear learning goals; all instruction and assessment are aligned to these because the strongest school-level influence on student achievement is opportunity to learn: students are unlikely to learn specific content without opportunity. Students are given multiple opportunities to demonstrate achievement because reading, math, social studies, and science should be treated like PE and music: poor initial performances do not receive low grades, but rather require repeated practice until students master the skills. Formative assessments, giving feedback and promoting growth, are emphasized because research shows effective feedback is the strongest single classroom instructional change increasing learning and achievement. Rubrics and scoring guides are consistently employed because they enable teachers to give students better, criterion-referenced feedback about specific skill and knowledge levels, not merely norm-referenced feedback via percentage scores. This helps teachers evaluate their learning objectives as well as advance student achievement. Teachers regularly report student progress toward learning goals because specific, formative, more frequent feedback than annual standardized tests critically affects teacher conscientiousness and effectiveness with initiatives developing new reporting practices and forms; with instructing, assessing, and encouraging students; and student success. Instructional activities represent the "how," standards the "what" and "why" of school programs.

The US Department of Education (ED) funds and supports high curriculum standards in public schools, but does not itself develop them; individual state education departments do. ED has given over $350 million in funds to a consortium of the Council of Chief State School Officers and National Governors Association for developing the Common Core State Standards (CCSS). Most US states have voluntarily chosen to adopt these standards. The CCSS has a website with information. Additional sites with information on federal support of other state educational initiatives include a site on the Every Student Succeeds Act (ESSA, replacing No Child Left Behind, or NCLB) flexibility, whereby ED enables states to develop their own accountability systems; sites about the federal Race to the Top initiative and its assessment; and a webpage with US Secretary of Education Arne Duncan's speech about high standards. CCSS are concepts students should know and understand;

school districts develop specific curricula, and teachers plan specific lessons, to help students master standards. Districts and schools have traditionally had printed copies of their state standards; today, these are typically also published online, the easiest way for teachers to access them—including any updates, which can be posted electronically more easily and frequently than printed.

While the abundance of federal-level and state-level curriculum standards might seem to facilitate teachers' preparing relevant classroom curricula, it can overwhelm educators trying to design standards-based learning units. However, teachers discover that standards enable more curricular focus, refinement of their previous work, clearer communication of expectations to students, and enhanced learning—provided some model and processes for classroom standards application, many of which are available today. Standards articulate clear expectations for what all students should know and be able to do—regardless of gender, minority status, socioeconomic status, history of academic success (or failure), and previous access or lack thereof to any kinds of educational opportunities—while addressing school constituencies' varying needs. Standards give states common referents for assuring coordinated functioning of educational system components across schools and districts; offer parents, businesses, and community stakeholders a common language for discussing educational processes and communicate shared learning expectations, enabling more effective partnering in education; provide impetus and focus for new school programs and innovations in organizing content, delivering instruction, and planning assessment; make teachers design more intentional, purposeful learning of important content; and for all students, clearly identify performance expectations and means for meeting them; promote more equitable, challenging, and rewarding experiences; and improve performance.

COGNITIVE, AFFECTIVE, AND PSYCHOMOTOR DOMAINS

The cognitive domain represents mental skills, i.e., facts, information, ideas, and concepts that one can learn, understand, and apply. Among knowledge, skills, and attitudes that a learner can acquire, the cognitive domain corresponds most to *knowledge*. The affective domain represents emotional *attitudes* that one can develop and apply, with respect to the self and others. The psychomotor domain represents physical *skills* that one can learn and apply. For example, when a student reads some information about physical exercise, understands it, analyzes it, compares it with other information sources, judges it according to established criteria, and writes a paper about it, these activities are in the cognitive domain. When this student finds value in exercise knowledge, demonstrates this by voluntarily participating in athletic events, and becomes an accomplished athlete in a certain sport, these activities are in the affective domain. When this student watches, copies, practices, and perfects the specific physical skills required for his or her preferred sport, these activities are in the psychomotor domain.

BLOOM'S TAXONOMY

Bloom's 1950s taxonomy originally included levels or categories of knowledge, i.e., recalling learned information; comprehension, i.e., grasping, restating, and explaining meaning; application of knowledge to new and different situations; analysis, i.e., separating components of material and showing relationships among components; synthesis, i.e., bringing separate concepts and ideas together to create new wholes and relationships; and evaluation, i.e., judging the value or worth of information according to established criteria. Anderson and Krathwohl's 2001 revision changed these nouns to verbs: remember, understand, apply, analyze, evaluate, and create—also switching the order of evaluate from after synthesis to before create. Instructional objectives should include learning activities that address each of these categories, sequenced correspondingly from remembering to creating to reflect the hierarchy's progressively increasing difficulty. Krathwohl and Bloom's taxonomy in the affective domain covers receiving, or attending to something;

68

responding, or showing new behaviors influenced by experience; valuing, or showing definitive commitment or involvement; organization, or integrating new values into priorities; characterization by value, or behaving consistently with new values. Dave (1970), Simpson (1972), and Harrow (1972)'s psychomotor taxonomies include observing a physical action or event; imitating another's action; practicing repeatedly; and adapting, i.e., fine-tuning performance. In all three domains, these taxonomies progress sequentially from basic to higher levels, as corresponding instructional objectives should.

OBSERVABLE BEHAVIOR

Educational interest in observable behaviors was influenced by behaviorist learning theory, which proposed that because internal mental or emotional states could not be externally observed or measured, the study and modification of behavior should be confined to observable behaviors, i.e., actions or states of being that others could outwardly observe an individual producing. However, because only observable behaviors could be accurately measured, these were the only kind that could be changed through behavior modification techniques based on operant conditioning principles. In applying Bloom's taxonomy to cognitive learning objectives, the same proposition is embraced in that only action verbs are appropriate. For example, under the second category of Understanding, the verb *understand* itself is not found because it is internal, hence impossible to quantify; action verbs under Understand include *describe, differentiate, discuss, cite examples of, demonstrate use of, identify, select, tell*, etc. Thus a good instructional objective would not require a student simply to know or remember something, which requires assuming the student knows or remembers, but rather to *recall, name, list,* or *repeat* it because these demonstrate the student's knowledge and memory in ways that others can observe.

MEASURABLE OUTCOMES

Learning objectives must be not only observable, meaning teachers and others can see, hear, or otherwise observe evidence a student has learned something; but also measurable, meaning there is some way to quantify the behavior demonstrating learning. Behaviorist learning theory pointed out only observable behaviors can be measured, therefore changed. As a corollary, it has demonstrated that by nature, observable behaviors can nearly always be measured because if people can observe another's behavior, they can also find a way of measuring it. To be measurable, outcomes or results must be specific. For example, "The student will use correct grammar" is not measurable because it is too vague, not specifying what or whether all or some percentage of grammar must be correct, etc. But the objective "The student, given a sentence written in the present or past tense, will be able to rewrite it in future tense with no contradictions (e.g., 'I will see them yesterday') or errors in tense" is a measurable objective, specifying the condition (given a sentence written in present or past tense) and behavior (rewrite it in future tense). These are elements of the ABCD method—*audience, behavior, conditions, degree of mastery* required (e.g. 100 percent, 95 percent, 90 percent, etc.).

EVALUATING TECHNOLOGICAL AND OTHER INSTRUCTIONAL RESOURCES

State education departments typically publish guidelines for their districts to evaluate instructional materials according to state criteria, aligned with state content standards and curriculum frameworks for each subject. In some instances, educators tasked with evaluating new instructional materials for certain subject domains (e.g., mathematics or science) and/or grade levels (e.g., preschool, elementary, middle, or high school), after studying various sets of evaluation criteria, found them all inadequate and decided to develop their own criteria instead. Some examples of elements found important to address and overlooked by existing criteria include: need for more authentic assessment practices within the materials evaluated; evaluation criteria focusing on technology's overall role in a specific instructional unit, rather than only criteria for evaluating individual pieces of technology; and criteria for evaluating whether an instructional unit is practical, e.g., whether teachers in schools with typical insufficient funding, overloaded classrooms, long hours, etc. can effectively implement the materials. Educators have consulted resources like standards published by national organizations for their discipline, e.g., the National Council of Teachers of Mathematics, National Council of Teachers of English; research articles and books on subject-specific assessment; local districts; and teacher and researcher experiences.

LEARNING RESOURCES VS. LEARNING MATERIALS

Teaching resources include locations and means for finding teaching materials, e.g., websites, libraries, stores, etc.; intangibles, e.g., theories of learning or education, published research articles and books, or support from colleagues; and materials. Teaching materials most often mean concrete objects, e.g., worksheets, workbooks, or manipulatives including tools and games that students can physically handle and interact with to learn new concepts and skills. For example, younger students can use blocks to learn counting. Teaching materials should ideally be customized to the subject content, students in the class, and teacher using them. Students achieve more when their learning is supported by materials. For example, students learning a new skill in class have significant opportunities to practice it using a worksheet. This not only affords necessary repetition, but also enables independent student exploration of knowledge. Learning materials help structure lesson planning and delivery, especially in earlier grades, by guiding teachers and students through regular routines, e.g., having a weekly vocabulary game relieves teachers of pressure while giving students needed practice with new words taught weekly, as well as fun. Materials also facilitate differentiating instruction for individual students. Some teachers make their own; many more are available online, most free.

THEMATIC INSTRUCTION

Thematic instruction reflects a holistic belief that learning is best in the context of a coherent whole, and connected to real life. Teaching thematically organizes curriculum around overarching themes—teaching around experiences, not isolated disciplines. For example, a teacher might design a unit wherein students explore a broad environmental theme including river basins, rain forests, communities, energy use, etc., simultaneously integrating reading, math, science, and social studies into each lesson. Thematic instruction's goal is teaching these cognitive skills within the context of real-world topics, combining both enough broadness to enable creative exploration and enough specificity for practical application. Teachers and students first choose a theme, typically around a broad concept—weather, democracy, etc.; or a large, integrated system such as an ecosystem, city, etc. They then organize their core curriculum's content knowledge and process skills learning objectives around the theme, e.g., with river basins, literature could include Mark Twain or other authors' books involving rivers; science could include floods, weather, etc.; social studies, the characteristics of river communities; math, calculating water volume and flow. Designing instruction includes combining subject hours, adjusting class schedules, inviting outside experts, planning field trips, team-teaching, etc. Teachers also encourage and assign student projects, which are naturally compatible with thematic units.

INTERDISCIPLINARY INSTRUCTION

Interdisciplinary or cross-curricular instruction applies knowledge, principles, and values to multiple school disciplines and subjects concurrently. Disciplines and subjects are often related through central themes—thematic units have been identified as interdisciplinary teaching's organizational structure—or experiences, processes, topics, problems, and issues. Schools first integrated listening, speaking, reading, writing, and thinking as language arts components, thereafter trending to more widely integrating all curriculum subjects through unifying themes. Cross-curricular instruction is often a remedy to recurring educational problems like instruction in isolated skills and fragmentary learning; and a means of supporting goals like giving students more relevant curricula, teaching reasoning and thinking, and facilitating skills transfer to other contexts. It enables students to apply and integrate knowledge across subjects, which isolated skills instruction does not; raises student motivation and engagement when, through participation, students realize the value of the knowledge; and supplies conditions for effective learning. Subject teachers collaborate, for example, a PE and math teacher may combine math skills of counting and graphing with PE skills of throwing, catching, hitting, and kicking balls, including student practice and teacher assessment of both physical and numerical techniques. Elementary classroom teachers may combine multiple subjects in one thematic unit, e.g., using a bean-growing project to teach science via botany, the life cycle, research questions, and observation; mathematics via counting and measuring; and English-writing reports.

Teachers of different subjects collaborate to plan interdisciplinary instructional units, generating topics, and developing instruction and assessment. For example, math and PE teachers have students count the number of times they can hit paddleballs consecutively, practice graphing them, and practice paddleball skills. Teachers might assess counting skills observationally, assess paddleball skills by observing student demonstrations, and assess graphing skills by reviewing handmade or computer graphing assignments. Elementary-grade teachers integrate English, math, and science, connecting classroom plant study to forest field trips, having students write about these connections. Vocational or technical high school students restored a historic landmark, integrating what they learned in math, journalism, and shop classes—applying learning to a real-life experience. Students also transferred learning, using creative, original thinking: after successfully completing the restoration project, they generated ideas for additional school and community service projects integrating various school subjects, presenting their ideas to teachers. A social sciences and math teacher co-taught students using ancient Egyptian computation techniques, comparing them to modern-day math. Students discussed ancient math in historical context, reflecting on past and present and what "modern" meant. Teachers find students gain more complex understandings of disciplines and their relationships through interdisciplinary instruction.

LESSON PLAN THAT BUILDS ON PRIOR STUDENT KNOWLEDGE

One model (Cunningham, ASCD, 2009) contains eight steps. (1) Introduction: state overall lesson reason or purpose. Introduce main idea, topic, and key concepts. "Hook" student attention with a challenge or a quirky or amazing fact, etc. Explain lesson relevance for extending prior knowledge and promoting future learning. (2) Foundation: confirm prior student knowledge, either by clarifying or double-checking. Connect the lesson to standards. Tell students precisely what they will know and be able to do from the lesson. Include additional information, preparing the main lesson. Introduce essential vocabulary visually, aloud, in reading, and in writing. (3) Brain activation: clarify concepts; add information through probing questions, engaging students and building background. Brainstorm concepts, ideas, and possibilities, enabling students to clarify and expand thinking. Plan activities revealing misconceptions; correct or clarify these. (4) Body of new information: present the main lesson via whole-class lecture, teacher-supervised small-group, or partner activity, including teacher input of new and key points, reading, problem-solving, and active student participation with specific goals. (5) Clarification: check for understanding with sample questions, problems, or situations; guide learning; give practice. (6) Practice and review: supervise practice; work with students. (7) Independent practice: supervise, selecting further strategies for small groups needing them; others work independently. (8) Closure: connect lesson steps and information; summarize; discuss lesson in larger learning context; have students write or explain learning, ideas, questions, and problems.

EIGHT STEP LESSON PLAN

Introduction – 5 minutes: teacher writes Lincoln's quotation of the Declaration of Independence's "All men are created equal"; students discuss potential 1860s meaning. Foundation - 5-10 minutes: brief discussion about slavery, men and women, educated and uneducated white men; the goal is explaining the significance of the Gettysburg Address to American history and today's voting rights. Key vocabulary words and phrases include *conceived in liberty; dedicated; proposition; equal.* Brain activation – 5 minutes: ask what the words mean, why Lincoln phrased it thus, what would happen today with this speech, what the speech informs us about 1860s America, how the phrase connects to the American history then and now, and how the first paragraph leads to the ideas in the second and third paragraphs. Body of new information - 10-15 minutes: referring to specified textbook pages and illustrations, discuss the Battle of Gettysburg. Teacher writes key ideas or notes on overhead; students add to history notes. Clarification - 5-10 minutes: students write reflections on text. Practice and review - 5-10 minutes: small-group discussions of the battle's and speech's significance, Lincoln's speaking on the battlefield, and its turning point in the Civil War. Independent practice - 10 minutes: students select and write brief summaries of two or three other key phrases from the speech. Closure - 5 minutes: students share phrases with partners, write favorites with short explanations on "exit passes," and the teacher collects these to assess understanding and inform tomorrow's lesson.

TECHNOLOGY APPLICATIONS WHEREBY TEACHERS CAN MORE EFFICIENTLY COMPLETE TASKS

Today, mobile applications abound to save teachers time, effort, and space on administrative tasks, freeing more of their attention for teaching and helping students learn. One example is an app for the iPad called Paperless Teacher (Evon Technologies). It automates and customizes processes of taking attendance, planning lessons, creating rubrics, and entering grades in grade books. It weighs each gradable element, e.g., attendance, participation, assignments, tests, and homework, according to teacher specifications, and then automatically calculates grades. It enables teachers to email these results directly to students and parents. This eliminates the repetition of entering names, calculating numbers, and entering them manually one at a time. Users can easily share common data using this app; hence teachers can exchange student profiles or lesson plans anytime, remotely and effortlessly. The app features an integrated Dropbox framework, preventing data loss and enabling users with various other devices to access data. Its Message User Interface enables exporting and emailing data sharing in format allowing other users to open data directly in their apps. This facilitates notifying students of tests, assignments, schedules, etc. Semester planning and grade setting are customizable for multiple semester plans or grading systems. A protection feature keeps data safe for separate users.

ROLES THAT SPECIAL EDUCATION TEACHERS CAN CONTRIBUTE TO COLLABORATIVE TEACHING ACTIVITIES

Special education teachers have great expertise in how to adapt curriculum and instruction and provide classroom modifications and accommodations for students with various disabilities who receive special education and related services. They can share knowledge with classroom teachers about instructional considerations for each category of disability, individual special education students, and their needs. Since the Individuals with Disabilities Education Act (IDEA) legislation first mandated education in the least restrictive environment possible for students with disabilities, inclusive education has increased and mainstreaming is more prevalent today. This presents challenges to regular classroom teachers, and advantages to collaborating with special education teachers, who can help integrate Individualized Education Program (IEP) goals into daily classroom instruction. In addition to knowing more techniques and strategies for teaching students with

72

special needs, they also are likely familiar with individual special education students at their school to inform classroom teachers from experience about particularly effective and ineffective specific techniques. They can show new teachers how task analysis, chaining, and shaping enable intellectually disabled students to learn complex behaviors; advise newly mainstreaming teachers on practical matters like classroom logistics with wheelchairs and assistive devices, teaching other students device and disability etiquette; and help teachers coordinate varied adaptations, modifications, or accommodations to prevent their interference with each other.

COLLABORATION BETWEEN LIBRARY MEDIA SPECIALISTS AND CLASSROOM TEACHERS

Library media specialists are experts at locating information and resources, among other things. As information specialists, they contribute skills for accessing and evaluating information resources in different formats for both students and teachers. They function as models for students, showing them strategies for finding, accessing, and evaluating information that is available in their school library media centers and outside them. Due to the impact of technology development on library media center environments, library media specialists also keep up with mastering the newest, continually evolving electronic resources, and pay ongoing attention to the quality, character, and ethical use of information in traditional and electronic formats. They are instructional partners collaborating with teachers, other educators, and administrators. They identify connections among school expectations for student learning, student achievement, school curriculum content, student information needs, and available information resources. They work closely and cooperatively with teachers in designing authentic learning activities and assessments. Collaborating with teachers, they help integrate information and communication skills to meet content standards. They have knowledge of current research literature in teaching and learning, and expertise for its application. They help students find information from multiple sources, evaluate it critically, and use it to support learning, problem-solving, and critical thinking.

GIFTED AND TALENTED TEACHERS

Teachers of the gifted and talented have specialized training in instructing this population. Considering mainstreaming requirements, increasing demographic diversity, school underfunding, staff shortages, and oversized classes, classroom teachers are challenged to meet all student needs in one class. They may have to spend large portions of time on differentiated instruction to students with disabilities, in addition to satisfying whole-class accountability requirements to cover enough required curriculum content and enable every student to perform to standards on high-stakes, large-scale tests to meet Adequate Yearly Progress (AYP). Some teachers having limited or no experience with gifted students may assume they can work more independently and need less teacher attention due to their high IQs and/or special talents. However, advanced students are frequently bored or impatient with the pace of instruction for average student abilities. They can demand more material to learn, at faster rates; more in-depth, extended, or enriched content; answers to their pressing questions; and advice, guidance, and feedback even as they work independently on projects. Teachers specializing in giftedness and creativity can help take some pressure off classroom teachers, by both working directly with these students, and giving teachers ideas for enrichment activities and coordinating these with classroom units and lessons.

COLLABORATION BETWEEN PARAPROFESSIONALS AND CLASSROOM TEACHERS

Teachers today not only must differentiate instruction for individual students with a diverse range of needs, they frequently must also do this with excessive class sizes. Teachers' aides and other paraprofessionals provide vital help with these demands. Their collaboration with teachers includes not only concrete assistance like taking attendance; physically setting up activities; helping with adaptive devices, distributing materials, snacks, etc.; but also scoring tests, grading papers; participating in training they receive from teachers, specialists, therapists, etc.; and then working

73

one-on-one with individual students to deliver differentiated instruction and help students needing individual supervision for classroom tasks. They may be trained by school psychologists to observe students and collect behavioral data, relieving teachers of these additional duties. In mainstreamed classes, teachers cannot always work with all individual students enough. Paraprofessionals are invaluable in making it possible for more students to receive more individualized attention, supervision, and instruction more regularly, for longer time periods, and more often. They can enable more students to achieve their individual educational goals.

INDIVIDUALIZED EDUCATION PROGRAM (IEP) TEAM MEMBERS

Student IEP team members can include any or all the following and more: parents; special education teachers; classroom teachers; audiologists; occupational, physical, speech-language, activity, and/or other therapists; American Sign Language (ASL) interpreters; orientation and mobility specialists; school social workers; school nurses; school psychologists; counselors; advocates, etc. Parents collaborate with teachers, sharing their experience with their children, children's histories, personal preferences, effective behavioral and learning techniques; and may volunteer to help in the classroom and/or at school functions. By advocating, they help teachers meet children's special needs. Special education teachers help address IEP goals by incorporating related instruction and activities into daily classroom lessons and routines; and offer expertise in differentiated instruction, teaching, and behavior management strategies. Audiologists contribute knowledge of hearing loss, hearing aids, classroom accommodations, and modifications. Therapists add expertise in their respective disciplines—physical therapists (PTs) make or adapt devices, provide targeted postural and large-muscle exercises; occupational therapists (OTs), fine-motor, ADL development; speech language pathologists (SLPs) incorporate language development into instruction; ASL interpreters translate between hearing and deaf or hearing-impaired students and families; orientation and mobility (O&M) specialists help blind and visually impaired students navigate classrooms, schools, and communities. Social workers provide student and family histories, coordinate special services, and help families locate and access resources. School nurses help with medications, monitoring diabetic diets and blood checks; school seizures, accidents, and emergencies, etc. Psychologists administer, score, and interpret IQ tests; provide behavior management plans and training; data collection and analysis, etc.

RESOURCES WHEREBY TEACHERS AND SCHOOLS CAN PROVIDE ENRICHMENT FOR STUDENTS

The Stanford Mobile Inquiry Learning Environment (SMILE) uses technology innovatively for educational enrichment. This interactive learning model includes mobile software for learning management, plus its own server, which can run on a battery and functions as a Wi-Fi connection, router, and storage device. At schools adopting SMILE, students can exchange questions and ideas with other students worldwide; and teachers can instantaneously collect summaries of learning data analytics. Another American enrichment resource is Students for the Advancement of Global Entrepreneurship (SAGE), a program emphasizing civic responsibility and duty for high school students, who form teams and develop social enterprise businesses (SEBs) or socially responsible businesses (SRBs), which compete in the annual SAGE World Cup. An American remediation resource is Teach for All, a model teaching lifetime educational advocacy and leadership foundations at both local and policy levels, training and developing effective leaders to change education for the most disadvantaged students; and promoting innovation by encouraging best practice sharing. PenPal Schools teach six-week courses about world issues, giving students global partners to share multicultural understandings. Its Pay-What-You-Want policy enables low-income student participation. Many other resources are available in other countries or are shared among the US and other nations.

74

VERTICAL ALIGNMENT AND HORIZONTAL ALIGNMENT

Vertical alignment is the process through which courses are sequenced across a curriculum. What a student learns in a 4th grade math course will prepare him or her for what he or she will learn in a vertically aligned 5th grade math course. Horizontal alignment is the process through which different sections of the same course are standardized such that what one student learns in a section of Biology with Ms. Smith is similar (though not exactly the same) as the material learned by a student in a section of Biology with Mr. Johnson. Typically horizontal alignment is addressed locally, perhaps through professional learning communities in coordination with district guidelines for course content. Vertical alignment is often developed on a state or even national level. School districts develop their course outlines in coordination with standards adopted from either the state or national level. Educators at the state level decide the general scope of the schools' curricula and choose yearly statewide assessments for students. Educators at the district level adapt the state course guidelines to fit local communities and teachers implement those curricula in their classrooms. The success of the entire system is dependent on educators at all levels working collaboratively in the best interests of the students.

COGNITIVE THEORY

In cognitive theories, e.g., Piaget's theory of cognitive development, the individual seeks to establish and maintain <u>equilibrium</u> or balance to keep things the same, i.e., homeostasis. When unexpected events occur and/or the individual encounters novel environmental stimuli, these disrupt equilibrium. To restore balance, the individual must adapt. The process of <u>adaptation</u> consists of <u>assimilation</u> and <u>accommodation</u>. In learning to understand the world, Piaget said children form <u>schemata</u>. A scheme is a mental construct about some aspect of the environment—people, things, events, and/or categories of these. A baby might form schemata for "things I can suck on," "things I can shake that make noise," and "people I know," for example. When a child encounters a new stimulus, s/he either assimilates it—fitting it into his/her existing schema for similar things; or accommodates to it—modifying an existing schema to accommodate some different characteristics of the new stimulus; or forming a new schema for it. Thus the process of learning, especially for children, involves frequently forming new schemata and changing existing schemata by adding to, subtracting from, or modifying the characteristics they include as experience and interaction with the environment progress.

COGNITIVE INFORMATION PROCESSING THEORY

As computers were developed to function analogously to the human brain in many aspects of receiving, encoding, storing, and retrieving information, so in turn computers were used as concrete models for information processing theory to describe how humans execute and sequence cognitive activities. Information processing theories characterize how people attend to environmental events, encode new information and relate it to existing knowledge, store new information in memory, and retrieve information as needed from storage. According to the computer metaphor, people receive sensory input in the sensory register or sensory memory; attend to it through the process of attention; "chunk" and rehearse it temporarily via working memory in short-term memory; encode it for transferring to long-term memory, where it may be stored indefinitely; and then retrieve it as needed, transferring selected data via working memory from long-term to short-term memory. Encoding includes grouping data into categories, outlining, establishing hierarchies, and developing concept trees as organizational mechanisms. It also uses imagery and mnemonics. Retrieval includes recalling information from memory independently, and recognizing provided information matching remembered information. Cognitive mapping (Tolman, 1948) mentally represents the literal physical and metaphorical environment according to relative importance of features for the individual, enhancing navigation, learning, and recall.

SOCIAL LEARNING THEORY

According to Albert Bandura, who originated social learning theory, students need not experience everything directly and personally to learn. Bandura found that children could observe other children engaging in certain behaviors and receiving desirable rewards (reinforcers) for doing so; they would then imitate the other children's behaviors in the hope of receiving similar rewards. Children not only imitate the actions of peers, but also the actions of adults, as all parents have observed. Bandura referred to these examples of behaviors provided by adults as modeling. He thus extended the behaviorist concept that an individual will emit a behavior to get a reward; once it is rewarded, the individual will repeat the behavior to obtain repeated rewards, by showing that because learners also emit behaviors they have observed others emitting, they can learn to produce behaviors based on their observation of others being rewarded for those behaviors. Bandura refers to this process as observational learning or vicarious learning.

RECIPROCAL DETERMINISM

Albert Bandura concurred with many concepts found in behaviorist learning theory, e.g., that individuals emit responses to environmental stimuli; that desirable consequences immediately following a behavior reinforce or strengthen the probability that an individual will repeat the behavior; and the deterministic nature of behaviorism in its attribution of behaviors to environmental causes. However, whereas behaviorism is sometimes called "learning theory," Bandura calls his theory "*social* learning theory." This name emphasizes a key difference in his theory: his orientation to the social contexts wherein learning occurs. Unlike behaviorists, Bandura finds social interactions vital to learning. This relates to Bandura's concept of reciprocal determinism. By this he means learning is a process involving the individual, the environment, and the behavior. The environment includes other people as well as physical surroundings and stimuli. The individual includes personality; cognitive factors; past experiences with reinforced behaviors; and psychological processes like beliefs, thoughts, expectations, etc. The environment and behavior mutually influence one another. Individual, personal characteristics and social factors reciprocally influence and are influenced by individual behaviors. Bandura identified the conditions of attention (observation), retention (remembering), reproduction (imitating or copying), and motivation (a good reason—past, promised, and/or vicarious rewards) for an individual to learn from a model's behavior.

CONSTRUCTIVISM

Constructivist philosophy and psychology view learning as a process whereby the learner actively constructs or builds his/her own knowledge and understanding of the world. Cognitive developmental theorist Jean Piaget was a constructivist. He proposed that children learned by interacting with and acting upon their environments. He likened them to "little scientists" who gathered information about the world, experimented with aspects of the environment by interacting with it, and drew progressively more informed conclusions about the world from observing their results. On the basis of this approach, children need experiences interacting with the environment to learn. Consistently with Piaget's characterization of young learners as scientists, problem-based learning is important to constructivist approaches: like scientists who conduct experiments to answer questions and solve problems, children develop higher cognitive capacities and learn more when they experiment with the environment and learn better trying to solve problems than only for obtaining external rewards or avoiding external punishments. Inquiry and discovery learning involves such active student questioning and inquiry and discovering answers or solutions. Vygotsky's zone of proximal development is the area between where a learner can accomplish something independently vs. with assistance, guidance, or encouragement, illustrating how more knowledgeable others (MKOs) enhance learning. Scaffolding is temporary needed support, gradually withdrawn as learners gain proficiency.

CLASSICAL AND OPERANT CONDITIONING

Pavlov discovered and described classical conditioning when he found he could condition dogs to respond reflexively to a secondary, previously unrelated stimulus by repeatedly pairing it with the stimulus originally producing the reflex. Ringing a bell every time he gave them meat powder, causing them to salivate, eventually enabled the bell alone to stimulate salivation without the meat. Skinner later described what he named operant conditioning. Based on Thorndike's law of effect that a desirable consequence increased the probability of repeating a behavior while an undesirable one decreased that probability, Skinner found through experiments that new behaviors could be established, existing behaviors made much more frequent, and other behaviors made less frequent or extinguished through controlling the antecedents (events or stimuli immediately before) and consequences (events or stimuli immediately after) each behavior. The key difference between classical and operant conditioning is that classical conditioning manipulates reflexive or involuntary behaviors, whereas operant conditioning manipulates conscious or voluntary behaviors. Both contribute to the behaviorist proposition that behaviors can be established, increased, decreased, eliminated, connected, and shaped through manipulating related environmental stimuli. Skinner called classical conditioning "respondent" to differentiate it from operant conditioning, which involves choice.

INTERNAL AND EXTERNAL REWARDS

According to behaviorist theories of learning, rewarding specific behaviors reinforces or strengthens the probability of their repetition. Rewards can be internal or external. Internal or intrinsic rewards originate within the individual, e.g., feeling gratification at learning or knowing something for the sake of additional knowledge, feeling self-efficacy for being able perform a given task successfully, feeling general competence or self-esteem for acquiring more knowledge or skills, engaging in behaviors congruent with one's self-image, etc. Both traditional and radical behaviorism ignored internal states as not outwardly observable or measurable, but many related theories, e.g., social learning theory, cognitive-behavioral theory, etc. incorporate sources of motivation and loci of control. External or extrinsic rewards are provided by other people or the environment. Research finds internal rewards more powerful for increasing and especially maintaining behaviors than external rewards. Behaviorism defines reinforcement as any consequence strengthening the probability of repeating a behavior. This can be positive reinforcement, i.e., introducing something desirable; or negative reinforcement, i.e. removing something undesirable. Positive punishment, conversely, is introducing something undesirable or aversive consequently to a behavior, making that behavior less likely to recur. Negative punishment is removing something desirable or removing a reinforcer, also decreasing the probability of behavior repetition.

HOWARD GARDNER'S THEORY OF MULTIPLE INTELLIGENCES

Gardner outlines eight distinct intelligences that people use in problem solving: namely, linguistic, musical, logical-mathematical, spatial, bodily-kinesthetic, naturalistic, interpersonal and intrapersonal, with a possible ninth: existential. Schools traditionally emphasize linguistic and logical-mathematical. Gardner placed emphasis upon learning skills in context, such as apprenticeships, rather than solely by textbooks. Traditional subjects, like English and math, should be taught in ways that appeal to all the multiple intelligences. History, for example, could be taught through dramatic reenactments, biographies, and architecture. He also thought that assessments should be tailored to different abilities and that student choice with assessments would ensure that

77

the students were completing the task to the best of their abilities and utilizing the intelligence in which they were most skilled.

CONSTRUCTING KNOWLEDGE

Knowledge is constructed via a dynamic process wherein learners assimilate new information into existing mental schemes or concepts; modify existing schemes to accommodate radically different or new ideas; reorganize ideas to connect them into coherent patterns; and draw on existing knowledge to make sense of new information, actively interpreting it based on established insights, attitudes, and beliefs. Four iterative learning processes (Timperley et al, 2007), one or more of which are involved in cycles for developing new skills and understandings, are: (1) cueing or retrieving previous knowledge; the outcome is an examination and/or consolidation of existing knowledge. (2) Integrating new skills and information into current belief and value systems; the outcome is an adoption or adaptation of new knowledge. (3) Creating cognitive dissonance with an existing belief, value, or position; the outcome is the rejection or acceptance resolving dissonance; reconstruction or repositioning of current belief and value system. (4) Developing self-regulated learning related to testing instructional effectiveness; the outcome is the monitoring of student proficiency; adjustment of teaching practices to maximize efficacy. Cycle (1) prepares the way for cycles (2) and (3).

ACQUIRING SKILLS

In early childhood, children acquire motor, cognitive, language, emotional, social and other skills through playing. Learners of all ages acquire skills through direct instruction from educators. Students in public schools learn academic content in required courses, and may also enroll in elective or outside courses to learn other desired specific skills. Students also learn by doing. Many skills, e.g., riding a bicycle, driving a car, dancing, all PE skills, art skills, etc. require hands-on learning and practice. Students may read books about a specific skill or skill set—not only required class textbooks, but on their own; not only to learn in more depth, breadth, and specificity about a school subject, but also learn other subjects. For example, a high school student interested in becoming a photographer might find his/her school offers art classes in drawing, painting, and sculpture but nothing in photography; and then enrolls in an outside course, and/or reads books on photography. Today, students have access to a plethora of YouTube video tutorials covering a diverse range of subjects. They can search a topic to find videos teaching specific skills. Internet searches also yield more information to read about skills. Apprenticeships and internships combine instruction, observation, imitation, and hands-on experience and practice.

METACOGNITION, SCHEMA, TRANSFER, SELF-EFFICACY, SELF-REGULATION, AND ZPD

Metacognition: thinking about thinking and understanding one's thought processes. Example: a student observes, "I learn better from a picture of something than words about it." Schema: coined by Piaget; a mental construct or representation of a concept. Example: a toddler has a schema for cows. Seeing a large, brown dog, she says "moo"—it fits her cow schema. Told this is a dog, she forms a new "dog" schema. Transfer: applying a learned skill to another activity or setting. Example: a child learns to make a clay pot in art class, then makes clay pots at home. Self-efficacy: coined by Bandura; a sense of competence for specific tasks. Example: based on experience, a student has high self-efficacy for getting an A grade in AP English, but low self-efficacy for passing calculus. Self-regulation: the ability to monitor, control, and adjust one's behaviors. Example: a high school student's grades are not high enough for his preferred college admissions; he watches less TV nightly and studies more. ZPD: coined by Vygotsky; the difference between what one can do unassisted vs. with what s/he can do with help or guidance. Example: a 4-year-old who can read a few words acquires more phonics rules and vocabulary from reading with her 6-year-old brother.

CLASSICAL CONDITIONING AND OPERANT CONDITIONING

Ivan Pavlov discovered and described classical conditioning. Experimenting with dogs, he placed meat powder on their tongues, causing them to salivate. At the same time he rang a bell. After repeatedly pairing the bell and meat powder, Pavlov found he could ring the bell alone without meat powder and the dogs still salivated by association. Classical conditioning involves evoking a reflexive response to a stimulus that did not originally evoke it through associating it with another stimulus that does trigger the response. Applying this to humans, if someone shines a bright light in your eyes, your pupils will reflexively contract. If someone says the word "contract" along with the light, after enough repetitions the person can say "contract" without shining the light and your pupils will contract. Based on Thorndike's Law of Effect, B. F. Skinner coined the term operant conditioning, differentiating it as "operant behaviors" from classical conditioning, which he called "respondent behaviors" (i.e., reflexive). Operant conditioning involves choice. Thorndike's law says actions followed by desirable consequences are likely to be repeated, while those followed by undesirable consequences are less likely to be repeated. Skinner found behaviors could be increased, decreased, or otherwise shaped through manipulating rewards and punishments.

DEVELOPING SKILLS AND MAKING SENSE OF THE WORLD THROUGH PLAY

Children and all humans learn through adaptation to the environment, as Piaget described it. Humans and other beings or organisms naturally seek to establish and maintain equilibrium, or balance. Adaptation seeks equilibrium, encompassing processes of assimilation and accommodation. If a young child can fit a new concept or experience into an existing schema—e.g., things I can eat, throw, or stack; people I know and trust, etc.—s/he assimilates it. If new information is radically different from any existing schema, the child accommodates to it by either altering the existing scheme or creating a new one—e.g., gum is something I chew but do not eat or swallow. Piaget also said children learn by interacting with and acting upon their environments. In play, children interact with the world at much earlier ages than academic activities. They learn physical concepts through their visual, auditory, tactile, olfactory, and gustatory senses. They learn and develop concepts—spatial, like under, over, through, etc.; temporal, like before and after, etc.; numerical and serial; sharing, taking turns, compromising, negotiating, and leading others, developing social skills; gross and fine motor skills through movement; language and literacy skills, including phonological awareness and conversation skills; self-esteem through demonstrating skills, accomplishments, and peer comparisons; and thinking, decision-making, independence, and cooperation and collaboration, including with diverse others, to prepare for adulthood and master life.

HUMAN DEVELOPMENT VIS-À-VIS BEHAVIORIST AND SOCIAL LEARNING THEORIES

Because psychoanalytic theories of human development, e.g., Freud's psychosexual and Erikson's psychosocial theories, made claims about internal processes that could not always be substantiated by empirical evidence, behaviorist learning theorists sought in response to restrict their examinations to outwardly demonstrated behaviors they could observe, quantify, and measure. As an example, a child who falls and feels some pain will initially cry as a natural reaction. However, when adults respond to the fall by rushing to help the child and expressing concern, this attention reinforces the crying behavior—not the fall, because the child associates the consequence immediately following with the most recent preceding event. The reinforcement of attention increases the probability the child will cry again next time s/he falls, whether it hurts or not, to reduplicate the attention. This is an example of what Skinner termed operant conditioning. In a related example illustrating Bandura's social learning theory, we have all witnessed a child falling, not feeling significant pain, and looking around at adults to gauge whether to cry or not. Bandura found children can learn by observing others' actions and their consequences (rewards and punishments), and can imitate others' behaviors that they observe.

The behaviorist approach to learning theory is justified in limiting its principles and practices to observable, measurable behaviors in that change cannot be proven nor accurately quantified unless existing behaviors can first be observed and measured to establish baseline rates; and subsequent behaviors following intervention can be measured again for comparison to assess changes from baselines. However, a primary limitation of this approach is that it fails to account for or explain maturational, hormonal, and other changes occurring throughout the human lifespan. For example, puberty, the major experience during adolescence, typically has many outward physical, social, and behavioral manifestations as well as many inward physical, cognitive, and emotional changes. These changes are primarily driven by hormones (though of course societal roles and expectations interact). This internal biological mechanism is not addressed by theories that behaviors are responses to external environmental stimuli. Hence human development has impact on learning theory: finding this theory incomplete, development demands explanation informed by additional biological, psychological, and sociological knowledge about how hormonal maturation, emotions, thinking, and social interactions are interrelated and interdependent, and how they ultimately combine to affect human behavior.

STUDENT TRANSITIONS FROM ELEMENTARY TO MIDDLE SCHOOL

Middle school students contend not only with pubertal changes in their bodies and feelings, but also changes from elementary to middle school, e.g., differences in location, learning environments, scheduling, activities, classmates, etc. While early teens become preoccupied and anxious about their appearances, behaviors, and peers' perceptions, they also become more independent, expressing more of their own personalities and interests and making more autonomous choices in friends, school, studying, sports, appearance, etc. Adults must realize this independence prompts greater privacy needs, as well as withdrawing from parents, seeking friends and other adults as role models, identifying their own peer groups, finding groups and friends more important, and experiencing peer pressure. Students' emotional and social development changes their self-perceptions, and educators should adjust instruction accordingly. The adolescent's "imaginary audience" causes self-centered hypersensitivity to others' perceptions; the "personal fable" is the belief their experiences and feelings are unique, and that nobody understands (Elkind). Educators should avoid overreactive discipline interfering with student self-regulation, overwhelming teens; establish safe classroom environments, discussing issues and emotions. Teachers can issue each student a (counterfeit-detecting designed) "leave me alone" pass—not applicable on test or quiz days—to excuse active participation or interaction during class on some days, promoting student empowerment, control, and stress management.

STUDENT GROWTH MODEL

A number of states use student growth models to track student progress. These models are statistical methods to gauge student progress on standardized tests, typically from the end of one school year to the end of the next school year. Statistical models allow students to be evaluated more appropriately, based on a dynamic growth measure instead of a static placement measure. A number of background factors (e.g., ELL status, learning differences, or student exceptionalities) may have contributed to low-achieving scores. Growth models incentivize BOTH progress toward proficiency in underachieving students and continued improvement in proficient students. Teachers and schools can be graded based, in part, upon success in facilitating student improvement and are not penalized for having students who begin an assessment cycle with low-achieving scores.

RESPONSE TO INTERVENTION (RtI) MODEL

The RtI model is a framework for providing high-quality instruction for all K-12 learners. RtI's three tiers are: 1) research-based **core** classroom instruction, 2) **targeted** instruction for students in need of additional challenge or support, and 3) **intensive** instruction for students whose needs are not accommodated by the first two tiers. The needs of all learners are addressed through the RtI framework with research-based instructional practices, curriculum adaptations responsive to students' individual backgrounds, and appropriate interventions including the extension of the standard curriculum toward greater rigor. The RtI model is data driven. Analysis of student data guides instructional decisions. RtI instructional decisions are made via collaborations of teachers and administrators. No one individual teacher or administrator is capable of implementing RtI. The best interests of the students are served by teachers and administrators teaming to interpret data and decide whether students are in need of additional tiers of (targeted or intensive) instruction.

UNIVERSAL DESIGN FOR LEARNING (UDL)

The Universal Design for Learning is a curriculum implementation/development framework for guiding educational practice that specifically addresses the "what," "how," and "why" of learning. The framework moves away from the "one-size-fits-all" nature of traditional curricula that teaches to the "average" student while overlooking exceptional students. The three principles of UDL are: 1) provide multiple means of representation ("what"), 2) provide multiple means of action and expression ("how"), and 3) provide multiple means of engagement ("why"). UDL embraces learner variability through flexibility in its methods and goals. Learners do not have to start from some predefined point. Rather, teachers are able to differentiate their curriculum implementations, maximize learning opportunities for each student, and empower all students to aim for the most appropriate levels of success.

Technology

PROBLEM-SOLVING LEARNING TASKS AND LEARNING PROJECT ACTIVITIES

Technology is an enormous asset to both teachers and students. For example, word processing programs, e.g., Microsoft Word, streamline teachers' work creating instructional documents like learning units, lesson plans, student handouts, worksheets, rubrics, checklists, progress reports, written parent communications, etc. Students can write essays, research reports, papers, short stories, plays, poetry, books, etc. They can type and save preliminary notes and outlines, then easily copy and paste portions into compositions. Students benefit from being able to delete and restore text paragraphs and sections instantly, and easily move paragraphs and sections to other locations as they learn how to organize their writing. Spell-checkers and grammar-checkers, while not substitutes for student knowledge, alert students to typing and mechanical errors for correction. Microsoft Excel and similar spreadsheet programs facilitate organizing numerical data and verbal information. Students can type in figures or lists with little or no editing and Excel displays and prints them in spreadsheet format. Databases give teachers and students large amounts of easily accessible information about specified topics, enabling them to search and sort it. Graphic tools enable students and teachers lacking artistic ability to create colorful, effective, professional-looking visual images to illustrate, organize, and understand information and concepts. Students and teachers can establish, use, and contribute to online communities to communicate and share information remotely, often instantaneously.

COMMUNICATING AND PUBLISHING INFORMATION WITH VARIOUS TECHNOLOGY TOOLS

Teachers and students alike can use available technology productivity tools to organize, share, and present information in different formats. For example, in preparing a lesson plan, a teacher might create a PowerPoint slide presentation to project while delivering a lesson. By entering summary statements of main ideas, important concepts, major facts, etc. on each slide, teachers call student attention to the most significant aspects of the lesson, reinforcing these even as they provide additional information and details through lectures, discussions, textbooks, etc. Not only are slide presentations good for identifying main points, they also reinforce information presented in other ways (speech, textbooks, handouts), providing the redundancy students need to learn and retain it. In addition to PowerPoints, slide shows are good ways to illustrate lectures, lessons, and student presentations with visual imagery that engages viewers. Teachers can make videos of class for objective feedback and analysis; students can produce videos for class projects. Teachers can create multimedia presentations to access different student learning styles, helping all students benefit from instruction. Teachers can write parent newsletters, and students can create and publish classroom or school newsletters. Students, parents, and school personnel can view documents via websites and programs on monitor screens and/or print copies.

ASSESSING LEARNING THAT STUDENTS DEMONSTRATE THROUGH TECHNOLOGICAL ACTIVITIES AND PROJECTS

Teachers newly integrating technology into student work often wonder how to grade it. Evaluating student processes and actions is the same as with traditional written work, though it differs with the divergent potentials and unique features of each medium. For example, a notebook contains handwritten notes and drawings; a blog can contain hypertext, interactive imagery, embedded video, etc. Teachers must distinguish a technology tool's capabilities from the performance of the student using it. For example, iMovie has built-in, user-friendly professional effects enabling anybody to produce visually impressive video presentations. Hence teachers cannot grade the end product but the process, i.e., the student's research, writing, image selection, and other activities. In this sense, assessment must be more formative than summative to avoid focusing only on flashy end products and observe learning activities throughout the project. Teachers can create assessment rubrics using online generators like Rubistar, Digital Media Scoring Guides, Matrix Rubric with Points, PBL Checklists, Scholastic Rubric Maker, and Common Core Rubric Creator; or use available rubrics designed for general assessment; student blogs, wikis, websites, digital portfolios, social media, effective technology use, videos, digital storytelling, podcasts, graphic organizers, programming, coding, and gaming.

PROVIDING UNIQUE GROWTH OPPORTUNITY FOR MODERN STUDENTS

Many technologies (e.g., calculators and iPads) are student-centered. They were developed to provide a one-on-one interactive experience with some form of learning. Research has shown that learning technologies act as cognitive amplifiers. Students can learn more efficiently and effectively with technology. Technology, however, is not a silver bullet. Simple access to technology will not empower students to learn better. Teachers will require training to learn how to properly implement classroom technology (in coordination with pedagogy) and students will have to learn to appropriately and responsibly use technology. In coordination with technology and new pedagogical innovations (e.g., flipped classrooms, collaborative problem solving, or inquiry-based learning), teachers are able to provide their students with engagement opportunities previously unavailable. Students who have access to technology are able to directly engage with concepts and contexts any time of day or night. No longer are teachers the sole facilitators of quality learning. With traditional pedagogies (e.g., lecture), technology may be more distracting and less helpful. Technology is not best utilized as a replacement for old modes of knowledge transfer (e.g., note-taking or board presentation). A professional educator can adapt to both the new devices and new modes of thinking that empower student learning at trajectories not previously attainable.

INCORPORATING SOCIAL MEDIA IN THE CLASSROOM

Social media is virtually ubiquitous in 21st century America. Our students are immersed in a society dominated by social media and this offers teachers an opportunity to model asynchronous (i.e., outside the time and vicinity constraints of standard class periods) learning processes that help students become lifelong learners. Examples of positive classroom social media outlets include *YouTube* where students can view or develop podcasts directly applicable to classroom topics. Teachers can use *Twitter* to post updates about assignments or deadlines. Teachers and students can blog about classroom experiences and practice academic writing skills. Students can receive more immediate feedback on academic pursuits with *Facebook*. Through all of these social media interactions, teachers can monitor students and model appropriate etiquette for online interactions as they help students become responsible and respectful citizens in a digital world.

Although there are a number of great benefits of social media in the classroom learning environment, these benefits do not come without the possibility of distractions. Students may try to tweet or snapchat with friends during class time. Teachers can always use less common social media tools to provide an opportunity for technologically empowered student engagement without the distraction associated with the most popular social networking platforms. For example, *Edmodo* enables educators to communicate with students, share materials, and distribute assessments in an efficient and non-distracting manner. Teachers and students can share work and gain efficient feedback through shared *Google Docs* that allow limitations on who contributes to social interactions. *Edublogs* allow teachers to share materials, encourage student contributions, incorporate videos, and facilitate online discussions.

ACCEPTABLE USE POLICIES

Like many businesses, most schools have acceptable use policies (AUPs) in place to stipulate the practices and constraints that users must agree to when accessing the Internet or local network. Many schools require students and staff to sign their AUP document before providing them with a network ID to gain access. AUPs are also required by Internet service providers (ISPs) of users when they sign up for the company's Internet access services. Users who sign AUPs agree to comply with such rules as not using the service to contribute to violating any law, not trying to violate any user's or network's security, not posting commercial messages to Usenet groups (sets of collected messages or notes on various topics submitted by users and posted to servers on a global network) unless they have obtained permission in advance, not trying to send spam or junk emails to anybody not wanting to receive it, and not trying to "mail-bomb" websites by flooding their servers with mass numbers of emails.

ELECTRONIC INFORMATION

To locate information on digital networks, many search engines exist, e.g., Google, Bing, Yahoo, Lycos, Excite, AltaVista, McAfee Secure Search (from the anti-virus program publisher), Trovi, and DuckDuckGo (a "trackless" search engine keeping search history and information private); and search engines offered by websites known as online marketplaces, social media, or information sources like eBay, Amazon, Twitter, Wikipedia, etc. These user-friendly sites create huge databases indexing millions of websites, locating sites relevant to the search terms (words or phrases) that users enter. Software applications enable accessing and manipulating information from remote devices. Similarly to how technical support agents access user devices remotely to resolve technical issues, users with applicable permissions and software can access information remotely. Both software programs and websites commonly include help features: the user clicks a *help* button loading a window, webpage, or website with information like step-by-step instructions, FAQs, and answers; indexes to look up specific Help topics; interactive tools; and chat windows. To evaluate e-information, first appraise author credentials, publication date, revision and edition, publisher, and journal title. Then critically analyze content, including intended audience, objective reasoning, coverage, writing style, and consult evaluative reviews.

EVALUATING ELECTRONIC INFORMATION CRITICALLY

Initial appraisal: what are the author's education, degree(s), experience, publications, and institutional affiliation? Is the institution reputable? Is the source about a topic in the author's expertise area? Look in the source's biographical information and/or *Who's Who* publications. Is the author cited frequently in multiple bibliographies or other sources? What is the publication date? Is the information current? Is the publication a first edition or a revision? Are revision dates given? Who is the publisher? University presses are typically scholarly and reputable. Is a journal scholarly or popular? These differ in complexity levels. Content analysis: read the preface, foreword, or abstract to discern author intent. For a broad overview of covered material, scan tables of contents, indexes, and bibliographies. Read chapters specifically addressing your topic. Is the intended audience general or specialized? Is the source too advanced, technical, or elementary? Or is it suitable for your needs? Is the information fact, opinion, or propaganda? Good writers can convince readers their interpretations are facts. Is information valid and well-researched, or questionable and unsupported? Are assumptions reasonable? Are ideas or arguments fairly consistent with other works on the topic? Is author viewpoint impartial, objective, and unbiased? Does it substantiate, update, or supplement other sources? Are sources primary or secondary? Is the style logical, organized, clear, and readable? Read critical reviews of the publication in online reviewing sources.

EQUITY ISSUES ARISING FROM DIFFERENCES IN TECHNOLOGY ACCESS AND USE

Although most schools have Internet access and some policies targeting minority, low-income and rural schools have succeeded, recent research still observes "digital divides" between poor and rich countries; differences in access among ethnic groups; unequal distribution of technology across regions and schools by socioeconomic status, minority enrollments, rural and urban vs. suburban schools; more access to computers in schools and homes for boys than girls; and slower Internet connections and unreliable, outdated hardware in poorer schools. Schools often poorly integrate and underuse available technology in classrooms. Even though technology can help students with disabilities access educational content, girls, disabled, rural, urban, poor, and minority students do not receive educational technology's full potential. Most homes have computers, but they are middle-class; in other families, lack of home access exacerbates gaps in school access when students with home access have more technology experience and confidence, dominate school technology, and reap more educational achievement and advancement. Parental support, modeling, and influence are also affected by socioeconomic status, lack of home access, and lack of parental digital knowledge. Girls use Internet and computer technology more confidently and often at home than in school. Even with apparently equal access, boys dominate home equipment, free access, and school computer clubs.

Instructional Practices

CRITICAL THINKING AND CREATIVE THINKING

Critical thinking includes the abilities to question, evaluate, and judge information or material. For example, students should learn to distinguish opinions from facts in what they read and hear; look for evidence supporting author or speaker arguments, or lack thereof; evaluate supporting evidence, e.g., consider whether its source is reputable, proven, accepted by experts in its field, etc.; judge the quality of information or material through comparison, experience, and intuition. Creative thinking includes generating original ideas, coming up with problem-solving alternatives that differ from usual solutions, applying knowledge in novel ways and contexts, and divergent thinking.

Traditional academics tend to emphasize and require convergent thinking, wherein multiple concepts, ideas, facts, and information come together or converge to yield the same answer or conclusion. Divergent thinking, by contrast, involves generating concepts, ideas, facts, and information that differ or diverge to yield varying answers or conclusions. For example, some informal assessments of divergent thinking include thinking of as many *different* categories of use for paper clips, or bricks, etc. (Bricks as projectiles represent *one* category, despite different targets and/or projection methods; bricks as building materials, also *one* category despite construction types or methods; using paper clips as fasteners is *one* category regardless of things fastened.)

QUESTIONING, INDUCTIVE AND DEDUCTIVE REASONING, AND PROBLEM-SOLVING

Questioning promotes inquiry learning; gives students purposes for reading; focuses attention on learning targets; fosters active thinking, metacognition, and self-monitoring; augments comprehension; and helps students review new material and connect it to their previous knowledge. Student question generation can help them identify important ideas in learning materials and synthesize information. Teacher and student questions help students clarify meaning, find new information; analyze information by wondering about author intentions, meanings, and choices of content, genres, and formats; and pursue personally interesting topics related to learning material. Inductive reasoning is a bottom-up, specific-to-general process, beginning from accumulating specific observations or information; identifying regularities or patterns; and ultimately drawing general conclusions or principles. Conversely, deductive reasoning is a top-down, general-to-specific process; beginning from a general theory, principle, or field of information; narrowing this down to more specific hypotheses; testing these by collecting observations, information, and data to confirm or refute the theory; and draw a specific conclusion. Problem-solving involves identifying a problem, generating alternative solutions, testing these through implementation, and evaluating their effectiveness. This requires focus for problem identification, divergent thinking to generate alternatives, and critical thinking to evaluate results.

PLANNING, MEMORY, AND RECALL

Planning is an essential cognitive process which many students fail to do before plunging into activities. It requires abstract thinking and imagination to envision the processes of a task before actually performing them. While many higher-order cognitive abilities seem located in the frontal lobe of the cerebral cortex, planning appears to be in the prefrontal lobe. It is high among the higher-order thinking skills. By planning before writing, for example, students are able to organize their compositions in advance, preventing many major problems, failures, and starting over from scratch. Students must plan projects before beginning them to give them organized structures, devote equal or appropriately weighted durations to different parts, stay on schedule, complete them within prescribed timeframes, etc. Moreover, planning academic tasks provides essential practice for planning in everyday life, which facilitates many activities in similar ways on a larger, even more practical scale. Students use working memory to rehearse information in short-term memory and move it into long-term memory for retention. They retrieve information from long-term memory by recalling it directly or recognizing it among provided alternatives. Without memory retention and retrieval, students could not demonstrate, apply, or build upon what they learn.

DIRECT INSTRUCTION VS. INDIRECT INSTRUCTION

Teacher-centered, direct instruction is the oldest, most widely used teaching model. Teachers give explicit, structured instruction using uniform lesson plans. Exploration, discussions, etc. are excluded. Most contemporary K-12 schools use updated versions. Examples include DISTAR, Hooked on Phonics, etc. Some longitudinal research shows Montessori, Waldorf, and other more flexible methods more effective. However, direct instruction is among the few scientifically

85

confirmed ways of improving curriculum. Siegfried Engelmann originated a more specific direct instruction (DI), comparing it with 21 other methods during the federally funded Project Follow Through (1968-1995), meant to extend preschooler education following Head Start programs. Although funding was discontinued when data showed little or no benefit for this purpose, empirical evidence proved DI most effective of 22 methods for teaching reading, language, spelling, arithmetic, and positive self-image—the only one producing positive results consistently. Indirect instruction is student-centered and interactive; teachers facilitate small-group and cooperative learning. Students construct or transform material into new or different, meaningful responses. Encompassing all Bloom's taxonomy levels, it includes reading for meaning, cloze, concept mapping, case studies, inductive and deductive reasoning, content organization, examples and non-examples, questions, student experiences, self-evaluation, and discussion. DI aids learning facts, rules, and sequences; breaking down textbook or workbook material; lower Bloom's taxonomy levels; piquing student interest. Indirect instruction aids learning abstractions, concepts, patterns, inquiry, problem-solving, and discovery learning.

INDEPENDENT STUDY

Independent study is not a single instructional method per se, but rather a type of instructional strategy that encompasses a range of different instructional methods. Teachers intentionally provide independent study types of methods for the purposes of developing initiative, self-determination, self-reliance, self-direction, and self-improvement in individual students. In addition to individual students working alone, the definition of independent study can also include paired, partnered, or small-group learning. In each case, the teacher functions as a facilitator and guide rather than directing or controlling the entire activity. Some advantages of independent study include giving students more choices of learning materials, topics, approaches, practices, and more autonomy in completing assignments. These increase student motivation. Another advantage is flexibility: teachers can use it with one, two, or several students and another strategy with the rest of the class; combine it with other strategies; or make it the main whole-class instructional strategy. An additional advantage is freeing teacher time. However, teachers must ensure students have developed skills required for it. Some examples of independent study activities and methods include doing homework, writing reports or essays, learning contracts, correspondence courses and lessons, computer-assisted instruction, research projects, learning activity packages, assigned questions, and learning centers.

EXPERIENTIAL LEARNING

Experiential learning is a student-centered, activity-oriented instructional strategy whereby students use inductive reasoning to discover information and insights. Process takes precedence over product. Activities involve "hands-on" learning. Rather than passively listening to teachers, only reading text, or viewing video or other visuals, students actively participate in direct experiences. This participation increases student motivation, as does communicating their activities to classmates so that, in effect, they teach one another. Critical components of effective experiential learning include formulating plans to apply learning to other contexts, and reflecting personally about learning experiences. Studies find student comprehension and retention are much higher through experiential learning activities than passive or receptive activities. Examples include administering surveys, building models, taking field trips, making field observations, conducting simulations, playing games, role-playing, synectics, focused imaging, and conducting experiments. Experimental learning involves the scientific method: asking research questions; formulating hypotheses regarding answers; testing hypotheses by experimenting, e.g., qualitative research like surveys and observations, or quantitative like randomly selecting participants, not treating a control group and manipulating independent variables with a treatment group to see if dependent variables are affected or unaffected to support or refute the hypothesis; reporting results; drawing conclusions and communicating these.

INTERACTIVE INSTRUCTION

Interactive instruction is a teaching strategy that enables a range of different interactive methods and ways of grouping students. It is interactive because it places a major emphasis on having students share and exchange ideas, questions, activities, and tasks, and engage in discussions of their work and learning with classmates. Students in pairs, threes, small groups, or whole classes may participate in interactive discussions, projects, or assignments. Some examples of activities involving interactive instruction include holding debates; participating in student panels; engaging in role-playing exercises, which are also used in experiential learning; discussion, which is also a feature of indirect instruction; group brainstorming to generate ideas; practicing academic skills and tasks with peers; cooperative learning groups, which are always interactive and sometimes also involve independent study; laboratory groups, which can also involve experimental and experiential learning; problem-solving activities; circle of knowledge group activity sessions; tutorial groups, including peer tutoring; and conducting interviews with peers and/or others.

ORGANIZING AND IMPLEMENTING EFFECTIVE INSTRUCTION

First review national and state standards, their course textbooks, supplementary materials, and any test preparation materials required, to ascertain which concepts they must teach. Create a plan of study based on this information. To visualize and organize instruction, make a personal lesson plan calendar. Using the plan of study and calendar, plan instructional units and timelines. Next, write detailed lesson plans for each unit. Effective lesson plans should include learning objectives; student activities; estimates of time needed; materials required; alternative plans for any students absent during lesson activities; and assessment methods, including tests, homework, and classwork. Transfer the general unit plan to a planning book, assembling all unit plans to get an overall picture of the school year, supporting organization, focus, and implementation. Write daily lesson outlines and agendas. Some teachers write detailed information and notes, while others make simple outlines including times. Being organized and making smooth transitions are important to maintain student attention. Collect or create required materials, e.g., lecture notes, overheads, handouts, manipulatives, any planned daily warmups, etc. Request media in advance. Create emergency lesson plans for substitutes and mini-lessons to fill extra or leftover time to plan for the unexpected.

CONTINUOUS MONITORING AND CHARTING OF STUDENT PERFORMANCE

Continuous monitoring and charting (1) gives teachers information on student progress with short-term, discrete objectives. They can respond flexibly to student understanding, engagement, lacks thereof, and feedback, adjusting instruction by re-teaching or reviewing skills and concepts immediately instead of only finding students did not learn certain things after having covered several topics; and (2) gives students visual depictions of their learning. Having students chart and graph their own performance can enhance their engagement in learning. Continuous monitoring functions as ongoing evaluation, visual representation, immediate feedback; a diagnostic tool; instructional planning guide; communication mechanism with students, parents, other teachers, and administrators; and an evaluation practice that can motivate and engage students. However, it is not an independent student practice activity. Critical elements are frequently assessing student understanding and performance of discrete skills and concepts; ability to replicate assessment procedures over several days; tally, graph, or chart student responses; and involve students in tracking that progress and setting goals. To implement, select a specific instructional objective; design an assessment sheet students can complete in a few minutes with items reflecting the target skill, and where indicated, concrete, representational, or abstract understanding level; administer and score; have students plot correct or incorrect responses on graphs; discuss; draw goal lines on graphs; repeat.

SCAFFOLDING

Scaffolding, in a metaphorical iteration of literal building construction scaffolding, is temporary support enabling students to complete tasks they cannot accomplish on their own at the time. As students master these tasks, the scaffolding can be gradually withdrawn until students perform the tasks independently without support. During this process, the role of the teacher is shifted from being the dominant expert on academic content to becoming more of a facilitator of learning and a mentor. As students learn how to perform tasks with support and gain increasing proficiency and independence, the responsibility for learning shifts from the teacher to the student. Scaffolded instruction establishes a supportive learning environment wherein students are able to give feedback, ask questions, and support one another in learning new material. Using scaffolding in teaching gives students motivation for adopting more active roles in their learning. Because teachers provide scaffolds for tasks students cannot initially achieve independently, scaffolding requires students to advance past their current knowledge and skill levels, sharing responsibility and taking ownership for teaching and learning.

Scaffolding can be implemented with individual students, small groups, or whole classes. It is useful whenever students cannot understand a certain concept or are not progressing in some aspects of tasks. Step 1: the teacher models how to perform a difficult or unfamiliar task, for example, how to use a graphic organizer when students have never done so. The teacher might prepare an incomplete graphic organizer with some parts completed for handouts and a projection. The teacher describes how the graphic organizer illustrates relationships, asking students to "think aloud" about this. Step 2: teacher and students work together on completing the graphic organizer. Students might suggest information to add. The teacher writes student suggestions on the board or overhead; students complete their copies of the organizer. Step 3: students work in pairs or small groups to complete a blank or partially filled graphic organizer. Teachers may need to provide multiple scaffolds at various times to help students master more complex content. Step 4: students practice independently, demonstrating mastery and gaining speed and automaticity. In each step, teacher and students have different roles and responsibilities.

INSTRUCTIONAL APPROACHES THAT EMPHASIZE STUDENT RESPONSIBILITY FOR LEARNING

In the inquiry-guided instructional method, students investigate to answer questions, attaining understanding of concepts independently. This not only promotes the development of lifelong research skills, but also places the responsibility for learning with the student. In the learner-centered teaching method, teachers are responsible for facilitating learning, while students take responsibility for learning. This shifts classroom power from teacher to student. In the instructional method of establishing learning communities, every member participates, taking responsibility for accomplishing learning goals. With shared learning, responsibility is collective, not individual. Participants include students, teachers, other educators, staff, administrators, parents, community members, and other stakeholders. Service learning is an instructional approach combining academic content with community service projects. Teachers are responsible for structuring and supervising learning, enabling student reflection. Students learn to take civic responsibility. In team-based learning (TBL), unlike other group activities, students participate as members of permanent teams; group meetings occupy most of class. Students are more responsible for and reliant on each other (interdependent) for learning, and more responsible for arriving to class prepared. Research finds TBL increases both student engagement and responsibility.

Mometrix

DEVELOPING HIGHER-ORDER THINKING SKILLS

Align learning goals, objectives, ideas, skills, content, tasks, materials, aids, and assessments. Create organized routines and activities: explain established routines, e.g., starting on time and following planned activity sequences; follow them. Conduct task analysis of a thinking skill to learn: identify the specific skill, prerequisite knowledge and skills, related sub-skills sequence, and student readiness with prerequisites. Prepare examples, sample problems and explanations. Prepare questions transcending simple factual information recall, addressing advanced understanding, e.g., how? How well? Why? Plan strategies for diagnosis, guidance, practice, and remediation. Establish a comfortable, non-threatening atmosphere. Communicate clear expectations, genuine topic interest, enthusiasm, and a businesslike approach combined with warmth. Prepare and organize thoroughly to minimize between-activity transition times. Clearly explain tasks: set goals at beginnings of assignments, and furnish finished product examples. Introduce tasks with clear, simple organizing frameworks like single-paragraph overviews, previews, charts, or diagrams. Introduce key terms and concepts before proceeding. Focus attention on important information using questions. Use written signals, repetition, nonverbal behaviors, and verbal statements for emphasis. Use demonstrations, models, pictures, diagrams, examples, etc. to make ideas vivid. Signal transitions between ideas. Give frequent feedback, including clarifying or correcting incorrect responses.

STUDENT DEVELOPMENT OF HIGHER-ORDER THINKING SKILLS

Cognitive and learning strategies include organization, elaboration, rehearsal; and metacognition for self-evaluating and self-regulating one's thinking, entailing mnemonics, visualization, diagramming, highlighting; or more complex strategies, e.g., the Multipass reading comprehension procedure. To help students develop critical and creative thinking and learning skills, intentionally design lessons expressly for teaching specific thinking and learning strategies. Teach self-reflection and self-evaluation: give students inexplicable dilemmas, paradoxes, etc., challenging pre-existing beliefs. Guide systematic student inquiry. Encourage reflection and making sense of new information by having students write or discuss in their own words how to integrate it with their existing ideas, approaches, and opinions. Encourage and guide students in forming hypotheses, brainstorming, guessing, speculating about consequences, and discussing how their thought processes have changed their ideas. Monitor inefficient strategies and correct them. Encourage continuous student reflection of beliefs about thinking, thought processes, and evaluating effectiveness. Use advance organizers and cognitive maps to show main parts or steps when approaching various thinking and learning tasks. Teach PQ4R (*preview, question, read, reflect, recite,* and *review*) with written materials. Instruction in abstraction, analysis, outlining, summarization, and generalization enhances both reading and reasoning skills. Stress broad algorithms, heuristics, and problem-solving strategies; give enough practice to overlearn for effortless, consistent use. Teach specific strategies using modeling, think-alouds, discussion, and practice. Students develop self-confidence from teachers modeling self-confidence in thinking and reasoning processes.

Name and define each cognitive skill for students; ask them for examples and synonyms. Model steps for applying each skill. Explain appropriate and inappropriate skill application contexts. Assign cooperative learning groups to practice skills. To improve comprehension, problem-solving, decision-making; and concept, principle, and procedure application: ask probing questions to diagnose existing student conceptions and misconceptions. Furnish hands-on experiences enabling students to explore generating new explanations or interpreting raw data. Give question stems or examples requiring higher-order thinking; have students answer in groups, pairs, or independently. Give practice in brainstorming, decision-making, experimenting, identifying and solving problems in art, music, and writing as well as math and science. Incorporate individualized options in lesson plans, e.g., assignment choices, modalities for multiple intelligences, varying instruction and application sequences, open-ended participation tasks with multiple alternatives, multi-ability

89

Copyright © Mometrix Media. You have been licensed one copy of this document for personal use only. Any other reproduction or redistribution is strictly prohibited. All rights reserved.

tasks and varied activities accommodating differences in abstraction, language proficiency, and emotional influences. Give opportunities to discover procedural knowledge; explain procedure goals, applicable situations or problems, and corresponding strategies and rationales; demonstrate stepwise procedure application; give students practice selecting and implementing procedures; give performance feedback. Promote internal locus of control by helping students perceive themselves as effective learners.

INTEGRATING TECHNOLOGY INTO INSTRUCTION

Instructional technology integration is effective when it supports curriculum goals. Technology must support four essential learning elements: active student engagement, group participation, frequent interaction and feedback, and connections with real-life experts. In the 1960s, MIT professor Seymour Papert collaborated with cognitive-developmental psychologist Jean Piaget, and then developed Logo, a programming language for children to use without advanced mathematical knowledge. Students using Logo could write and debug programs to control robot movements with minimal instruction. They learned more in-depth geometry concept understanding and programming skills—and were more engaged in learning than in traditional classroom exercises. Papert pointed out the ample overlap of education and fun with computers for promoting all students' internal motivation. Today technology learning tools abound; almost every US public school has Internet connection. When technology is used for more ambitious learning goals than basic skills, studies find it helps students develop creativity, research skills, and higher-order thinking.

Technology can further learning through building local and global communities including students, teachers, administrators, parents, scientists, and others; giving students and teachers more opportunities for reflection, feedback, and revision; offering learning tools and scaffolds, e.g., visualization tools and modeling programs; giving classrooms exciting, real-world problem-based curricula; and expanding teacher learning opportunities. Social media support collaboration, reinforcing learning's social nature. Technology enables learning communities and improves learning cultures. Students learn concepts in ways impossible or impracticable with other instructional methods through social networking, simulations, and digital gaming. Educational technology complements what exemplary teachers naturally do. Experts note that digital games, instead of separating instruction from assessment, constantly assess student problem-solving progress, giving students feedback and further practice. Letting students teach them how they engage with digital media both informs teachers about technology and develops student metacognition. Integration means using technology to learn content and demonstrate content understanding, not simply digital expertise. Students need guided practice and exploration to achieve this.

COMPUTER MEDIATION

Communicating using computers gives students opportunities to access remote data sources, collaborate with students in other places on group projects, and share their work with other students to obtain their responses or evaluations. Research finds that computer-based instruction (CBI) and computer-assisted instruction (CAI) combined with regular classroom instruction enhances student motivation, academic achievement, and attitudes. Moreover, the increasing prevalence, even requirement, of computers in workplaces demands student preparation; and federal and state standards increasingly require integrating technology into instruction and student computer literacy. Studies have shown that the following computer-mediated communication applications are effective for enhancing student learning of prerequisite skills and higher-order cognitive skills: building skills in logical reasoning, inductive reasoning, deductive reasoning, and making verbal analogies; practicing and drilling procedures that incorporate tests or probes; and

90

practicing problem-solving strategies and skills in making inferences. In addition, interactive learning software programs give students more autonomy in learning, allow them to learn at individual paces, engage student interest, and often make learning more entertaining. Moreover, students need immediate, specific, corrective feedback on their learning progress, which interactive software programs can give more consistently than single teachers with large classes.

ACTIVE TEACHING AND LEARNING STRATEGIES

Active teaching and learning strategies make students active participants in learning. Rather than passively listening to teachers discuss, read about, or observe others perform skills, students practice skills to gain proficiency. Many students learn best by doing. Hands-on activities take students out of books and sometimes their seats, classrooms, schools, or even familiar thinking habits. In addition to engaging student interest and giving actual practice, they have the benefit of integrating subject-area content with all four language and literacy domains—listening, speaking, reading, and writing. Though research consistently shows students learn better through active content engagement, some teachers avoid active learning. Objections and dilemmas include: concerns they will never cover required content; losing class control by not lecturing; having trouble getting students to work in teams—some doing all the work, others none; students' not knowing how to answer higher-order questions; student resistance to active learning or a preference for habituated listening and note-taking; what to do with ELL or special education students during active learning and group activities. Guidelines include: vary partners and small-group teams via randomization, specific rotation schedules, or other systematic schemes. Vary required team tasks and techniques. Clearly identify team member roles, task purpose, outcome, and time allotted. Prepare all needed materials. Determine how to grade tasks. Start small or brief activities early. Establish a signal for students to stop discussion.

Giving students choices among assignments enables them to decide how to demonstrate their learning. For example, some might choose to write compositions, some to make spoken presentations, some to draw illustrations, and some to construct models to demonstrate the same knowledge. A language strategy is A-Z Taxonomy: small student groups write the alphabet vertically on paper and think of vocabulary terms in the content they are studying that start with each letter. This technique is effective as both pre- and post-instruction. Pairing students to debate some controversial issue related to learning content, having pairs explain pro and con positions to each other and agree to an overall recommendation gives students practice in negotiating and compromising skills, plus listening and speaking opportunities. Brainstorming evokes creativity, originality, and quantity: ask open-ended questions; never criticize ideas. Providing a suitable target number of ideas sometimes helps. Some linguistically diverse students may feel more comfortable responding as members of a small student team or group.

In a "carousel questions" strategy, the teacher writes several questions about a content topic being learned on large posters or paper stations posted around the classroom. Small student groups, each with a different color marker, rotate every few minutes among question sets. At every station, teams add ideas, responses, or answers not already included. Then the class shares all student responses, gaining multiple and varied answers to the questions. In case studies, students are given real-world stories about things that happened to an individual, family, school, or community; students apply their content knowledge and skills to authentic situations. In critical explanation, teachers ask students to consider reasons or factors that might explain some content-related issues or problems. Use "might" and "could," not "why" to avoid implying right, wrong, or only one correct answer. In discussion webs, students consider a content-related issue or problem in small groups, then regroup and share their work and information with classmates from other groups. In field studies, students have opportunities to learn about and study issues in their community related to the content they are learning. Health classes might study community nutrition, disease, safety, environmental issues, consumer health, or healthcare services; earth science classes might collect rock samples, identify them, and determine local distribution patterns; social studies classes might study local landmarks and associated history, etc.

LONG-TERM GOALS, SHORT-TERM OBJECTIVES, INSTRUCTIONAL OBJECTIVES, AND LESSON PLAN OBJECTIVES

Long-term goals typically are mastered over a school year and are stated in very broad, general terms. Goal areas typically correspond to content areas like reading, writing, math, and other subjects. Teachers derive short-term objectives from long-term goals. Short-term objectives can be completed in shorter time periods, ranging from two weeks to three months. Teachers then derive instructional objectives from short-term objectives. Students can generally master instructional objectives within one lesson. From smaller numbers of long-term goals, teachers should be able to generate a larger number of short-term objectives and even larger numbers of instructional objectives from short-term objectives. As an example, if a long-term goal is for students to read at grade level, then related short-term objectives could include recognizing vocabulary sight words; using phonics, context clues, and structural analysis to identify unfamiliar words; and demonstrating text comprehension on literal, inferential, and critical levels. From these, a teacher could break down phonics into rules for short and long vowels, digraphs, initial and final single consonants, and consonant blends to write individual instructional objectives.

Correctly written objectives include: student orientation, behavioral terminology, a criterion, and a condition statement. "Review long and short vowels in one-syllable words" or "teach fire safety" are teacher-oriented. To clarify their significance and use for students, they should be student-oriented: "correctly read aloud words containing long or short vowels"; "identify fire safety rules." Behavioral terminology is observable and measurable. This is why Bloom's taxonomy supplies action verbs for each complexity level in the hierarchy and each domain. Experts remark that while knowledge-level objectives, e.g., to read sight words aloud or recite multiplication tables, are prerequisites for more advanced learning, teachers should still not dwell primarily on these as most easily observable or identifiable, but ensure they give equal time in their lessons to higher-level cognitive skills. Experts also remind teachers not to confine objectives to Bloom's cognitive domain, but include the psychomotor and affective domains as well. Objectives can include all three. For example, an instructional objective for a student to answer comprehension questions orally with 90 percent accuracy after silently reading a passage from a grade-level basal text can include requesting assistance by raising one's hand, using a person's name to get his or her attention, asking a question, and saying "please" or other social amenity.

SWOT

SWOT analysis stands for *strengths*, *weaknesses*, *opportunities*, and *threats*. While frequently used by anyone analyzing market trends, identifying target markets, and/or developing marketing plans (which includes not only salespeople, but also therapists and other practitioners who must promote their services), it is also useful to apply to education. For example, teachers can use it with high school students in career counseling to identify the job-relevant skills they possess (strengths) and those they lack (weaknesses); jobs open, job growth probabilities, and chances for advancement in a student's preferred career field (opportunities); and competition for jobs, dead-end positions, and downsizing probabilities (threats). Accompanying the SWOT analysis, a gap analysis tool identifies employer needs and job requirements; student and candidate knowledge and skills; differences between these, which represent gaps; an action plan to fill gaps; a timeframe to complete the plan; and people who can help. For example, an employer might require knowledge of Excel or other spreadsheet software; the student might only know Word or other word-processing software. The action plan is to learn Excel or other spreadsheet programs through a short community college course, school enrichment program, library-offered class, interactive computer tutorial, etc. Teachers can also use these tools to identify and address other, non-career-related academic gaps.

HYPOTHETICAL SITUATION WHEREIN A TEACHER IDENTIFIES AND ANALYZES STUDENT KNOWLEDGE GAPS

Suppose a teacher has designed a unit on a content subject and has taught the class a number of individual one-day lessons within this unit. The teacher's regular practice is to conduct formative assessments, e.g., pop quizzes, oral Q&A sessions, whips (going around the room quickly, having every student answer an open-ended content question), etc. near the end of each day's lesson. So far, each formative assessment has shown 80-100 percent of students grasped main lesson concepts, facts, and points. But on this day, the teacher finds 90 percent of the students fail to demonstrate knowledge or understanding of lesson content. It is highly unlikely 90 percent of students did not pay attention or lacked cognitive ability to comprehend the lesson, and highly likely the lesson was ineffective. Also, the 10 percent displaying knowledge and understanding may have been the most conscientious students and/or had the highest cognitive ability levels; and/or some, most, or all of the 10 percent may already have had existing knowledge of the lesson topic. Therefore the teacher re-teaches this lesson, using different instructional strategies than the first time. This time the formative assessment shows 95 percent of the class knowing and understanding key concepts and information.

TEACHER ASSESSMENT LITERACY, PRACTICES, AND NEEDS

Various research finds teachers viewing learning as memorization assesses student information recall; teachers viewing learning as constructing knowledge and understanding use formative assessment to create continuous information flow about student understanding and adapt instruction to be more effective. Studies also show assessment-literate teachers do not limit assessment to multiple-choice or true-false questions but apply many, varied strategies, selecting those strongest and most relevant for specific learning goals. Pre-service teachers are found having inadequate repertoires of assessment strategies. One study showed the teacher asking the most conceptual questions and having the biggest variety of ways to adapt instruction according to assessment results had the highest student performance level. Also, some researchers (Gottheiner and Seigel, 2012) conclude others frequently overlook how teachers interpret formative assessment data in their studies, and more resources for doing so are needed. Teachers in their study reported that, although student group discussions of questions could contribute to new misconceptions, they also triggered discourse—building on classmate ideas and enabling concept discovery and construction before even learning corresponding terminology.

ADDRESSING STUDENT CONCEPTIONS, MISCONCEPTIONS, AND PRECONCEPTIONS

Multiple teachers agree to the value of having students discuss scientific concepts and struggle to define these on their own before teachers supply them with the scientific terminology. They find this process enables students to construct and own their knowledge. Teachers also observe students from diverse cultural backgrounds may have different ways of making sense of problems, making it important to provide real-life contexts giving them personal relevance to students and accessing prior student knowledge for understanding them. Teachers emphasize structured activities, which afford students chances to develop their thoughts before sharing them; and allowing each student time to share ideas increases participation. Starting with small groups and progressing to whole-class discussion allows teachers to circulate, monitoring or assessing many more student responses; allows students to exchange and develop ideas in smaller, non-threatening groups; and improves subsequent whole-class discussion levels. Teachers emphasize needing to address previous student knowledge. They realize misconceptions can be based on cultural beliefs and personal experiences, making them resistant to change. Researchers report that, although teachers can often predict common student misconceptions, students frequently give wider response ranges than teachers can predict; and that many teachers propose re-teaching for preconceptions, but more experienced teachers try different instructional strategies.

DIFFERENTIATED INSTRUCTION PRACTICES EFFECTIVE FOR ENHANCING STUDENT LITERACY

Teaching experts advise using common instructional texts for read-alouds to facilitate differentiation. Teachers can use teaching text read-alouds to build background knowledge, demonstrate strategy application to students, introduce issues and invite student journal responses, and assure every student access to the information and skills they need to improve their reading. Researchers find that using multiple texts at varied reading levels—not just one—to teach units enables all students to obtain information from materials they can read best. Rather than teaching "the textbook," teachers need to organize every individual instructional unit around a topic, issue, or genre. This applies whether teachers assign students to small-group work, or use whole-class differentiated instruction approaches. By organizing for instruction this way, teachers can meet all student reading levels. Because students can only become better readers if they understand how to construct meaning while they read, teachers must show them this process by modeling the ways in which they think about texts during read-alouds; work with small reading groups; and one-on-one instructional conferences with individual students. This gives students multiple opportunities to learn how to construct meaning from text.

Expert teachers find discussion particularly important when differentiating reading instruction. Student discussion effectively builds on every individual student's factual knowledge and understanding, and gives students opportunities to build comprehension and clarify meaning. Students deepen recall and understanding when teachers ask them to progress past fact memorization to discussion applying those facts to problems and issues. In-depth small-group or whole-class topic discussions demonstrate how classmates think and reason, build background knowledge, and can make information relevant to students' personal lives. Teachers must never assume every student absorbs the same information from a lesson or demonstration; also, students not having absorbed lesson content can write little or nothing about it because they can only write what they know and understand. Writing strengthens comprehension and enables thinking, exploration, and learning. Teachers can glean insights from reading student journals about student text analysis and inferential thinking skills, supporting intervention planning. Ongoing assessments enable teachers to reveal individual student need areas and successes and target instruction accordingly to support every student. Experts also advise teachers to think through every unit to determine what they want students to learn about genres, issues, and reading strategies; carefully plan units accordingly; and assemble appropriate read-aloud texts, plus reading materials to meet every student's needs.

CULTURALLY RESPONSIVE TEACHING

Culturally responsive teaching utilizes diverse students' cultural background knowledge, previous experiences, and performance styles, increasing the effectiveness and appropriateness of learning for them by teaching through and to their strengths. Culturally responsive instruction recognizes various ethnic groups' cultural heritages as legitimate—both as legacies influencing student attitudes, approaches, and dispositions to learning; and as content worth including in formal curricula. Culturally responsive approaches establish meaningful connections—both between students' school and home experiences, and between abstract academic concepts and the sociocultural realities that they live. It employs a broad range of instructional strategies addressing different student learning styles. It teaches students not only knowledge about their own and others' cultural traditions and heritages, but moreover to praise one another's cultural legacies and practices. Instructional practices that are culturally responsive incorporate multicultural information, materials, and resources in all skills and subjects schools routinely teach. Classroom environment considerations include using literature reflecting various literary genres and ethnic perspectives; incorporating everyday living concepts like jobs, economics, and consumer behaviors of different ethnic groups into math instruction; and activities that reflect a range of visual, auditory, tactile, and other sensory experiences to accommodate different student learning styles.

Culturally responsive teachers maintain cultural identity and heritage as well as academic performance. They teach the whole student, using cultural references to develop cognitive, affective, social, and political learning. Students develop interpersonal relationships, acting as extended family members supporting, encouraging, and helping one another. Group accountability makes individual success everybody's responsibility in academic communities. Teachers satisfy student needs regarding human dignity, sense of belonging, and individual self-concepts. Multidisciplinary teacher teams may collaborate, teaching single cultural concepts; students can actively participate in their own evaluations. Classroom climate, learning context, student-teacher relationships, curriculum content, instructional techniques, and assessments are included in culturally responsive teaching, which is multidimensional. It empowers students as learners and people by sharing teacher and student authority; relating personal growth to public life; developing critical curiosity and inquiry habits as well as strong knowledge and skills; and treating individual development as a social, cooperative, active process wherein students explore society, power, inequality, and change. It uses varied cultural experiences, not traditional practices, as teaching and learning resources. Students learn reflection, decision-making, and effective action—personally, socially, economically, and politically; more humane, caring interpersonal understandings and skills; more insightful, clearer thinking; and continual knowledge criticism, revision, renewal, and sharing.

COOPERATIVE LEARNING

Cooperative learning requires positive interdependence (students sink-or-swim together): assign assembly line-style and synergistic task completion. Establish collective goals, resources, and rewards; assign group roles; arrange group furniture and environment; have groups compete against each other. Face-to-face interaction entails seating groups in circles or pairs facing each other. Promote individual accountability through checking with random group members, assigning individual tasks, bonus group credit or rewards if all members perform well individually, and having students bring individual work to their groups. Social skills including decision-making, communication, trust-building, leadership, and conflict management must not be assumed but taught. Teachers should record their observations of students on observation forms to provide feedback. Social skills include categories of group formation and assembly, group functioning, and the formulation and fermentation of ideas and knowledge. Group processing can be accomplished orally and/or in writing by small group reflection; teacher provision of feedback to small groups or whole classes; teacher and small group observations; and goal-setting, by students with teacher guidance as needed, for students' next work sessions, e.g., regarding further social skills development.

PROMOTING STUDENT USE AND REFINEMENT OF HIGHER-ORDER THINKING SKILLS

To get students to explore ideas from diverse perspectives, plan and ask questions prompting them to use their imaginations. For example, during a lesson on agriculture, ask students what they would think and feel about certain policies and practices if they were, respectively, legislators, corporate executives, factory farmers, small farmers, migrant farm workers, consumers paying for groceries, families eating groceries, etc. In a history lesson, ask students to take the perspectives of

Native American tribes and of European settlers; or consider both the viewpoints of American revolutionaries and British colonial governors, etc. To promote problem-solving, instead of telling students how to solve problems—mathematical, scientific, economic, logistical, creative, etc.—ask students how, also promoting inquiry; have them brainstorm to generate many ideas as a group; guide their consideration of alternatives and speculation about potential consequences; and let them practice implementing solutions, analyzing and discussing results. Rather than "yes" or "no" questions, asking open-ended questions allows for many varied responses. To develop research skills, have students form research questions, guiding revision of overly broad or narrow questions; guide them through steps of formulating hypotheses, conducting experiments testing hypotheses; collecting, analyzing, and interpreting data; reporting results; and drawing and communicating conclusions.

AREAS OF EXECUTIVE FUNCTIONING THAT COMMONLY POSE CHALLENGES FOR STUDENTS

Parents frequently identify <u>time management</u>, <u>planning</u>, and <u>organization</u> as challenges for their children. These are three among many areas involving executive function. Executive function skills start developing during infancy, continuing development into adulthood. Considering this duration for full development, children need solid foundations. Executive functioning involves cognitive skills utilized for executing tasks. A single task requires several executive function skills. For example, to get dressed for school, a student must plan ahead for the weather, sustain attention long enough for task completion, manage emotions regarding wanting or not wanting to go to school, and start and finish the task in a timely fashion. Students use executive functioning skills to help them do homework and chores, keep track of belongings, follow rules, save money for things they want, and many other things. Some signs that a student may be experiencing difficulty developing and/or applying executive function skills include: the student has trouble estimating how long it will take to complete a school project, and/or planning the project; telling a story with the details sequenced correctly; or remembering information while performing an activity.

HELPING STUDENTS DEVELOP TIME MANAGEMENT, PLANNING, AND ORGANIZATIONAL SKILLS

<u>Time management</u>: have students color portions of a clock face using dry-erase markers to represent time segments, e.g., five minutes, 15 minutes, etc., helping them visualize elapsed and remaining time; and check in halfway through time allotted. Give students halfway-point questions, e.g., are they halfway finished? Are they still focused on the task's goal? Are any distractions robbing them of on-task time? Must they speed or slow their work pace? <u>Planning</u>: one application is helping students plan homework. Ask them what a given homework assignment would look like; have them sketch it on paper divided into two columns, e.g., with a vocabulary assignment, students write vocabulary words and definitions in the left column, and draw pictures illustrating each definition in the right column. This helps them identify where to start, what they need, and how completed homework will look, promoting more independent work. Post-it note calendars help students visualize longer-term assignment due dates, and divide assignments into more manageable chunks. <u>Organization</u>: workspaces with Post-it notes or baskets labeled "Prepare," "Do," and "Done" support both planning and organization. Dual-pocket folders, one pocket for homework or materials to take home and another for completed homework to turn in, facilitate organization.

Instructional Strategies

PROCEDURAL STEPS FOR TEACHING THAT FOLLOW DIRECT INSTRUCTION PRINCIPLES

(1) <u>Introduction and review</u>: get student attention to introduce new information, or review or build on previously learned information. Identify the lesson's learning goal and relevance or significance. (2) <u>Development</u>: model the skill, knowledge, or behavior students will need to demonstrate. Clearly explain and give sufficient examples of material to be learned. Check for understanding by asking key questions or otherwise eliciting student questions. Use visual aids, multimedia presentations, or other prompts to facilitate successful student information processing. (3) <u>Guided practice</u>: once students respond positively to modeling, explanations, and examples, assign tasks for student practice and monitor them closely. Offer help and additional direct instruction (repeating the second step) to students not having mastered the material yet. (4) <u>Closure</u>: conclude the lesson, recapping what it covered; remind students of the learning goal; prepare them for the next step: (5) <u>Independent practice</u>: assign tasks or activities to students who demonstrated proficiency and competency in step (3) to eliminate any teacher prompts and assess degrees of student mastery. This can include homework. (6) <u>Evaluation</u>: assess progress formatively through classroom assignments, worksheets, etc.; and/or summatively through projects, tests, etc. Determine if learning goals are met or need revisiting in future lessons through evaluation feedback.

INDIRECT INSTRUCTION STRATEGIES

Indirect instruction is student-centered. Students actively discover or construct knowledge through inquiry, hands-on exploration, experimentation, and problem-solving activities. Teachers are facilitators assigning and guiding student activity selection, supervising and supporting work. In inquiry learning, students formulate, ask, and answer questions and solve problems rather than teachers' giving answers or solutions. Students apply content knowledge and skills analyzing and explaining teacher-supplied case studies—detailed, in-depth histories and observations of individual real-life persons, families, groups, schools, communities, etc. Concept mapping facilitates students' visualizing, organizing, and applying learned concepts. Teachers guide student project and assignment preparation, identifying focus, participants, schedules, etc.; idea generation and listing; idea sorting and rating for structure; developing maps using software for multidimensional scaling, cluster analysis, etc.; interpreting; and applying maps. Reading for meaning involves active reading, previewing and predicting before, seeking relevant information during, and reflecting after reading. Students identify explicit textual messages; make logical inferences; identify main themes and ideas; analyze development, connection, interaction of people and characters, events and plot, and ideas; evaluate purpose or viewpoint influences on text content and style; differentiate objective and subjective; integrate and evaluate visual and numerical as well as verbal content; comparatively analyze multiple text topics, themes, approaches, and information. Cloze procedures—requiring student meaning determination from context to supply missing words— teach sequencing awareness, linguistic relationships, searching, prediction, and reconstruction.

Independent instruction promotes individual student autonomy, initiative, self-determination, self-direction, self-reliance, self-improvement, self-confidence, self-efficacy, and self-esteem. Students can pursue individual interests using individual styles and paces. Its applications are highly flexible and adaptable. One caveat is that teachers must ensure students have acquired the skills necessary before beginning. In learning contracts, students agree to complete specified tasks within designated conditions and schedules and sign them, promoting accountability and responsibility. In research projects, students independently develop research questions; locate, access, and consult multiple information sources; use the information to answer research questions; and write reports or papers organizing and communicating results (with teacher guidance as needed). Learning centers are self-contained areas within classrooms containing easily accessible, varied learning materials where students independently engage in self-directed learning activities. They include skill development centers, exploratory and interest centers, and enrichment centers. In computer-mediated instruction, students interact with software programs rather than teachers or classmates, working more autonomously at their own paces. In distance learning, students access information remotely, eliminating restrictions from geographic locations.

FIELD TRIPS, EXPERIMENTS, SIMULATIONS, ROLE-PLAYS, GAMES, AND OBSERVATIONS

Students generally love field trips for getting them out of classrooms and providing real-world adventures, experiences, and materials. However, they also benefit from applying knowledge and skills acquired in classrooms to real-life situations for authentic, hands-on learning experiences. For example, in a geology lab, rock samples are usually distributed equally; but on field trips, students discover some rock types (e.g., quartz) are far more plentiful; find samples with mixed types; and enjoy independence and excitement in seeking and procuring samples—while additionally interacting with nature. In experiments, instead of reading or hearing about scientific concepts and procedures, students practice these, encountering and solving involved problems and challenges first-hand. They experience direct ownership of their learning. Instead of abstractions, concepts become real to them. Simulations, while not real, are realistic, enabling students to engage in activities not experienced in real life, e.g., developing military strategies, planning battles, and fighting wars; working in various occupations; marrying, raising families; building and managing cities, farms, corporations, etc. Technology makes simulations increasingly accessible, interactive, and vivid. Role-plays enable students to envision different perspectives, developing understanding, empathy, and social interactions. Games apply skills and knowledge in entertaining contexts, structured by rules. Observations develop student perception, detail-orientation, and objectivity.

INTERACTIVE STRATEGIES

All interactive strategies promote interpersonal and social skills. Brainstorming eliminates or minimizes student inhibitions and promotes self-expression, originality, and creativity by asking students to generate and express as many different ideas as possible without teacher or classmate criticism, censure, or rejection. Quantity supersedes quality. Students acquire more ideas from classmates than they could produce alone. Cooperative learning groups promote both collective and individual accountability, responsibility, and teamwork. They access and utilize the cooperative, noncompetitive orientations of students from collectivist cultures; and enable ELL and LEP students to ask classmates questions their cultural backgrounds might inhibit their asking teachers. Interviews help students learn about one another, show them they can serve as helpful resources for one another, and develop student communication skills. Discussions let students exchange ideas, information, and opinions; ask and answer questions; consider problems, questions, or ideas classmates propose that did not occur to them; use evidence to support their arguments; learn to disagree civilly; and consider differing perspectives. Peer practice affords classmate support, interaction, and greater comfort levels and identification than individual or teacher-led practice. Debates teach students to apply logic, support arguments with evidence, attend and respond to opponent arguments, take turns, follow rules, and interact formally.

HELPING STUDENTS DEVELOP COMPLEX THINKING PROCESSES

When students learn concepts, they are not merely memorizing facts, the lowest level of Bloom's taxonomy. They also understand ideas, which is the next level. Problem-solving involves multiple steps: first, students must identify the specific problem, requiring observational and analytical skills. Then they generate multiple possible alternative solutions, requiring understanding relationships between needs and actions, plus independent and divergent thinking. Third, they anticipate various potential consequences of different alternatives, requiring abstraction, imagination, relating hypothetical situations to their own background experiences, and speculation.

The next step, implementing solutions, requires active, hands-on, experiential learning. Then students evaluate solution results, requiring analytical thinking, cost-benefit analysis, judging effectiveness, value, etc. Analysis is Bloom's fourth level, evaluation Bloom's fifth. Metacognition involves thinking about one's own thought processes, requiring objectivity, analytical skills, reflection, and application—using metacognitive insights to inform, self-improve, and refine one's own learning strategies and processes for greater effectiveness. Critical thinking requires intellectual standards; discipline; open-mindedness; fairness; empathy, humility, and integrity; distinguishing objective from subjective information; evaluating and judging information and sources for validity and quality; applying logic and reasoning to unfamiliar or new ideas; informing thought with evidence; accuracy, clarity, precision, relevance, consistency, depth, and breadth. Transferring knowledge and skills requires application—Bloom's third level—to different contexts and situations.

The directed reading and thinking activity (DR-TA; Stauffer, 1969) helps students analyze text, determine purpose, question, clarify, and predict in all content subjects. Students examine the title to predict text subject matter. Following reading, open-ended questions elicit student predictions, opinions, and opinion-text connections. Comparison-contrast: make students develop questions about similarities and differences, writing them in graphic organizers, e.g., students might ask, "If circles were squares, what would happen?" "How are dogs and cats different and similar?" "How are gloves like hands? How are they not like hands?" Inferring: provide political cartoons or comic strips, and ask students to infer meaning. Student pairs or small groups identify inferences and connections they must make to interpret the cartoonist's point. Categorizing: with younger students, play 20 Questions or "animal, vegetable, mineral"-type games; provide manipulatives, having them sort objects into three different category containers. Give older students a controversial question or statement; have small groups research the topic; sort information into columns headed "Pro," "Con," and "Interesting Facts"; form opinions, and discuss. Summarizing: model first; have student partners or small groups read, stopping regularly to paraphrase; have them summarize key ideas in three or fewer textbook sections in no more than 20 words. Synthesizing: have students contribute to an idea web mural, adding and connecting ideas and comments about a central topic or question.

MODELING, DEVELOPING SELF-REGULATION SKILLS, SCAFFOLDING, GUIDED PRACTICE, AND COACHING

Modeling: many students learn better from witnessing demonstration than only hearing or reading verbal description, particularly when learning procedures they must execute physically. Modeling also allows teachers to demonstrate correct techniques and sequences. Additionally, modeling helps students develop self-regulation skills including managing emotions, overcoming discomfort, taking turns, listening, demonstrating, and communicating. Teachers modeling appropriate behaviors show students how to perform tasks, and use self-regulation to complete them. They also teach self-regulation through hints, cues, and scaffolding: temporary support students need to complete tasks that are gradually removed as students gain skills. Differentiating instruction: teachers recognize diverse student experience and expertise levels in content knowledge, thinking, problem-solving, listening, speaking, reading, and writing; through ongoing assessments, develop differentiated lessons to meet each student's needs. Having students learn in pairs or small groups promotes meaningful discussion, observation, and learning from each other. Differentiation focuses on concepts and issues, not chapters or books, encouraging students to expand concept understanding and explore so-called "big ideas." Choices of experiences and tasks or projects motivate students. Guided practice: after modeling, explaining, and examples, assign tasks or activities, monitoring closely; offer assistance as needed. Coaching: helps students understand impacts of time management, organization, and disorganization on studies; examine and strengthen study skills, problem-solving, strategic thinking, and effective interaction and collaboration.

Phases of Self-Regulated Learning

One popular model of self-regulated learning defines three phases. (1) <u>Forethought and planning</u>: students analyze learning tasks, setting specific goals for completion. Students learning new or unfamiliar material may not recognize appropriate goals, best task approaches; teachers instruct them about these. (2) <u>Performance monitoring</u>: students apply strategies for task progress, monitoring strategy effectiveness and their motivation to continue. Students may react to discomfort with new strategies by falling back on more familiar, less effective strategies. Teachers help students overcome frustration and gain fluency with new strategies through close monitoring and specific feedback. They also support self-monitoring by having students keep records of how many times they worked on specific tasks, amounts of time working, and strategies they used, enabling students to visualize progress and make needed changes. (3) <u>Reflections on performance</u>: students evaluate strategy effectiveness, their task performance, and manage emotions regarding outcomes. Self-reflections influence subsequent planning and goals. Encouraging setting short-term goals helps students track progress. Goal-setting and planning are complementary: planning includes and supports establishing goals. Teaching students to approach tasks with plans promotes self-regulation and learning. Self-monitoring involves goal-setting and planning. Instructional strategies promoting self-regulation include direct instruction, guided and independent practice, reflective practice, social support, and feedback.

Instructional Grouping Configurations

The whole-class group configuration is the traditional, most widely used model. Teachers deliver lectures or lessons, assign classwork to, ask questions of, and lead discussions with the entire class at once. Small-group instruction, a more recent development, divides classes into groups, usually three to six students each. Each group collaborates, researching and discussing topics. Group members may be assigned different group roles, e.g., leader, facilitator, recorder, summarizer, timekeeper, presenter, errand monitor, etc. Teachers may assign individual tasks to each group member or have everyone contribute to a larger task. Students benefit from sharing, discussing, developing, and preparing their ideas in less threatening smaller groups before doing so in the whole class; and learning and practicing social interaction skills with fewer classmates under more controlled conditions. Small groups can benefit ELL/LEP students culturally intimidated about questioning teachers by enabling questions of classmates, and students with autism spectrum disorders (ASDs) overwhelmed by larger group interactions. Independent learning allows proceeding at students' own paces, using their own learning styles and strategies. One-on-one instruction benefits students needing intensive, direct instruction, remedial intervention, and/or personal student-teacher interactions and relationships. Think-pair-share structures student discussion, limiting off-task thinking and behavior, and builds in accountability through reporting to partners and the class.

Cooperative learning groups are very structured, typically containing three or four students working several days or weeks. Teachers clearly define assignments, goals, and plan of operation, and spend time teaching member roles, e.g., questioner, reporter, recorder, etc. Within designated roles, team members share leadership. All must contribute for team progress: group interdependence dictates groups win or lose together. End products represent whole teams. Cooperation, goal achievement, task completion, and group process awareness are equally important. Highly individualistic or creative students may chafe at restrictions and students preferring whole-class anonymity feel pressured, but learn cooperative teamwork skills. Collaborative groups feature three to six students working days, weeks, or months on open-ended problems or tasks which can cover much content. Flexible student roles can change throughout assignments and projects. Students help others, observing, evaluating, critiquing, explaining, and suggesting improvements. Team goals, product, and collaborative communication process awareness is constant; meeting goals justifies changing direction. Students honestly discuss ideas, information, resources, procedures, results, their own and/or others' work; multiple approaches and open communication are important. Students needing structure may prefer cooperative teams, but collaborative groups learn flexibility and communication. Homogeneous groups may feel more comfort and commonality than heterogeneous, gender-inclusive and multi-age groups, but lack their exposure to diverse perspectives expanding experience. Multi-age grouping can facilitate helping and mentoring relationships.

SHORT-TERM, WORKING, AND LONG-TERM MEMORY

When we temporarily retain information for about three to 20 seconds, this involves short-term memory—a receptacle for visual and auditory information we rehearse, consider, analyze, interpret, or otherwise manipulate using working memory. For example, repeating a phone number to oneself silently or under one's breath until dialing or telling it to someone is in short-term memory. When we encode or consolidate and transfer information from short-term memory to long-term memory, that information is stored for an indefinite time period. Depending on individual cognitive characteristics, relative importance and meaningfulness of information, its affective impacts and associations, whether and how often one accesses the information, etc., long-term memories can last a lifetime, years, or less. Via top-down processing, prior knowledge in long-term memory strongly influences sensory perceptions; expectations about sensory experiences influence their interpretation, contributing to bias. Instructional design implications include making information sufficiently meaningful and relevant for transfer to long-term memory; and dividing information into chunks to facilitate transfer. Chunking enables the brain to automatically group some items for better retention and learning. Long-term memory, organized into interrelated schema networks, enables recalling relevant knowledge and relating new information to existing knowledge, which teachers activate using curiosity-piquing questions, graphic organizers, video, etc.

TEACHABLE MOMENT

Teachable moments, unlike instruction teachers plan in advance, are unplanned situations arising in classrooms, offering teachers ideal opportunities to impart some understanding or insight to students regarding some concept or topic. Teachers cannot design or plan for teachable moments. They occur momentarily; therefore, teachers must be observant, notice them, and seize the opportunity to take advantage of them. Because they are unexpected, making use of teachable moments can insert temporary detours into a teacher's original lesson plan in order to explain some idea which has aroused collective student curiosity and/or captured their interest. As an example, a teacher describes a morning class meeting wherein one student asked why the previous day had been a school holiday to observe Veterans Day. The teacher took advantage of this question as a teachable moment to discuss military service personnel's historical and current sacrifices on behalf of our country. Students were so fascinated with this topic, they discussed neighbors, relatives, and friends serving and the meaning of the military to the country's future for 20 minutes. The benefit of following such tangents is their maximal impact on students through their natural timing. Teachable moments can ultimately develop into complete lesson plans or instructional units.

USEFUL FEEDBACK

Useful feedback must be consistent, formative, timely, and ongoing to enable student performance adjustments. It must be user-friendly: students must understand feedback to apply it, so it must be age-appropriate or developmentally appropriate, not containing excessive or overly technical information for students to handle. Expert educators communicate observation of one important behavior, which changing can produce noticeable improvement immediately, not offering advice until ensuring students understand the significance of observations. Effective feedback is actionable: grades, "wrong," and "good job" are not feedback. Inferences from data without presenting data are not descriptive enough. For example, "Many students were bored in your class" is judgment, not observation. "Twelve of 25 students texted or passed notes during your lecture; only one did during the small-group activity" is less arguable, more neutral and useful. Feedback must include explicit goals and tangible, goal-related results. Students can be too occupied with performing to attend to results: video recordings help. Most school district "formative" test grades refer to recently taught objectives, not final performance standards. Evaluating fall and winter performance against spring standards, measuring progress using more pre- and post-assessments, and using item analysis to identify individual student performance improvement needs are more effective.

DIVERSE STUDENT BACKGROUNDS AND NEEDS

Today's classroom diversity includes students with different native languages, cultural backgrounds, previous educational and personal experiences, and knowledge. Disabilities are also a possibility. Regardless of background, gender, or other characteristics, all students need teachers to behave and communicate in considerate ways. Teachers who consider how peers and faculty may misjudge some students and how this affects them, and are aware of stereotypes and their consequences, can develop true awareness of others' perspectives. Using language, examples, and behaviors to treat students with interest and consideration and encourage others to follow suit facilitates establishing welcoming environments where students feel comfortable participating, enabling their success. Even though teachers may have student records, they need to inform themselves of individual students' background knowledge. They can begin school years surveying student knowledge prerequisite to their subject or class; give students lists of basic content-area vocabulary they expect students to understand, asking them to identify unfamiliar or problematic words; consult Individualized Education Program (IEP) information, special educators, and parents about how student disabilities can affect attendance and participation; and ask students, parents, school social workers, and/or others about student religion, family obligations, and other unique factors to consider.

Assessment

STATISTICAL RELIABILITY AND VALIDITY

Reliability: whether a test gets consistent results over repeated administrations. Test-retest reliability retests the same respondents with the same test, e.g., two weeks or a month later. Difficulties include having to write different questions on the same material, etc., to control for memory and practice effects. Internal consistency reliability compares two versions of a test concurrently, evaluating whether they correlate or measure the same construct. Validity: whether a test measures what it purports or intends to measure. Criterion validity: whether a test reflects certain abilities. One type is concurrent validity: whether a test correlates with benchmark or criterion tests. Another type is predictive validity: how well a test predicts abilities by testing respondents for a given construct, then comparing future results. Content validity: whether a test represents all of a given construct. Construct validity: whether a test measures its identified construct and not others—e.g., depression, not stress or anxiety. Convergent validity: whether constructs we believe are related are actually related. Divergent or discriminant validity: whether constructs we believe unrelated are unrelated. Bias: subjective slant toward expected results.

Example: IQ test item "cup and (a.) saucer, (b.) fork, (c.) table," presumed student familiarity with cup-and-saucer sets; but low-income students chose "table," having experience only with cups on tables, not cups in saucers.

FORMAL AND INFORMAL ASSESSMENTS

Standardized tests are a primary example of formal assessments. They have been used to test large numbers of students; data from results are mathematically calculated and summarized; standard scores, percentiles, or stanines are provided. Statistical analyses support conclusions based on test results, e.g., a certain score range is the average for representative samples of the student population in a given grade, hence other scores can be defined as above or below average and by how much. These are typically norm-referenced tests. Informal assessments are performance- and content-driven, not data-driven. For example, a running record of how well a student is reading a particular book is an informal assessment. Typical scores are most rubric scores; percentage of words read correctly; 15 correct answers out of 20 questions, etc. These are typically criterion-referenced or performance-based tests. To compare students to peers their own age, compare student strengths and weaknesses with those of peers, or assess overall achievement, formal assessments suit these purposes. To inform and improve ongoing instruction, as in formative assessment, informal assessments meet those purposes. Formal tests, statistically proven, are good for summative, not formative assessment and generalized data, not individualized data. Informal tests, more individualized, are good for ongoing assessment but less objective or statistically supported.

Formal assessments all include standardized methods for their administration, scoring, and interpretation of the scores. Some examples of formal assessments include all standardized achievement tests, which are often national or statewide; so-called high-stakes examinations; standardized intelligence or IQ tests; many standardized screening tests; and many standardized diagnostic measures. Standardized testing instruments have been statistically proven valid, i.e., they test what they are meant to test; and reliable, i.e., they yield consistent results across repeated administrations. Their manuals include statistical methods for scoring and interpreting the scores, and tables or charts showing the average scores of samples of students that represent the test-taking population, plus other scores and how many standard deviations these are from the average. Quizzes and exercises at the ends of educational textbook chapters, sections, and units are also examples of formal assessments. Informal assessments do not typically include standardized instruments, though some exist, e.g., standardized reading fluency measures. Teacher observations, class or student question-and-answer sessions, running reports, student projects, presentations, and experiments, student portfolios, and performance assessments are examples of informal assessment measures. Some find peer teaching and debates informal assessments as well.

Formal assessments provide quantitative data because they are standardized and report standard scores. Informal assessments provide qualitative data because they are not standardized, so the results reported by teachers using them are more subjective. Formal assessments enable comparison of individual students with peer groups, but typically not specific details about individual students. Informal assessments can give more detail about an individual student's strengths, needs, and performance; but less objective comparison of individual student performance with age, grade, or peer performance. Formal assessments are norm-referenced tests comparing student performance to norms for their developmental level, age, or grade. Informal assessments are typically criterion-referenced tests comparing student performance to pre-established criteria students are expected or intended to achieve and teachers are expected or intended to teach. Some students experience significant test anxiety when standardized formal tests are administered in whole-class or group settings. Some students also experience significant anxiety, even panic, when teachers single them out to answer questions in class as informal assessment. Hence it is important that teachers obtain sufficient results from both formal and informal assessment, and multiple forms of each, to develop more comprehensive pictures of student abilities and achievements.

Student scores from standardized intelligence scales and standardized scales of adaptive functioning are often used to inform student placements into specific schools, grades, and types of classes most compatible with their educational strengths and needs. While tracking is generally unpopular these days, educators seek to place students into groups where ability levels are similar and teachers can offer material (even if via differentiated instruction) that is sufficiently challenging, neither impossibly, inappropriately, or overwhelmingly difficult nor overly easy or boring. For students with certain disabilities, e.g., autism spectrum disorders (ASDs), many formal assessments exist to inform educators where a student is on the spectrum; intellectual and adaptive functioning levels; individual interests, difficulty areas, and specific behaviors, which can be both typical of the disorder and vary widely individually. Formal assessments are given at ends of school years to measure student achievement. These results are used for purposes of individual student grade promotions; to compare year-end student performance to baseline scores to assess student progress toward instructional objectives; and school accountability, to compare school effectiveness by comparing rates and percentages of student achievement to those of other schools, inform school improvement plans, and secure or continue government school funding.

One of the most valuable and prevalent uses of informal assessment findings is to inform ongoing instruction. While teachers plan instruction based on initial student assessments, during implementation they may find some students are not responding to their methods or having difficulty learning new material. With new students and large classes, teachers can discover new individual student characteristics throughout the school year. For example, by using informal measures regularly as formative assessments, teachers may find early on a student(s) not progressing at the rate(s) projected. They can then either (1) change the timeframe when the student is expected to achieve certain objectives; (2) change objectives to represent smaller increments, amounts, or lower levels to achieve within the timeframe; or (3) change the instructional approach, techniques, or strategies to be more compatible or effective with particular students. Conversely, when students progress much faster than anticipated, teachers can adjust instruction to provide higher difficulty, enriched content, etc. Formative assessments also monitor and document on-target student progress. In addition to formative assessment, informal measures afford alternative ways of evaluating student performance that formal standardized tests cannot measure, e.g., performances, portfolios, creative projects, etc. Some students cannot respond to objective examinations but demonstrate their competencies in different formats.

ESSAY QUESTIONS VS. SELECTED RESPONSE QUESTIONS AND WRITTEN TESTS VS. PERFORMANCE MEASURES

Essay questions have one obvious advantage of testing composition and writing skills as well as subject content knowledge when testing subjects other than English composition. They also enable students to go into depth and detail about topics, showing the extent of their knowledge. Essays afford students choices of subtopics, points they make, examples they use, how much they emphasize certain subtopics and points, how they organize their essays; allow them to persuade or convince readers through argumentation; require recall, not recognition; and showcase student higher-order thinking skills. Disadvantages include being more time-consuming to administer and write; requiring writing skills, which if deficient can obscure a student's other subject knowledge; and requiring far more time and subjective judgment to grade. Selected-choice questions are much faster to administer; can cover larger numbers of smaller points; allow teachers and testers more control of subject matter; are easier for students, requiring recognition, not recall; have more clear-cut right and wrong answers; are graded more objectively, and far faster, even electronically or automatically. Disadvantages include less information about individual students' overall knowledge; lacking elaboration or depth; and enabling some correct answers from sheer guesswork through probability. Written tests can be more objective; performance measures enable students to show what they can actually do, an advantage for those who do not write well.

PORTFOLIO ASSESSMENTS

Portfolio assessments involve reviewing a collection of student work products gathered cumulatively over a period of time, e.g., a semester or school year. One of their advantages is that they can provide clear evidence of student progress, growth, and other longitudinal changes that a written test or single term paper will not show as clearly. Another is that products may be artworks, models, and other concrete objects, not just test answers, written essays, or papers. These are more individualized, demonstrating more student skills than tests or papers, including nonverbal skills like artistic ability, creativity, divergent thinking, spatial awareness, mechanical ability, nonlinguistic organization, etc. Students with different learning styles, who may not use the linear thinking needed for objective tests and/or lack organizational, language processing, and/or verbal skills for writing, but excel in other areas, can produce evidence of those strengths in portfolios. Another advantage is avoiding test anxiety for many students. Students also have less time pressure and can devote more total time to creating things more gradually. Portfolios can be used for both formative and summative assessment. Some disadvantages include more subjective teacher grading, time required to accumulate portfolio products, teacher time and effort to match products with learning objectives, and lack of standardization.

CONSIDERATIONS FOR SELECTING ASSESSMENT FORMATS AND INSTRUMENTS

When choosing assessment instruments, educators and testers should first always remember that any comprehensive assessment must include multiple and varied methods, instruments, tools, and (when feasible) formats. They should never rely on a single test. One test might be most indicated for assessing a very specific skill, but even for single domains, e.g., language or adaptive functioning, multiple tests are better, as responses and scores can differ and some reveal abilities others overlooked. Age-appropriateness is important. For example, to use Wechsler's IQ scales with a young child, one would administer the Wechsler Preschool and Primary Scales of Intelligence (WPPSI), not the Wechsler Intelligence Scales for Children (WISC) or Wechsler Adult Intelligence Scales (WAIS). (If a gifted child exceeded WPPSI's top levels, administering the WISC would be interesting, though other giftedness instruments would also be indicated.) Students who are nonverbal—e.g., some with autism spectrum disorder (ASD), cerebral palsy (CP), intellectual disability (ID), or other disorders—can be evaluated using the Leiter, Raven's Progressive Matrices, UNIT, etc. Young and/or disabled students with receptive language understanding but absent or limited expression can respond to the Peabody Picture Vocabulary and other receptive tests.

A student's age or grade level are not the only factors to consider for selecting assessments. The educational context is also a key to format and instrument choice. For example, while intelligence scales give an idea of a child's intellectual capacity for purposes of educational placement, curricular and instructional design, individualized or differentiated instructional planning, etc., intelligence testing is not necessarily relevant or even significant to define adaptive functioning levels. Some children, due to innate characteristics, life experience, and training, function significantly higher in daily living and social skills than intellectually. Other children function adaptively much lower than their intellectual capacities would suggest due to behavior disorders like attention deficit hyperactivity disorder (ADHD), autism spectrum disorders (ASDs), learning disabilities (LDs), major mental disorders, etc. To ascertain daily living activities a child can perform compared to age peers and inform instructional design for developing adaptive skills, tests like the Vineland Adaptive Behavior Scales are indicated. When developmental delay is suspected in young children, tests like the Bayley Scales of Infant and Toddler Development help evaluate developmental levels. Because many school districts model their goals on their state education department's standards, the best way to align assessment with campus and district goals is often to administer standardized tests provided by statewide assessment systems.

ALIGNING INSTRUCTIONAL DESIGN AND GOALS WITH STATEWIDE ASSESSMENTS

Teachers need not view the process of aligning their instruction with assessment as "teaching to the test." Instead, they first need to read the standards on which the statewide assessments are based. As an example, many states are now basing their statewide assessments on the Common Core State Standards (CCSS). This means that what students in the state are expected to learn to know and do via the instruction they receive is encapsulated within the CCSS. A teacher whose students will be taking a test based on the CCSS would need to first review the standards and align their teaching to ensure that everything included in those standards is also included in their planned curriculum for the year. Because the state tests are written to align exactly with the standards on which they are based, teachers can be assured that students who are adequately instructed in the knowledge and skills outlined in the standards will be measured appropriately by the exam, without the need for focusing on the test itself.

MONITORING STUDENT UNDERSTANDING AND GUIDE INSTRUCTION

Rather than teach an entire unit and administer an end-of-unit test, only to discover most or all students did not understand key or major points the teacher wanted to convey, it is more useful to monitor student understanding early and often. For example, at any grade level, after a teacher makes introductory statements in a lesson, s/he can stop and ask the class questions whose answers should reflect whether they heard and remember the few main points, whether they can repeat one or a few key definitions the teacher gave, whether they understood the concepts communicated, etc. Seeing few or no volunteers or many students looking perplexed indicates a need to reteach and/or explain or demonstrate concepts differently. Quizzes at ends of lessons within units also monitor student understanding of shorter segments. When teachers assign small-group projects, they may have a member of each group orally report current group or project status and progress to the teacher or class periodically. Teachers can offer time-management strategies if they are falling behind schedule or advise reducing project scope, information amounts, etc. Teachers who find the majority of students not understanding or learning need to revisit and revise their instructional levels, approaches, methods, and/or techniques.

FORMATIVE AND SUMMATIVE ASSESSMENT

Formative assessments are conducted during instruction. Teachers use them to obtain feedback that they and their students can both utilize for improving the teaching and learning that will occur as it continues. For example, after giving a lecture, a teacher might ask middle or high school students to write down a sentence or two that identify the lecture's main point(s). Similarly, kindergarten and first-grade teachers can review an orally taught lesson by asking students to repeat one or two key vocabulary terms included, and/or one or two main points. When a teacher has told older students they will be assigned a paper as part of a unit, once the class has completed enough reading, teacher lessons, lectures, classwork, discussions, etc., the teacher can have students write and turn in outlines for the papers they will write. Summative assessments are conducted after instruction. They may evaluate learning from a unit, semester, or school year. Teachers use these to determine course grades, student grade promotion, and evaluate class, grade, and school achievement compared to those of other schools for accountability purposes. For example, grading final exams, critiquing senior music recitals or art projects, etc. help determine final course grades.

Research finds that formative assessment reduces learning gaps. It also helps teachers design instruction targeting specific learning goals; supporting student learning; monitoring student progress; identifying strengths, needs, learning gains; differentiating instruction; evaluating instructional effectiveness; informing and adjusting ongoing instruction; promoting effective teaching practices; enhancing learning for struggling students, ELLs, and students with disabilities; improving all student learning outcomes; augmenting coherence through alignment or connection with state comprehensive assessment systems; and reforming curricula. Hence federal legislation like the Every Student Succeeds Act (ESSA), replacements for the ESEA and NCLB Acts, the Individuals with Disabilities Education Act (IDEA), and state policies promote using formative assessment to narrow learning gaps. Researchers find: (1) to identify learning gaps, educators must understand differences between what students know and need to know to design instructional support enabling student progress toward learning goals. (2) Teachers must give clear, detailed feedback designed to close instructional gaps. Reciprocal teacher-student feedback informs student learning status and next instructional steps. (3) Active student involvement in learning and assessments, and student-teacher collaboration to develop shared knowledge regarding current learning status and actions needed for progress develop student skills for self-monitoring and knowing when they need help. (4) Teachers must break down major learning goals into smaller learning progression components to locate students on the skill set continuum required for mastering learning standards.

DIAGNOSTIC ASSESSMENT

Whereas formative assessment is conducted during instruction and summative assessment is conducted after instruction, diagnostic assessment is conducted before instruction. Also called pre-assessments, these frequently focus upon one domain or area. Administering diagnostic assessments can give educators information about previous knowledge each student has about a subject. This informs teachers where to begin their instruction for all students in the same class to access it without experiencing either significant knowledge gaps or significant repetition of things they already know. Pre-assessments also inform teachers of existing student misconceptions to correct during instruction. And they establish student knowledge baselines to compare knowledge following instruction to assess learning and instructional effectiveness. Teachers can use diagnostic assessment results to inform their development of lesson plans, and also differentiated instruction for individual students within classes to meet their specific needs best. Pre-assessments also gauge student preparation during sequential learning, e.g., after teaching the Coriolis effect, teachers might determine student concept retention through diagnostic pre-assessment; and refresh or reteach as needed, before they proceed to begin teaching a unit about ocean currents.

MULTIPLE-CHOICE TESTS AND ORAL QUESTIONING

Multiple-choice tests have stems—usually questions, sometimes statements—and several answer choices. One answer is correct, others incorrect; in some formats, there is more than one correct answer. These are efficiently, easily administered to large classes. They can be scored by teaching assistants, machines, or computer programs. These are effective to measure memory, knowledge, convergent thinking, and problem-solving in convergent subjects; but not when "correct" answers are equivocal, ambiguous, or disputable. Writing wrong answers reflecting common misconceptions or errors enables diagnostic value from wrong-answer pattern analyses. However, students cannot elaborate on topics. High-quality tests are harder to write than some teachers realize. Overuse can lead students to memorize separate pieces of information instead of developing overall subject understanding. Oral questioning is the most common classroom assessment. Teachers can use hypotheticals ("What would you have done if...?"), get explanations and reasons for specific student practices, challenge practices, and check understanding of underlying concepts or principles not directly observed. Not requiring reading and writing is often more inclusive and less discriminatory. It applies highly to assessing spoken, not written language. It is more valid than reliable, and time-intensive, indicating standard questions for summative assessments or multiple assessors. Recording is required for permanent documentation, which has its own considerations. Experts advise asking students' opinions of lessons and activities before questioning, for highest information quantity and quality.

DIFFERENT ASSESSMENT FORMATS

For making preschool and kindergarten placement decisions, developmental scales are useful for assessing their developmental levels in various domains. These tests are also helpful in comparing developmental levels to age norms for diagnosing developmental delays. Developmental scale results then also become useful for designing instructional objectives whereby teachers can help children with developmental delays to reach or approximate normal development. When assessing students with significant disabilities, it is important to assess their adaptive well as intellectual functioning, as these sometimes differ widely. This also informs the levels, types, and weights of instruction for each. When older students are new to a school, diagnostic pre-assessments help educators evaluate their prior knowledge to determine classroom placement and where to begin instruction. When educational records are incomplete or unavailable, new assessments help determine intelligence, literacy levels, strengths and difficulties in specific academic subjects, etc. Standardized tests like ACT and SAT differentiate student verbal vs. quantitative abilities. For example, when a student more verbally than numerically gifted used a 166-point gap between verbal and quantitative SAT scores to justify her math struggles, her guidance counselor responded that her quantitative score nevertheless indicated she should be performing better in math.

STUDENT SELF-ASSESSMENT

Self-assessment promotes student reflective and metacognitive skills development, critical thinking in analyzing and judging effectiveness of teacher instructional practices and student learning strategies, and helps teachers identify and understand individual student differences to make their instruction more responsive to student needs. Having students create or contribute to rubrics defining success in group discussions, multimodal presentations, reading response tasks, etc. augments learning levels. Having students create and agree to learning contracts when beginning units engages students in defining learning goals, agreed activities, and products as evidence of learning. Teachers have students revisit contracts frequently during units to document new learning, identify points needing clarification, and obtain teacher or classmate feedback. Teachers can designate a classroom area for "muddy points," questions, or topics that students want the class to revisit. Teachers can build student learning ownership by periodically asking students to choose an item from this board. In the "nameless voice" method, teachers have students submit work samples anonymously for class sharing and discussion of similarities and differences with their understandings. Having students write end-of-unit letters to future students explaining what they learned, tips for learning, working with difficult texts, etc. This promotes both reflection and feedback on student thinking and learning.

Because student needs vary widely, educators must differentiate content, processes, and products of learning for individual student readiness, learning styles, and interests. Also, because of this student diversity, more than one record and voice are needed to recognize and report student growth, development, and learning needs. Moreover, research finds both conducting ongoing assessment and engaging students as partners in their learning and assessment vital. When students must analyze their own thinking and learning critically, they become more motivated to learn; they develop metacognitive skills, enhancing their engagement across subject areas and supporting lifelong learning motivation. When ongoing assessment is used to inform and adjust ongoing instruction, both students and teachers reap benefits of additional knowledge about what students do and do not understand from student feedback. However, students commonly lack the experience, training, and expertise to conduct assessments as teachers can. They obviously are less objective than others when assessing themselves. Individual student differences cause corresponding self-assessment differences, whereas one teacher's assessments of all students may be more uniform. Teacher assessments must accompany self-assessments, to standardize evaluation across students and mitigate self-interested, self-destructive, or overly subjective results.

PEER ASSESSMENT

Constructivist and active learning theories provide foundations and support for peer assessment. By assigning peer assessment, teachers can empower students to take responsibility for and manage their own learning. They can help students learn assessment techniques and develop lifelong assessment skills. Peer assessment leads to exchanges of ideas and diffusion of knowledge among students, enhancing all individual students' learning. Teachers can also motivate students to engage in more depth with course materials by having them assess one another's learning. Teachers can incorporate peer assessment by identifying activities and assignments wherein peer feedback could benefit students. They can include peer assessment opportunities at different stages of larger assignments, e.g., an outline, first draft, second draft, etc. of a paper. Teachers should create rubrics or guidelines defining tasks clearly for students conducting peer reviews; and use learning exercises to introduce rubrics to assure student abilities for effective rubric applications. Peer reviews can be in-class, homework, online, etc.; teachers should determine these. Teachers must also model constructive criticism, appropriateness, and descriptive feedback in their own responses to inform peer assessment. Including small-group feedback sessions enables recipients to question, and peer reviewers to explain, written comments to recipients.

Before assigning peer assessment, teachers should explain to students the benefits and expectations of the peer review process. One disadvantage is that student relationships and interactions can influence peer review to be personal or subjective. Teachers can keep student work anonymous for peer review, making feedback more objective. Students inexperienced with peer assessment may not know what kinds of feedback are or are not useful and why or why not. Teachers can address this by giving students feedback on their feedback to classmates. They can also give examples to students of feedback with different levels of quality, and discuss with students which are more or less useful and the reasons why. To impart structure, norms, and appropriateness, teachers should provide time limits and clear direction for in-class peer review, and define deadlines for homework peer review assignments. Peer assessments are more valid when students are more familiar with and take more ownership of criteria, so teachers should engage students in discussing designated criteria. Teachers should offer necessary input and guidance during group feedback discussions. Peer assessment is better assigned for academic tasks that students have experience with, not professional tasks. To encourage more individual responsibility, avoid letting multiple students assess identical tasks.

INTERPRETING STUDENT ASSESSMENT SCORES

In general, a student's raw score on a statewide assessment equals the number of items that a student answered correctly. Raw scores can only be meaningfully interpreted relative to both the total number of items on the assessment and the raw scores of other students in the same grade. Raw scores must not be compared among different test administrations since minor variations in the test can result in widely varying average performances. With the limitations of the raw score, many assessments use a horizontal scale score allowing score comparison by adjusting for varying test form difficulty in different administrations. Using the horizontal scale score, educators can compare student cohorts (age and grade groups) taking the same subject or grade assessment in different years, compare individual students taking the same subject or grade assessment, and identify satisfactory or advanced performance. A vertical scale score, meanwhile, allows educators to measure student progress across subjects or grades.

COMMUNICATING ASSESSMENT RESULTS TO STUDENTS AND PARENTS

Experts recommend two steps in reporting assessment results to students: an initial briefing for the whole class or group tested; and then follow-up meetings with individual students, focusing on how teachers will meet their needs. Briefings should include an overview of the assessment program and instruments; how teachers, school, and districts use test results; the process for reviewing results with individual students; which results students receive; and any plans for recognizing outstanding assessment performance. Follow-up meetings should include assessed student strengths and needs, how these relate to other student information from other tests and/or teacher observations, and the plan of action recommended for addressing individual student needs. Teachers and school administrators should jointly report results to parents to build active partnerships for student learning. Individual parent-teacher conferences are ideal for explaining individual student results, reporting school-wide performance, answering parent questions, and explaining instructional improvement initiatives. If these are impossible, teachers can provide written reports carefully describing assessment processes and procedures, explaining how to interpret results, and including contact information for questions. Parent group meetings are alternatives if individual meetings are impossible. Parent newsletter articles describing assessment, scoring, overall school placement, improvement initiatives, FAQs, etc. are additional communication options.

GETTING STUDENTS ENGAGED IN CLASS ACTIVITIES AND INCREASING THEIR ON-TASK TIMES

Seating arrangements appropriate to the specific activity enhance engagement and on-task time. Choosing course materials relevant to students, and emphasizing how they can apply the learning in real life, enables students to connect activities with prior knowledge and their lives. Students view schoolwork meaningful to them as more valuable, important, and worth the effort. Giving students some control and choice in learning, e.g., self-monitoring and self-evaluating progress or choice of paired or individual work, increases sense of autonomy, hence engagement. Assigning achievable yet challenging tasks for all students, including those with disabilities, at-risk, remedial, etc. enable students to feel successful, and to believe that they earned their success. Repetitive, rote tasks and seemingly impossible ones both discourage engagement. "Mystery" approaches give students partial or contradictory information and require they develop hypotheses based on available evidence, piquing their curiosity. This also fulfills needs for autonomy, competence, self-directed inquiry, and independent discovery. Assignments only teachers will read are unilateral: teachers typically do not need the information that students submit. Contrastingly, designing cooperative learning and other projects enabling students to share new knowledge with peers promotes reciprocal relationships, making learning activities more engaging.

UNANTICIPATED LEARNING OPPORTUNITIES

According to some experts, effective early childhood development programs combine adult-guided and child-guided educational activities. Adult-guided activities include active, significant roles for children; child-guided activities include intentional adult roles in which adults take advantage of both learning experiences they planned, and unexpected opportunities for learning. For example, consider the preschool teacher whose class collected acorns outdoors and brought them back into the classroom. The teacher observes two children playing with the acorns. One child divides the acorns into two halves. She spreads her half out into a long row and clusters the other child's half into a pile. The second child becomes upset that she has more acorns than he has. The teacher asks the children how they could find out whether they each have the same number of acorns. Prompted by this intentional question, the second child gets the idea of counting both groups of acorns. The teacher observes, gives supportive comments, and asks thoughtful questions. The children discover they have the same number of acorns despite their arrangements and appearances. This teacher used an unexpected opportunity, helping two children normally in Piaget's preoperational stage of cognitive development to achieve an insight associated with Piaget's later concrete operations stage.

PROGRESS MAPS

When teachers find traditional test results do not give students the feedback they need to understand and correct their errors, they can design classroom assessments to help students organize their learning goals. This involves establishing benchmarks to use as criteria in rubrics; identifying transfer levels as referents for rubric expertise levels; making individual student progress maps, plotting their scores over time, and giving them feedback customized according to their developmental or expertise levels; plotting collective student scores on aggregate progress maps, and planning future learning opportunities in response to score clusters and deviations; and informing student self-reflection and personal goal-setting by embedding these progress maps into students' electronic portfolios. Progress maps describe knowledge, skills, and understandings in their typical developmental sequence, depicting longitudinal improvement in specific subjects and domains by organizing longitudinal assessment data according to subject knowledge and skill continua. They include initial baseline assessment data, e.g., at the beginning of a school year, relative to associated standards; and subsequent formative assessments throughout the year according to developmental benchmark criteria. Their visual nature enables quick, easy appraisal of student progress toward subject content standards. Technology makes data collection, organization, and storage most efficient.

INTEGRATING TECHNOLOGY

Examining patterns of teacher and student use of technology can show whether and/or to what degree technology is integrated into their teaching and learning environment. For example, an indication related to teacher activity is use patterns, e.g., the percentage of teachers using computer technologies for a variety of instructional and instruction-related tasks, including locating instructional resources; accessing resources and libraries online; downloading curriculum materials; communicating and networking with colleagues and other professionals; using computers to create instructional tasks, visuals, and/or materials; collaborating with remote teachers and classrooms on projects; communicating with parents; and publishing instructional materials online. Student use patterns, e.g., the percentage of students using computer technologies for various learning and instruction-related tasks, is another indicator of technology integration in the learning environment. Student instruction-related tasks include performing calculations; gathering information from varied sources; information organization and storage; collecting experimental or investigational data; making measurements; analyzing, interpreting, or manipulating data and information to draw conclusions, generate questions, discover relationships; reporting or communicating results, information, or conclusions; creating visual information or data displays; interacting or communicating with classmates, schoolmates, and others outside school; producing audiovisual presentations; composing, editing, and publishing text; creating original art, music, or graphics; publishing materials or projects remotely; and developing understanding of abstract or complex concepts and materials.

Assessment Tools

RUBRICS AND ANALYTICAL CHECKLISTS

A rubric defines in advance a specific behavior(s), skill(s), or task(s) to perform. It supplies basic guidelines for performing task components and criteria for successful performance of each component. Rubrics also typically define general performance ranges and levels, e.g., unsatisfactory, satisfactory, or excellent, briefly describing each level's characteristics. Teachers and/or students can create rubrics or select from existing ones. The teacher should first go over the rubric with students, explaining what each part means, demonstrating when necessary. Then the teacher directs students to follow the rubric as a guide in performing the task. Finally, the teacher uses the rubric's criteria to assess student work. Advantages include combining learning objectives, associated tasks, performance guidance, and task evaluation criteria; and brevity, conciseness, and clarity. Disadvantages include assigning performance levels, not more precise grades or percentages; and perhaps not lending themselves to more detailed assignments. Analytical checklists pre-define certain behaviors, skills, and tasks; teachers check observation of their presence or absence. Advantages include saving time and effort by pre-listing tasks, behaviors, and skills, enabling quick and easy assessment; and making assessment uniform across students in terms of tasks and components. Disadvantages include not identifying additional valuable accomplishments observed (without additional notes); and sometimes limiting assessment to Yes/No formats, though some checklists do incorporate performance levels like rubrics.

SCORING GUIDES, ANECDOTAL NOTES, AND CONTINUA

Scoring guides are typically issued by authors of specific standardized assessment instruments to help teachers and testers score their tests. An obvious advantage of such a scoring guide is that it instructs scorers to follow procedures and interpretations designed by the authors, minimizing chances that scoring will be inaccurate, inappropriate, or interpreted incorrectly. Also, scoring guides do not force assigning specific responses specific scores, but allow some flexibility to use judgment according to individual student responses and test conditions within a reasonable range. Disadvantages include guideline misinterpretation or misapplication by users lacking experience or good judgment. Anecdotal notes have advantages of recording teacher observations of individual student behaviors often not included in standard checklists or test instruments; and collecting information outside of as well as during assessment, which can contribute to valuable insights. Disadvantages include lack of standardization, norms, or criteria for comparison unless a recording teacher includes these; and often, lack of supporting context. Continua offer the advantages of avoiding the limitations of discrete grades, percentages, and numbers, enabling more precise and individualized evaluative description; and more realistic, accurate performance ranges than exact numbers or cutoff scores. Disadvantages include difficulty comparing scores within or among students, classes, and schools without exact numbers, making continua more applicable to individualized than standardized assessment.

STANDARDIZED TESTS OF ABILITY AND OF ACHIEVEMENT

Some standardized tests measure abilities, such as intelligence quotient (IQ) tests, which are the most prominent examples; tests of creativity, of divergent thinking (considered a key element of creativity); and more domain-specific abilities, e.g., verbal, numerical, quantitative, spatial abilities, memory, etc., which are often included as subscales on standardized IQ tests. Ability tests do not indicate or necessarily even predict student school grades. They only indicate what a student is capable of, i.e., they gauge competence, not performance. In addition to abilities, some tests measure levels of mental health constructs, e.g., Beck's Depression Inventory and Anxiety Inventory. In contrast to ability and competence or mental and emotional states, standardized achievement tests measure what students actually achieve rather than what they are capable of achieving. Standardized achievement tests are summative evaluations typically given at the ends of school years, not formative evaluations made during instruction. They test what students have learned and can demonstrate knowing and doing. This allows educators to compare individual student progress across years, compare students to peers, and compare their school to others.

STANDARDIZED APTITUDE TESTS

One thing that most standardized aptitude tests share in common with most standardized ability tests is that both types of instruments measure potential rather than accomplishment. For example, IQ tests measure intellectual ability in various cognitive domains, but not how students perform academically—i.e., what grades they actually get in school. Similarly, aptitude tests measure student interest and ability for certain subject areas and domains—not specifically IQ or cognitive levels, but how inclined a student is toward certain activities or areas of interest. Some tests evaluate broader domain aptitudes, e.g., for numerical or mathematical thinking and activities, verbal or literary thinking and activities, etc. Others evaluate interest and ability for more specific activities, e.g., preference tests often used in career counseling with high school students. While these identify discrete interest areas, when some tests combine responses, they may produce strange results not accurately reflecting the whole person or even applicable career directions, e.g., a student whose responses indicated liking books and nature received results recommending careers of librarian or forest ranger—neither was appropriate. Aptitude and preference tests, like IQ tests, differ from achievement tests by testing competence, ability, and interests; achievement tests evaluate learning a student has achieved and can demonstrate.

NORM-REFERENCED TESTS

Norm-referenced tests are standardized tests that provide pre-established norms for student scores on given tests. Before publishing or marketing standardized tests, e.g., national or statewide achievement tests, test authors typically administer their test to groups of students they have selected as samples representative of the larger intended test-taking student population. They then conduct and publish statistical analyses of the scores received by students in the sample groups. These show what the average score or range of scores is, the proportion of students receiving this average, and the distribution of all other scores on the test. Once a test is statistically proven valid and reliable and is published, educators who administer it can compare their students' scores to the established norms supplied with the instrument. This enables school administrators and teachers to compare their students' average and individual performance on the achievement test to the performance of the students in the norm samples. Because the sample students were selected as representative of the national or statewide student population, their scores provide norms against which educators can compare their students' performance. Such comparisons are typically used to satisfy federal and state legal accountability requirements for all schools receiving federal funds to educate their students adequately.

CRITERION-REFERENCED TESTS

Whereas norm-referenced tests provide established norms in the form of average scores, all scores, and score distribution of students selected as samples representative of the larger student population, to which educators can compare their own students' scores, criterion-referenced tests do not compare student results to norms or other students. Instead, they compare student results to some pre-established criterion or criteria. Test authors have selected criteria to indicate successful student performance on each item tested. Criteria can include minimum percentage or number out of a total of correct items; minimum number of attributes included in responses; descriptions of required detail, clarity, and/or other features which responses must match or approximate; in some tests, rates of speed, e.g., assessments of oral reading or speaking fluency; or other criteria specific to the skills or learning being evaluated. Student result data from criterion-referenced tests can be used for formative assessment to monitor student progress, evaluate instructional effectiveness and adjust instruction; and/or as parts of summative assessment to demonstrate students have achieved pre-defined learning objectives, in addition to norm-referenced measures.

VALIDITY, RELIABILITY, RAW SCORES, AND SCALED SCORES

Validity in testing means that a test instrument measures what it intends and/or claims to measure. For example, a test validated for educational diagnosis and/or placement could be completely invalid for determining high school graduation. However, the same test might be used for both purposes on the condition that the test has been validated for both. Reliability is consistency, i.e., whether a test yields similar results over repeated administrations. Internal consistency is reliability determined by administering two forms of the same test concurrently and finding they correlate. If one such form is given to students and the other form to the same students a month later—eliminating practice and memory effects from giving the same form both times—and they achieve similar scores in both administrations, this establishes test-retest reliability. Tests can be valid but not reliable, or reliable but not valid. Raw scores are students' actual scores on test scales, e.g., number or percentage correct. Scaled scores convert raw scores to common scales permitting numerical comparison, of individual student progress across semesters and years, among students in subject areas, etc. Scaled scores typically vary within tests among different content-area subscales.

STANDARD DEVIATION, MEAN, MEDIAN, MODE, GRADE-EQUIVALENT SCORES, AND AGE-EQUIVALENT SCORE

Percentile is a statistical ranking method indicating a score or value below which a specified percentage of scores falls within a group. For example, if a student's test score is in the 90th percentile, this means s/he scored higher than 90 percent of other students in the group tested. Standard deviation (SD or σ) is the "mean of the mean," measuring score, data dispersion, variance, or spread. Numerically, SD equals the square root of variance. SDs nearer to 0 indicate all data points clustered close to the average; higher SDs indicate wider distribution. The mean is the average of a data set or score distribution. The median is the middle score in a distribution. The mode is the value or number occurring most frequently in a distribution. Grade-equivalent (GE) scores indicate where on a continuum a student's test score falls. For example, if a 9th-grade student scores a 10.5 GE, this represents the raw score typical of a student in the fifth month of 10th grade. Age-equivalent (AE) scores are based on student age, not grade. For example, for a student aged 7.5 years, a 6 AE score indicates performance typical of a 6-year-old. GE and AE scores should only be used as comparative or relative, not absolute assessment measures.

> **Review Video: Standard Deviation**
> Visit mometrix.com/academy and enter code: 419469

ANALYTIC SCORING

Analytic scoring separately evaluates and scores discrete writing features, e.g., concise concept expression, creativity, grammar, punctuation, etc. Teachers may average these scores, but more often weigh them by relative importance. Analytic scoring helps teachers consider all writing elements, preventing them from, for example, giving too low a grade because of poor mechanics to an essay with excellent concept expression or problem analysis. By enabling final score breakdowns and teacher comments, it diagnoses areas needing improvement to guide further student efforts. Disadvantages include being time-intensive for teachers, not all students reading their teacher comments, and not using those teacher comments to benefit future assignments. Also, negative feedback, particularly combined with unclear or confrontational comments, can be counterproductive to student development. Written analytic scales define grading criteria and expectations for students. Teachers should weigh criteria by importance, e.g., if an assignment's goal is learning course information, then ideas, organization, and/or logic outweigh grammar and mechanics. Comments should balance challenge with support. Teachers should avoid confrontational practices like sarcastic comments; crossing, scribbling, or blocking out student work; etc.

HOLISTIC SCORING

When teachers have many essays to grade, holistic scoring is less time-consuming than analytic scoring, which divides writing into various components to score separately, deriving the composite score by weighing components according to assignment goals and purposes. Holistic scoring also enables multi-grader scoring. The original teacher chooses at least three student essays which, according to the teacher's criteria based on the learning objectives for the assignment, represent average, high, or low achievement. Using these as models, the teacher and other graders assess many essays written by a class (or classes) of students. Holistic scoring is found highly reliable and consistent as a method of scoring student writing. Because it takes so much less time than analytic scoring, holistic scoring is more efficient. Disadvantages include that, although scores are reliable, individual students are not necessarily informed of specific reasons for their grades. Most teachers write some final comment to give students some idea why their essays were worse, better, or similar to model essays. However, detailed comments throughout as formative feedback for student improvement are not provided as with analytic scoring. Holistic scoring is also most useful for two or more graders and can be impracticable for single instructors.

EXPLAINING TESTS AND RESULTS TO PARENTS AND STUDENTS

A common parental question is why their children were tested. Educators can explain to parents that standardized tests can identify their child's school strengths as well as areas where their child may need to improve. They can also evaluate and improve their child's school and the entire school district to provide better education. Educators should also tell parents their children are never evaluated based on a single test, and any assessment program is one among multiple tools evaluating student performance. Some parents are bewildered by scores like percentiles, stanines, grade-equivalent scores, etc. Teachers can help clarify these. For example, "stanine" refers to "standard nine," meaning that on a scale from 1-9, a score of 1-3 is below average, 4-6 is average, and 7-9 is above average. Percentiles tell what percentage of students scored below that percentile. Teachers should explain to parents that a score in the 75th percentile does not mean their child got 75 percent of test items correct; rather, it means their child scored higher than 75 percent of other students in the test group. If a student gets an 8th-grade-equivalent score on a 5th-grade reading achievement test, parents may think their child is ready for 8th-grade material; however, teachers should explain this means their child reads 5th-grade material as well as a typical 8th-grader.

When educators explain the meanings of scores like stanines, percentiles, and grade-level equivalents to parents, they should also explain that these are derived by comparing their child's scores with those of a comparison group, which may be a sample of students representative of the national population or the other students in the school district who took the test at the same time. Discussing a student's test scores relative to other students' scores makes test results most meaningful for parents: teachers can tell them how their child is different and/or similar to others in the group. Parents most often want to know what test scores mean. Teachers should compare student test scores with daily classwork before parent conferences to ensure scores match. Differences can be attributable to subscale scores. For example, a student's overall reading test score may seem adequate in the 75th percentile; but the student's subscale score in comprehension might be in the 85th percentile but in the 65th percentile for vocabulary, indicating need for vocabulary improvement. To track progress, teachers should compare students' present to past scores with parents whenever possible.

When explaining test results to younger students, teachers should avoid technical terms that the students will not understand. They can simplify while preserving general accuracy. For example, rather than telling a young child s/he scored in the 95th percentile, a teacher can say s/he did better than most of the other students. Even among parents, audiences vary, influencing how teachers should communicate test results. For example, if a parent is an educator and/or psychometrist, the teacher can likely give percentiles, stanines, grade-level and age-level equivalents without having to explain them. Such knowledgeable parents may only want to know which comparison group was used; or how their child's score compares to a larger, national comparison group, etc. However, for parents with completely unrelated backgrounds, occupations, or little formal schooling, teachers may omit technical terms entirely or give parents concise, clear definitions of them; either way, be prepared to offer a common-sense equivalent, e.g., their child is doing similarly, better, much better, or worse than most other students in the class, group, or school.

Some parents' cultures and/or countries view education as more unilateral and authoritarian than in America. They may punish children for low test scores; and/or avoid helping children with homework, studying, or getting involved in school, viewing these as inappropriately challenging school and teacher authority. In some cultures, students typically receive few years of formal education; parents from these cultures may have lower expectations for children's educational achievement. Regarding English language proficiency test results, some immigrant families want to abandon their native languages as soon as possible to acquire English, discouraging children from using L1s. When these children are still too young for verbal fluency, this can hinder their proficiency in either language. Educators can explain how L1 proficiency contributes to L2 acquisition. Some parental attitudes positively influence English learning. Parents in communities lacking opportunities for independent English learning have positive attitudes toward English acquisition. Most immigrants, viewing literacy positively as key to succeeding in America, want to learn how to help their children in school. While preserving native cultures and languages, many parents also want to participate in mainstream US culture. Many cultural family structures are stronger and more involved than in America; collective commitment to family exceeds individual motivations.

The Professional Environment

Partnerships and Collaboration

PARTNERING WITH STUDENTS' FAMILIES TO SUPPORT EDUCATION

Family involvement improves student attitudes, test scores, grades, post-secondary enrollment, self-esteem, attendance, and behavior. Research finds teacher practices and school policies predict parents' educational involvement more than race, marital status, or education levels. Avoid preconceptions or judgments about families; respect and make them allies in helping students. Contacting and building rapport with families at the beginning of the year, communicating the importance of their contributions and partnership—not meeting only if or when problems arise—sets an inviting tone. Give all families information about ways of creating positive home learning environments, e.g., limiting TV, creating homework spaces, scheduling homework times, and making homework-checking plans. Contacting families at the first signs for concern shows teachers care and respect family contributions. Regular communication—via newsletters, phone calls, meetings, individual and mass emails, etc.—sustains partnerships. Ask about family expectations for children, how they currently support them with schoolwork, how you and the school can help, if hardships are emotionally affecting students, and sibling childcare or other student home responsibilities. Encourage family questions about students, classroom practices, and contacting you. Include families and students in goal-setting, problem-solving, and creating student consequences and rewards. Focus not on inadequate-appearing family involvement, but helping students succeed. Encourage collaboration among parents and families, particularly considering time constraints.

HELPING STUDENTS, TEACHERS, AND FAMILIES WITH EDUCATIONAL PROCESSES

Guidance counselors can help parents and families by interpreting student scores on standardized tests, identify individual student strengths and needs, counsel students on school programs and career paths, collaborate with teachers on programs supporting student career interests, listen to student academic and social problems and concerns, and make suggestions to improve and support student study habits and social interactions. IEP team members can offer ways to incorporate classroom activities enabling students to address IEP goals and objectives, contributing expertise from their respective disciplines and knowledge about individual students. Special education teachers provide ways of adapting and modifying curriculum and instruction to accommodate special student needs, strategies for inclusive and differentiated instruction, and knowledge about assistive devices. Speech-language therapists can inform teachers of student therapy goals, therapeutic techniques, and how to integrate or connect these with classroom instruction. Physical therapists inform teachers of exercises for gross motor skills development, and make or adapt devices. Occupational therapists inform teachers of fine motor skill development and daily living skills activities. Library media specialists help students and teachers locate, access, and evaluate information resources in various formats, and keep them technologically current. Teachers of the gifted and talented provide accelerated and enrichment activities and compressed and streamlined curricula. Para-educators can complete many routine classroom duties and work one-on-one with individual students.

FACTORS THAT IMPEDE SCHOOL-HOME COMMUNICATION AND PARENT AND FAMILY PARTICIPATION

Collaborating with families makes teachers' jobs easier and raises student odds of succeeding. Higher family involvement in children's education correlates with higher student achievement.

117

Teachers impede communication when they only tell parents and families what to do; they facilitate communication when they spend equal time listening to families, share teacher and parent or family expertise equally, and brainstorm together for strategies that best support each student. Diverse family member educational backgrounds can impede communication and participation when parents and families had poor school experiences, feel ineffectual due to their own histories as unsuccessful students, feel alienated from school processes by differing cultural or linguistic backgrounds, and/or experience language barriers to communicating. Parental availability and participation can be affected by family dynamics including number of children, work schedules, transportation, custody arrangements, etc. Teachers who collaborate non-judgmentally can address such constraints with appropriate solutions. Teachers should initiate positive parent and family communication when school years start, not wait for problem-related contact; not wait for problem escalation to contact parents; give every family suggestions for establishing positive learning environments at home; maintain regular communication using phone calls, conferences, meetings, emails, and newsletters; inquire about home conditions and parent and family expectations; encourage family questions; and collaborate on student goals, effective reinforcers, and consequences.

STRATEGIES FOR EFFECTIVE PARENT-TEACHER CONFERENCES

Experienced teachers advise always starting with some positive student aspect, working into needed improvements, and sandwiching criticisms between positives. Some teachers send conference invitations with forms requesting parents write and return questions or concerns before meeting; and include lists of major topics covered and expectations for each student, so parents are prepared for collaborating during conferences on plans to help students. Keeping student work samples handy for conferences is another strategy. Some teachers design games and ideas parents can use at home with their children. Some write pre-conference notes on student strengths and needs. Teachers emphasize the importance of thanking parents for attending conferences and listening to parents. Administrators also encourage teacher conference preparation, including having specific suggestions prepared for parents asking how they can help. Teachers advise reviewing two or three things students can improve, and asking parents to contact them in the weeks following conferences to report whether students have improved. Tactful phrasing prevents antagonizing parents and students. Some teachers include students in parent conferences. Some agree on one or two goals with students and parents early, then stay in communication throughout the year about goal progress and future plans. Some include student-led conferences about report cards, portfolios, etc.

BENEFITS OF TEACHER PARTICIPATION IN SCHOOL AND DISTRICT COMMITTEES AND ACTIVITIES

By participating in school functions and projects, teachers access opportunities to work with professional colleagues. Collaborating on committees enables teachers to solve problems for both their students and themselves. Committees work both during school days and during extracurricular events and activities, e.g., PTA (or PTO) nights and school open houses. Teacher participation in such events and committees enables both communication with parents and demonstration to students their interest and support for them beyond academics. Whether students have extracurricular activities frequently depends on teacher support. Numbers and types of committees available for teacher participation expand opportunities for professional development; keep teachers engaged in school activities; and benefit those with whom teachers share their time, individual expertise, and special interests. In addition to traditional department, faculty, staff, and PTA meetings, teachers help other committees decide school rules; disciplinary actions; furnish leadership for athletic and intramural events, concerts, recitals, plays, musicals, book fairs, carnivals, field trips, talent shows, awards, hospitality, holiday programs, and

118

fundraising; safety maintenance and crisis management, child abuse prevention, gang and/or drug awareness and prevention; multicultural awareness; tutoring; new teacher mentoring; technology; school spirit; special population admission, review, and dismissal; instructional continuity; curriculum design, textbook identification and adoption; needs assessments; and faculty professional development and individual content-area training.

TEACHER APPRAISAL SYSTEMS

Experts maintain that reflective teachers fear neither self-evaluation nor evaluation by others, but seek experienced other educators' opinions to inform their self-improvement to serve students best. Teacher performance appraisals are typically conducted annually by trained administrators who observe individual teachers throughout the school year and apply established criteria for identifying acceptable performance. Appraisal systems evaluate teachers in areas including: student-centered instruction; successful, active student participation in learning; student progress evaluation and feedback; time, material, instructional strategy, and student discipline management; professional communication; professional development; requirement, policy, and operating procedure compliance; and improvement of all students' academic performance. Administrators evaluate and score teachers separately in each area. In addition to scores and teacher observations, documents and procedures can include teacher self-reports, annual printed summative appraisal reports (which administrators share with teachers), and annual summative conferences. Typical rules include not making classroom observations right before holidays or at the very beginning or end of the school year, time limits for assessors to provide feedback following observations, and time limits for teachers to dispute assessments in writing. Teachers receiving unsatisfactory ratings typically must follow growth or improvement plans. Teachers can prepare by requesting mentor observation and feedback, and planning lessons according to prescribed formats aligned with appraisal systems.

WORKING WITH MENTORS

Mentors provide newer teachers insights, resources, and strategies developed through years of experience, reassurance regarding challenges, and non-judgmental support. In student relationships and classroom management, they help teachers identify ineffective and inconsistent responses to student misbehavior, arrange classrooms for lesson activities, and organize material distribution and collection. They help with gaps in subject-area content knowledge, specialized vocabulary, information-accessing resources, and content-area emphasis decisions. They also help with unit planning addressing performance standards; incorporating lifelong learning skills; connecting lessons coherently; and including varied challenges, activities, and experiences for extending and applying text and teacher information. Mentors help teachers understand appropriate per-lesson material amounts and student need for clear directions, spiraling material, and regular review; include techniques activating and building on existing student knowledge and relating content to student experiences and interests; activities related to real-world experiences that apply learning; challenges with gradually increasing difficulty requiring individual and cooperative student discovery and work; and questions requiring higher-order cognitive skills. They help teachers implement lesson plans effectively by timing activities properly, anticipating and incorporating student responses into additional questions and discussions, and determining when to diverge from plans regarding student responses; and design, select, and refine and manage assessments. They help teachers contact and interact with supervisors, school staff, and parents; meet supervisor expectations; self-evaluate and pursue professional development.

FINDINGS ABOUT THE BENEFITS OF TEACHER COLLABORATION

Evidence is mounting of positive correlations between teacher collaboration and student achievement. Researchers have found lower rates of turnover among new teachers at schools

119

providing support through induction and mentoring programs. Teachers report strong collegial relationships, decision-making involvement, and self-efficacy beliefs afford greater personal satisfaction. Though all teachers' sharing responsibility for all students' success and support for new teachers enhance teacher satisfaction and retention, this occurs at the minority of schools. In the majority, teachers plan and teach alone; even in states that fund mentoring programs, new teachers are not guaranteed the support they need or want. Experts recommend school leaders earmark resources for supporting collaboration in classroom observations, planning, and mentoring; engage experienced teachers in both professional development and inducting and mentoring new teachers; and cultivate shared responsibility. Studies find teacher collaboration often dramatically turns around student achievement at chronically low-performing schools within a few years. Case studies find teachers collaborate by meeting to review student work relative to standards and target instructional improvements, form teams for aligning lessons across grade levels and self-plan professional development, receive regular lead teacher and coach support, access data guiding instructional decisions and planning, and share planning time.

TEACHER ROLES IN SHAPING POLICY AND ADVOCATING FOR THE TEACHING PROFESSION

Teachers play important roles in nurturing and preparing not only students, but also the next generation of teachers. Secretary of Education Arne Duncan stated public education for coming decades will be shaped by attracting and retaining "the best talent... to elevate and strengthen the teaching profession," which he said would require "massive cultural change" but have "extraordinary" long-term impacts. The US Department of Education (ED), in efforts to enlist this next teacher generation, started the TEACH.org project, subsequently reforming it as a public-private partnership with Microsoft. ED's related Project RESPECT (Recognizing Educational Success, Professional Excellence and Collaborative Teaching) temporarily employs active classroom teachers for input about federal budget proposals, widespread teaching reform efforts, and redefining teaching in the global economy. Elements include attracting and preparing diverse, high-performing talent; creating a professional career continuum with competitive compensation; creating conditions for success; supporting and evaluating teacher and leader development and success; providing highest-need students with the best educators; and transitioning to a more effective educational system beyond the project grant. Duncan identified RESPECT goals as elevating teacher voices in federal, state, and local education policy; collaborating with educators to rebuild teaching; and making teaching "not only America's most important... but most respected profession."

BENEFITS, CHARACTERISTICS, AND ELEMENTS OF SCHOOL PARTNERSHIPS WITH COMMUNITY MEMBERS

Schools' broad-based community involvement, and development and implementation of strategies promoting effective partnerships strengthen schools, families and communities and improve all students' learning. When schools share responsibility for student learning with families and communities, students can see how school curriculum and skills required in the real world are connected. They have more opportunities for engaged, meaningful learning. Schools can use meetings, interviews, and surveys to identify not perceived, but true family and community strengths and needs to develop policies and programs for involvement and partnership. Community needs assessments help school action teams develop involvement program goals leading to full policies reflecting supported involvement levels and types, school priorities for formal partnerships with community businesses and agencies, outreach approaches, and developing parent education and support programs. Some partnerships include learning compacts ensuring shared stakeholder responsibility for education and defining school, parent, family, and community goals, expectations, and responsibilities. Local needs, resources, and interests determine each specific community's most applicable strategies. Important elements include identifying varied means of community member involvement; activities mutually valuable and meaningful to students, schools, and community; emphasizing two-way communication; school outreach soliciting community constituencies' involvement and support; and redefining schools as community learning centers.

RESEARCH VS. PRACTICE

Educational researchers and educators alike agree that the gap between research and practice, while varied and complex, requires more cooperation between researchers and practitioners. Some researchers propose professional learning communities, and/or design-based research models (rather than only research-based design) as solutions. Some, distinguishing research-based knowledge published in journals vs. classroom teachers' pedagogical knowledge, perceive researcher-practitioner tension attributable to researchers' seeking new knowledge vs. practitioners' seeking new solutions to operational problems. Others distinguish fundamental gaps, i.e., disagreements about vocabulary, reward systems, and the nature of theory and knowledge; from practical gaps, i.e., different time and resource allocations, authority issues, and lack of cross-organizational collaboration. From literature reviews, some researchers have identified four interrelated issues characterizing research-practice gaps. (1) Education research yields insufficient valid, reliable, or conclusive results. (2) Education research has limited practical applications. (3) Teachers find educational research not meaningful, conclusive, or practical. (4) Teachers either lack the skills to apply research findings, or seldom apply it appropriately. Proposed solutions include more researcher-educator cooperation and collaboration; more educator involvement in research processes; including research training in educator preparation; and replacing top-down, linear models of disseminating research knowledge and developing and disseminating educational innovations with mutual, two-way, circular models.

INTERPRETING THE RESULTS, DATA, AND CONCLUSIONS OF RESEARCH

Authors of educational journal articles, speakers at teacher education conventions, and others frequently cite research in support of opinions about learning and teaching. However, as researchers themselves point out (e.g., Ediger, 2000), apparently those citing or even quoting research do not necessarily determine a particular study's quality. For example, a study may examine teaching practices and student outcomes in only one school district, county, or state, but not nationwide. If a study references a conclusion "according to" a specific standardized test, the conclusion stated by that instrument was contextual; different instruments could reach different conclusions. Hence to interpret educational research, teachers should consider researchers clearly state their study's purpose without pre-study opinions or vague assertions. They must remember study participants vary in intelligence, motivation, reasons for learning, achievement capabilities, socioeconomic levels, etc.; researchers cannot always control for all variables. Hypotheses must also be stated clearly. Teachers may need to accept statistical formulas, e.g., for determining significance levels, on faith as these are often too difficult for non-statisticians to understand. Experimental study averages, such as those of student scores, do not reflect individual high and low extremes. Student scores on specific tests and in studies may contradict their typical performance.

PURPOSES, CHARACTERISTICS AND BENEFITS, AND TEACHER USES OF EDUCATIONAL RESEARCH

Purposes: research informs educational policy and practices; supports high-quality instruction for all students; and stimulates discussions among educators, parents, business leaders, legislators and other stakeholders. Characteristics and benefits: teachers do not passively receive research findings; they actively decide its implications for classroom practice, give researchers guidance, and conduct their own classroom-based research. Research explicitly describes its guiding beliefs and assumptions, enabling teachers to inform instructional practices with varied theoretical orientations and viewpoints, e.g., research into writing as an individual cognitive process and a social process, respectively. Research also explicitly describes its methodology and explains how methods address classroom realities, enabling teacher insights. Research benefiting teaching and learning is trustworthy and plausible via utilizing methods appropriate to research questions and applying those methods rigorously enough. Such research must also be ethical. <u>Teacher uses</u>: teachers study research to inform instruction, critique research by asking evaluative questions, strategically select research most promising for enhancing teaching and learning based on their knowledge about theory and the relationship of theory and research, apply research to their own classroom practice, and conduct research to answer their own classroom questions and concerns systematically.

TEACHER SELF-ASSESSMENT MODEL

One teacher self-assessment model (Silver Strong & Associates, 2011) synthesizing much of the best instructional design research from constructivist perspectives has nine dimensions, resulting from combining two main component categories: (I) Instructional Design and Delivery, containing five elements; and (II) Four Cornerstones of Effective Teaching, containing four elements. The five elements for category (I) are: (1) preparing students for new learning (knowledge anticipation), (2) presenting new learning (knowledge acquisition), (3) deepening learning (practicing and processing new knowledge), (4) helping students reflect on and celebrate learning (reflecting on new knowledge), and (5) applying learning (knowledge application). The four elements for category (II) are: (1) organization, rules, and procedures; (2) positive relationships; (3) a culture of thinking and learning; and (4) engagement and enjoyment. Teachers rate themselves on each dimension using a four-point scale of (1) novice, (2) developing, (3) proficient, or (4) expert (or "NA" for self-assessment questions not applicable to an individual teacher's work). The model includes checklists of student behaviors indicating teacher effectiveness in each dimension. For example, for category (II), element (1), organization, rules and procedures, student behaviors include demonstrating respect for the classroom and one another, understanding and following rules and procedures, access to needed resources, using time well, self-direction, responsibility for learning, positive attitudes, and conflict-resolution techniques. Teachers also write ideas for improvement.

SCHOOL AND COMMUNITY

No single person educates a child. Everyone in a child's community (both inside and outside of school) helps that child develop into the citizen he or she will be as an adult. Although schools have the primary responsibility of educating children, community engagement is a vital aspect of any truly successful school. Teachers can always use additional classroom resources to improve the effectiveness of education inside of the classroom. That might entail borrowing a book from a local library or bringing in a professional guest speaker from the community. In a large number of ways, community resources contribute to the development of students each year. One characteristic of a successful teacher is his or her ability to build and maintain positive partnerships with members of the community. Effective school-community partnerships are marked by a sense of ownership and pride of a school, its students, and its successes. A supportive community will come out to support its school at athletic contests, musical/theatre performances, and other events throughout the year. An involved school can give back to its community through service and volunteer projects in coordination with local institutions (e.g., hospitals, nursing homes, shelters, and soup kitchens).

Professional Organizations and Development

PROFESSIONAL ORGANIZATIONS

In addition to research, mentors, supervisors, and colleagues, professional development resources for educators include professional organizations. Discipline-specific and other organizations enhance educator knowledge, expertise, and skills through conventions, conferences, workshops, trainings, publications, online courses, networking, local chapters, etc. Organizations include: the American Association of School Administrators, National Association of Elementary School Principals, National Art Education Association, American Counseling Association, American School Counselors Association, National Association for the Education of Young Children, American Library Association, International Reading Association, National Council of Teachers of English, American Council on the Teaching of Foreign Languages, Teachers of English to Speakers of Other Languages, Council for Exceptional Education, National Association for Gifted Children, National Council of Teachers of Mathematics, American Association of Physics Teachers, National Association of Biology Teachers, National Science Teachers Association, National Council for the Social Studies, Council for Exceptional Education, National Association for Sport and Physical Education, American Educational Research Association, Association for Educational Communication and Technology, American Federation of Teachers (AFL-CIO union), National Education Association (union), Association for Childhood Education International, Association for Supervision and Curriculum Development, National Middle School Association, National PTA, National School Boards Association, and National Staff Development Council.

DETERMINING PROFESSIONAL DEVELOPMENT GOALS

US states typically certify or license college graduates to teach in public schools for two years or similar periods with the expectation they will attain master's degrees or some other additional certification during that time. Teachers meeting state-established goals earn more advanced licensure. Even teachers with advanced graduate degrees must continue throughout their careers to set and achieve goals. Mentor teachers help new teachers set personal goals, develop personal development plans (PDPs), and document ongoing professional activities. Goals can include reading professional literature, attending educational conferences and seminars, etc., as well as taking college and graduate courses, accruing continuing education units (CEUs), etc. School district professional development committees (PDCs) work with new teachers and mentors to assure goals meet established district guidelines, sometimes paying workshop tuition. Teacher PDP approval by PDCs gives state licensure boards documentation of new teacher efforts to meet state requirements. PDCs and district administrators collaboratively set district-wide professional teacher goals, both subject-specific and interdisciplinary—e.g., aligning curricula with state standards and raising standardized test scores. PDCs offer all teachers training that targets district goals. Teacher, mentor, and PDC goal-setting must meet state education department standards. Goals should also be SMART—*specific, measurable, attainable, relevant/result-oriented*, and *time-limited*.

PROFESSIONAL DEVELOPMENT RESOURCES

Educational research studies often evaluate the effectiveness of various instructional practices. Educators benefit from many available literature reviews, meta-analyses, compilations, or other syntheses identifying consensus on effective practices to implement. Federal and state education departments, boards, and local school districts frequently adopt research-based instructional practices for individual teachers to follow. Professional organizations also disseminate research findings and provide courses, workshops, and conferences where members can learn additional information, insights, skills, and techniques to improve their teaching and student learning. A common route for teachers to improve knowledge and practical expertise is through graduate courses. Some teachers begin with bachelor's degrees, then complete master's degrees while

Copyright © Mometrix Media. You have been licensed one copy of this document for personal use only. Any other reproduction or redistribution is strictly prohibited. All rights reserved.

working, obtaining more advanced knowledge of pedagogy and specific subject-area content, higher-level teaching certification, and salaries. Some certified in general education subsequently complete graduate courses in educational specialties. Some get degrees or certificates in additional subjects and specialties, e.g., math plus science, multiple languages, English plus ESL, special education plus early childhood education, etc. Mentors personally and individually advance PD, helping educators with PD plans; observing and providing feedback; sharing their knowledge, experience, and expertise; and providing reassurance, encouragement, and support. Pre-service internships provide closely supervised on-the-job practice and experience. Study groups and learning communities enable information sharing; learning communities also allow workshop and presentation collaborations, etc.

HELPING EDUCATORS UTILIZE AND INTEGRATE TECHNOLOGY INTO INSTRUCTIONAL DESIGN AND DELIVERY

Contemporary technology not only greatly facilitates and enhances instruction, learning, and education overall, but integrating technology into instruction has become a necessity now that society depends on and requires its use so heavily. Among many available resources, one is the International Society for Technology in Education (ISTE), offering consulting services and helping educators develop customized PD learning programs. Workshops include one providing in-depth examination of worldwide educational initiatives using technology. Another, for teachers and educational leaders with advanced technology skills, teaches ISTE Standards and how to teach others these in schools or through peer coaching. A virtual workshop gives lead teachers hands-on experiences in designing learning activities embedding ISTE Standards, measuring activity effectiveness, and working district-wide with faculty teams to integrate these standards across the curriculum. A three-day onsite leadership academy provides in-depth PD knowledge and understanding of ISTE Standards; and instruction from experts in these standards regarding the conditions essential to implementing them at district, school, and classroom levels. ISTE mobile learning support services help educators and stakeholders apply prevalent (and popular with students) mobile technology for learning. ISTE's classroom observation tool measures effective classroom technology integration. ISTE offers school administrators and principals digital citizenship, technology leadership institutes, a standards readiness workshop, and essential conditions readiness Survey.

REFLECTION

Reflection enables teachers to gain some distance and objectivity to analyze their instructional practices and interactions with students, which in turn enables them to identify, plan, and implement measures to improve these for improved student learning. To track their effectiveness in the classroom, teachers should establish baselines early in the school year. They can keep journals, writing their reflections about classroom interactions as often as possible. Selecting one high-achieving and one low-achieving student in a class and charting how the teacher's professional relationship with each student develops can often accurately reflect learning opportunities the teacher provides for all students. Writing honestly and rereading previous entries regularly help teachers change their behaviors to improve student-teacher relationships, hence learning. Many pre-designed self-assessment checklists, questionnaires, and tools help teachers evaluate their practices systematically and use their responses to reinforce or expand teaching strengths and address weaknesses. Through peer assessment, teachers have colleagues observe and provide feedback on their instruction: others often see behaviors and omissions we cannot, and/or provide alternate perspectives. The "critical friend" method is similar. Systematic incident analysis enables teacher insights into student behaviors and teacher-student interactions and how changing teacher behaviors can change student behaviors. Portfolios enable teachers to review work development and changes longitudinally.

REFLECTION QUESTIONS THAT A TEACHER MIGHT ASK HIM OR HERSELF AFTER A CLASSROOM ACTIVITY

1. What were the learning objectives for this experience? Did I expect too much or too little of the students?
2. Did this experience work well? Did the students react positively or negatively? What data do I have that this experience was (un)successful?
3. What can I change about this lesson? Is it possible to better prepare my students for this lesson next year?
4. What questions should I have asked before the experience? Which questions should I have asked after the experience?
5. What student behavior was most notable? Did any circumstances from outside the classroom affect this behavior?
6. How do my students learn? Would my students learn better in some different way?
7. Were all my students actively participating in this experience? How can I adapt my lesson to make it more student-centered?
8. What data do I need to make an informed decision about this activity's effectiveness? What plans should I make to get this data in the future?
9. What do my data tell me? How can I adjust my expectations and my activity based upon the data I got?
10. Can my students meet the objectives in a more efficient manner? Does this activity need less time or more time? How can I adjust for next year?

PRACTICES THAT APPLY RESEARCH DATA FINDING THEM EFFECTIVE FOR INSTRUCTING STUDENTS

Cognitive research studies have established that comparing, contrasting, and classifying help students understand complex concepts. Teaching students to identify idea similarities and differences applies these findings. Research shows students' higher-order cognitive skills for analysis and synthesis, in-depth analysis, and reading comprehension improve through effectively summarizing information and note-taking. Teaching students how and assigning them to summarize and take notes efficiently applies research to improve instruction and achievement. Educational achievement motivation research demonstrates the impact of recognition for reinforcing and monitoring student effort, e.g., symbolic or abstract recognition is more effective than concrete rewards; rewards contingent on meeting some performance standard are most effective; 8-year-olds' learning strategies differ radically from 12-year-olds' and adults' strategies; and 8-year-olds learn mainly from positive feedback, not negative. Teachers raise student achievement by recognizing, rewarding, and praising specific goal achievements. Studies show learning occurs linguistically and non-linguistically; visual or other non-linguistic representations help students understand, retain, retrieve, connect, and apply knowledge; and the more students combine linguistic and non-linguistic systems, the better they learn and think. Teachers apply these findings using multimodal instruction. Additional research-based effective teaching practices include practice, homework, objectives, feedback, generating hypotheses, testing hypotheses, advance organizers, questions, cues, cooperative learning, and teaching and assigning nonfictional writing.

FEEDBACK

Teachers receive feedback from a number of sources (e.g., students, parents, colleagues, department leaders, and school administrators). Some (but not all) of the feedback will be useful. Feedback like "I don't like your class" does not give a teacher the opportunity to improve his or her classroom practice. Other feedback like, "Try to allow more wait time between asking a question and calling upon a student to answer" is more specific and teachers can act on this. Helpful feedback and less helpful feedback both provide a teacher with the opportunity to initiate a conversation on his or her pedagogy. In response to non-anonymous feedback, a teacher can ask follow-up questions to clear up any vagueness. Feedback can be something to talk over with a mentor, an invitation to initiate a discussion within a professional learning community, or even a starting point at which to begin a process of action research in the classroom. Unfortunately the feedback a teacher receives (particularly from students) is not always helpful and in some cases can be hurtful. A beginning teacher must remember not to take feedback personally. A professional teacher is only expected to do the best that he or she can to improve based upon the appropriate feedback he or she receives.

CHARACTERISTICS ASSOCIATED WITH HELPFUL FEEDBACK (TOTAL)

1. **Targeted**: Feedback should be targeted towards a goal and allow the subject of the feedback to adjust his or her actions in an effort to improve. Vague or imprecise feedback is not only unhelpful but can also be misleading.
2. **Ongoing**: For feedback to be useful, individuals must have the ongoing opportunity to improve.
3. **Timely**: Feedback must be timely. Late arriving feedback deprives an individual of the opportunity to improve recent behavior or efficiently affect better results.
4. **Actionable**: "Great Work" or "This is not right" are not examples of good feedback. Both lack the specificity necessary to be useful. Good feedback can be acted upon. Adjustments can be made in response to specific and useful suggestions on how to improve.
5. **Level-Headed**: Feedback must be genuine, trustworthy, and not overly ambitious. Improvement in any endeavor is an incremental process that is best accomplished slowly, in short increments over long intervals of time. A feedback recipient must be able to trust that a critique is both sensible and prudent.

RESOURCES AVAILABLE TO HELP PROFESSIONAL DEVELOPMENT AND ENHANCE EFFECTIVENESS

Every educator in the world (at universities, colleges, and schools of every type) is a part of a professional learning community, in the broadest sense of that phrase. The growth of the internet and data resources have made teacher professional development more available than it has ever been before. Websites like *Edutopia* can help a teacher stay current with the latest technology or innovative pedagogy. National organizations (e.g., NCTE, NCTM, NCSS, and NSTA) offer memberships for teachers in every field and each offers publications and web based resources. National and state-based organizations organize conferences at which educators come together to share and collaborate. Numerous research journals are published regularly and are searchable via indexing services (e.g., ERIC and JSTOR). Journals regularly publish peer-reviewed articles featuring the best new ideas in teaching and learning in their fields. A virtually innumerable amount of resources is available for every teacher who wishes to stay current. A modern professional teacher is one that is open to new ideas and is willing to put forth the effort to learn about new pedagogical methods. A modern professional teacher is willing to try to implement new classroom methods based upon new learning about the best practices.

IMPLICIT TEACHER BIAS

Implicit teacher biases are stereotypes or attitudes that are manifested unconsciously in the classroom. In some cases these biases may adversely affect student learning. One pervasive stereotype is that girls are not able to do mathematics as well as boys. A math teacher may subconsciously call on boys more often or praise girls less often. Boys may do better in this math class because they are given more opportunities or praise, which may not be available to girls because of a stereotype. As a teacher, awareness of potential biases is the first step in overcoming them. Teachers should reflect on their teaching practice and collect/analyze classroom evidence (data) to determine if biases are present. In order for each student to have a fair chance to succeed, teachers must recognize each as an individual, rather than a member of some stereotypical group (e.g., athletic team, ethnic group, gender, or those with past behavioral issues).

MENTORS AS A RESOURCE FOR STRENGTHENING TEACHER KNOWLEDGE, SKILLS, AND EFFECTIVENESS

Collegial collaboration is the basis of quality educational practice. No individual can reach every student or solve every problem. In recent years, a number of school systems have begun formal programs to help train veteran teachers to serve as mentors for younger teachers. A mentor is a veteran teacher who is accepting of a new teacher, is effective in a variety of different interpersonal contexts, and adept at providing instructional support. A mentor is empathetic, optimistic, and open to development in new aspects of the teaching profession. A mentor is a resource who can provide insight into the culture of a school, share tips and tricks that he or she has picked up over the years, and talk about how to resolve challenging circumstances. A mentor is a colleague who can put issues into their proper perspective and reassure a new teacher who may feel isolated or overwhelmed.

PROFESSIONAL LEARNING COMMUNITY (PLC)

Although the phrase "professional learning community" can have multiple meanings, PLCs are most often small groups of educators who meet on a regular basis to discuss and collaborate to improve teaching skills and student academic performance. Professional learning communities might discuss the creation or editing of class materials, completed student work as exemplars of student learning, data from student assessments, or professional literature pertinent to classroom experience. The focus of professional learning communities is learning: student learning and teacher learning about student learning. Professional learning communities can offer an opportunity for teachers to engage in reflection on teaching practice and cycles of action research or other evidence-based adaptations of classroom activities/assessments towards better student performance.

PROFESSIONAL VERSATILITY

Education has never been and will never be a one-size-fits-all endeavor. No two learners are exactly the same and no two classes are exactly the same. What works for one student or class may not work for another. Given the diversity of students in the classroom, open-mindedness and a willingness to adapt are arguably the most important characteristics of successful teachers. Both as an individual in the classroom and as a part of a professional learning community outside of the classroom, an openness to the possibility of a new approach allows a teacher to persevere through the most challenging of circumstances. Challenges encountered might arise due to: behavioral problems, learning differences, student exceptionalities, technology, and any of a number of possible distractions originating inside or outside the classroom. A versatile teacher open to collaboration with colleagues, creative problem solving, and trying new methods can overcome almost any challenge.

ACTION RESEARCH

Action research is a process of reflective classroom inquiry performed by the teacher. Action research is a technique through which a teacher might refine his or her teaching practice by using available data to inform new methods or mechanisms of student learning. The four generic stages for action research are: Plan, Act, Observe, and Reflect. A teacher plans a learning experience for his or her students and then puts that plan into action. The teacher observes his or her students' reactions during the experience and the learning results (positive or negative) through either formative or summative assessment. After analyzing the available quantitative and/or qualitative data, the teacher formulates a new plan of action for future student learning experiences and the action research process begins again. Action-based research is the most natural mechanism of classroom study for the teacher. The teacher is using the evidence available in a scientific process to improve his or her educational practice. Action research is one example of the evidence-based educational practice advocated by the standards.

INVESTIGATING A PROBLEM USING A MIXED METHODS STUDY

Quantitative methodologies are adept at answering "if" questions. Numerical-based methods can help answer questions regarding whether there is evidence that a particular pattern is occurring. For example, a study of test scores will tell you **if** your students understand a given concept. Qualitative (text-based) methods are adept at answering "how" or "why" questions. For example, qualitative (text-based) methods would be required to determine **why** students have not learned a given concept well. Mixed method inquiry (including both quantitative and qualitative aspects) can greatly benefit an educator seeking to grow as a professional by providing both direct verdicts and indirect contexts to questions of pedagogical effectiveness.

QUANTITATIVE AND QUALITATIVE RESEARCH METHODS

Quantitative methods are deductive in nature. Quantitative investigators will collect and analyze numerical data with mathematical and statistical tools. An example of a quantitative method would be to compare the results of a pre-test (before a lesson) and a post-test (after a lesson) to determine **if** a lesson was effective. Quantitative methods are commonly applied in scientific fields in which numerical data is available (e.g., biology and physics).

Qualitative methods are inductive in nature. Qualitative investigators will collect and analyze textual data collected from interviews, observations, or conversations. An example of a qualitative method would be to discuss a lesson (after the fact) and ask the students for their perceptions about the effectiveness of the lesson. Qualitative methods will help determine **why** students were or were not successful on a given assessment. Qualitative methods are commonly applied in fields studying human behavior (e.g., marketing and sociology).

Pros and cons of quantitative and qualitative research methods:

- Quantitative methods are number-based. Qualitative methods are text-based. Numerical methods can determine **if** students are learning about a particular concept. Qualitative methods would be required if a teacher wished to understand **why** students were not learning a given concept.
- Quantitative methods are more objective; numerical data is gathered using unbiased measurements. Qualitative methods are more subjective. Researchers must interpret the results of interviews or discussions and can be susceptible to implicit or explicit biases.
- Quantitative methods tend to require more planning time before implementation while qualitative measures require more time after the implementation. Numerical data are more straightforward to analyze but more difficult to collect. Textual data are more challenging to analyze but less cumbersome to collect.
- Quantitative methods are stricter in their design; collected responses must be numerical. Qualitative methods are more open-ended in their design; a greater variety of responses can be accepted and analyzed.
- Both quantitative and qualitative methods can be shown as valid and reliable.

Roles, Expectations, Ethics, and Legal Concerns

LEGAL RIGHTS AND RESPONSIBILITIES OF TEACHERS, STUDENTS, AND PARENTS

Teachers have Fourteenth Amendment rights to due process receiving termination notice; protection from discrimination based on race, gender, and nationality; privacy; setting student behavior rules and directions, training students to follow rules, requesting support with student behavior; First Amendment academic freedom of expression, limited by student age and grade level, teacher experience, subject content—specifically prohibiting political or personal class discussions; rights and responsibilities to correct, guide, or punish students to meet educational objectives; student custodial responsibilities; training students in moral values and civilized citizenship. Federal rights include for students with disabilities to free, appropriate public education in the least restrictive environment under the Individuals with Disabilities Education Act (IDEA), which gives parents due process rights to advance notice and refusal of identification, evaluation, and placement for special education and related services; to appeal school decisions about their children, etc. Other student rights and responsibilities vary by state and district. An example (Fairfax County Public Schools, Virginia) includes rights to attend safe, welcoming schools; property safety; fairness, respect, and courtesy from school staff and other students; freedom of expression; advocacy for change in laws, regulations, and policies; complaint and response; expulsion and suspension disputes; responsibilities for timely attendance, dress, rule-following; respecting others' rights, property, beliefs, and differences; staff authority; peaceful dispute resolution; not bullying, hurting others, or using violent, obscene, disruptive, or disrespectful words, gestures, and images; and reporting dangerous behavior to staff.

TEACHER ROLES AT PROGRESSIVE LEVELS OF QUALIFICATION, EXPERIENCE, AND EXPERTISE

While specific districts and schools must determine teacher roles and responsibilities, ED provides an example: <u>resident</u> teachers are beginners—not teachers of record, but paid; not student teachers, but completing a (typically 1-year) Master teacher-supervised residency or practicum. <u>Novice</u> teachers are certified, but still developing; paired with master teachers; not tenured, but may receive tenure; typically promoted after two to five years, possibly after two consecutive years' of effective ratings. <u>Professional</u> teachers are tenured, lifelong learner exemplars, academic coaches and advocates. Many teachers spend whole careers at the professional level. <u>Master</u> teachers, key school leadership team members, work in classrooms, lead school teams, and are teaching resources for the whole professional team, modeling effective teaching practices for resident and novice teachers, teaching both students and colleagues—sometimes dividing hours between classrooms and faculty support. They typically have worked at least five years in classrooms, being rated highly effective at least three years. <u>Teacher leaders</u> also divide time between classrooms and working with leadership teams and principals, e.g., sharing distributed leadership, designing peer evaluation and review systems, and developing communities of practice. They have at least five classroom years, demonstrating effectiveness at least three consecutive years. Each level earns more. With development, master teachers and teacher leaders may become principals.

INSTRUCTING SPECIAL-NEEDS STUDENTS

With legal mandates for inclusive education and mainstreaming being today's prevalent trend, special education students frequently end up in regular education classrooms, whose teachers are required to instruct them. This can happen even when students are found eligible for special education and related services, assigned a special education teacher, educational specialist, various therapists, other service personnel based on individual student needs, or Individual Education Plans (IEPs) and learning goals. Teachers collaborate with special educators, who provide knowledge and expertise about classroom accommodations and modifications, differentiated instruction, etc. However, teachers are still responsible for special-needs students' instruction

129

unless student IEPs specify otherwise. Diverse student needs including disabilities; ELL or LEP status; and varied cultural, racial, ethnic, and socioeconomic backgrounds require teachers to ensure all students receive educational equity by making curricular, instructional, and classroom environmental modifications and/or accommodations, including selecting or adapting materials to reflect multicultural perspectives; differentiating instruction; consciously avoiding bias, offering equal opportunities, and treating all students fairly. Teachers are both legally and ethically required to keep student records confidential and protect their personal information's privacy. By copyright law, teachers must also request and obtain author or publisher permission to use copyrighted materials as teaching resources.

FAMILY EDUCATIONAL RIGHTS AND PRIVACY ACT (FERPA)

FERPA applies to all schools receiving federal funds under applicable ED programs. Parents and eligible students (aged 18 or attending post-secondary school) have rights to inspect and review schools' student education records; to request school corrections of misleading or inaccurate records; to formal hearings if schools refuse to amend records; and if schools still refuse following hearings, to file statements contesting information with records. Schools must generally obtain written parent or eligible student permission to release information from student education records. However, records disclosure without consent is allowed by FERPA to these parties or under these conditions: school officials having valid educational interests, schools where students transfer, specified auditing and evaluating officials, appropriate student financial aid-related personnel, accrediting associations, those conducting certain studies on school behalf, by legal subpoena or judicial order, appropriate personnel in safety and health emergencies, and by specific state laws and local juvenile justice system authorities. FERPA allows schools to disclose student names, addresses, phone numbers, birthdates, birthplaces, attendance dates, honors, awards and other "directory" information without consent. However, schools are first required to inform parents or eligible students and allow them enough time to request non-disclosure. FERPA requires schools to notify parents or eligible students annually of their FERPA rights.

EQUAL ACCESS ACT (1984)

The federal Equal Access Act (1984) prohibits discrimination against student religious groups in public high schools receiving federal funds. Such schools having at least one non-curriculum, student-led club meeting outside class hours ("limited open forum") must allow organization of additional such clubs and equal access to school meeting places and publications. Groups interfering with orderly school activities are exceptions. Technically, schools can prohibit all non-curriculum clubs to "opt out" of this law. In *Westside Community Schools v. Mergens* (1990), the Supreme Court declared this law constitutional, ordering the school let a Christian student group meet. It has been invoked in lawsuits against school administrations denying Gay-Straight Alliance assembly and privileges. State Supreme Courts have always ruled in favor of these alliances, saying schools must either allow them or ban all non-curriculum group assembly. Two major legislative acts governing privacy and confidentiality of student education records in schools are the Family Educational Rights and Privacy Act (FERPA, 1974) and Individuals with Disabilities Education Act (IDEA, formerly PL 94-142, 1975). Both grant similar rights to parents and eligible students (aged 18 or attending post-secondary schools) to review or inspect records, request correction, have formal hearings, document contested information, and advance notice and non-disclosure of directory information.

AMERICAN ASSOCIATION OF EDUCATORS (AAE) CODE OF ETHICS FOR EDUCATORS

Principle I: Ethical Conduct toward Students – Educators interact justly, considerately with every student, resolving disciplinary and other problems by school policy and law; eschew intentionally exposing students to disparagement; protect student information confidentiality unless laws require otherwise; constructively endeavor to protect students from conditions harming safety, health, or learning; and seek to present facts without bias, personal prejudice, or distortion. Principle II: Ethical Conduct toward Practices and Performance – Educators meet appointment or contract terms and apply for, accept, and assign positions and responsibilities based on professional qualifications; maintain physical and mental health and social judgment to perform professional duties; continue professional growth; follow laws, regulations, and school policies; avoid intentionally misrepresenting official school or educational organization policies; distinguish these from personal opinions; account for all funds in their charge; and never use professional or institutional privileges for partisan or personal advantages. Principle III: Ethical Conduct toward Professional Colleagues – Educators protect colleague information confidentiality except required by law, make no willful false statements about colleagues or school systems, do not interfere with colleague free choice, and fight coercion violating professional integrity. Principle IV: Ethical Conduct toward Parents and Community – Educators work to communicate to parents all information in student interests; respect diverse cultural values and traditions in classrooms and communities; and take active, positive roles in school and community relations.

SUSPENSION OR REVOCATION AN EDUCATOR'S CERTIFICATE

The Education Practices Commission may suspend an educator certificate for up to five years, or revoke it for up to 10 years or permanently for: fraudulent certificate pursuit or acquisition; knowingly not reporting suspected or actual child abuse, alleged administrator or instructional staff misconduct affecting student safety, health, or welfare; proven incompetence to teach or perform duties in public school or teach in or operate private school; acts of moral turpitude or gross immorality; suspension, revocation, or surrender of certification in another state; conviction or guilty plea to a felony, misdemeanor, or any criminal charge except minor traffic violations; being found guilty of personal conduct seriously decreasing district school board employee effectiveness; breach of contract; Department of Revenue notice or court order of certificate suspension due to noncompliance with a written agreement, subpoena, or order to show cause or child support order; violation of Principles of Professional Conduct for the Education Profession according to State Board of Education rules; other law provision violations penalized by certificate revocation; violation of any Education Practices Commission order; plea agreement or court order in any jurisdiction requiring permanent certificate surrender or relinquishment, pursuant to commissioner probable cause finding; or disqualification from educator certification under any of the felony or misdemeanor offenses prohibited under any section of the statute on disqualification from employment (s. 1012.315). There are six additional provisions, three with two, three, and two respective subsections.

PROVISIONS INCLUDED IN MOST SCHOOL DISTRICT POLICIES FOR USING TECHNOLOGY IN SCHOOLS

Individual school districts establish policies for technology use. For example, district policies may include Internet safety terms like software filters blocking access to material that is pornographic, obscene, harmful to children, otherwise inappropriate, or disrupts the educational process. Typical disclaimers include that filtering software may block access to other materials, may not succeed in blocking access to all inappropriate or disruptive materials, and does not cancel user obligations not to access such materials. Terms and conditions of use for curriculum and instruction include using district technological and telecommunications resources consistently with district curriculum and diverse student developmental levels, abilities, instructional needs, and learning styles; adhering to selection criteria for instructional and library media center materials; and permission for school staff to use technology and Internet resources throughout the curriculum, consistently with district guidelines and goals. Terms and conditions may define district electronic resources as part of curriculum, not a general-use public forum; stipulate that staff give students developmentally appropriate guidance in using digital information resources for district curriculum-related study and research; and inform students of their network user rights and responsibilities before giving them access. Acceptable use prescriptions and proscriptions, including regarding copyright laws and software licensing agreements, are typically parts of these policies.

USE AND MAINTENANCE OF STUDENT RECORDS AND INFORMATION

Permanent, cumulative student records—physical or electronic—can vary by school district in kinds of information they contain. Student records include student information, curriculum information, annual standardized test scores, Individualized Education Program (IEP) records, ELP levels, academic background, recent report cards, conference information, teacher comments, and other pertinent information. Teachers should check their school's policy and procedures regarding student records; check cumulative records first when they have questions about individual students; open and update cumulative records when school years start; update IEPs, ELP level changes, and conference information throughout the year; add final attendance, curriculum covered, report cards, comments, and close records at years' ends. Every student cumulative record is a confidential, legal record. Parents and students aged 18+ can request access to their records in writing. Otherwise, only school officials whose professional responsibilities require it can legally view cumulative records. Keep all information safe, intact, and confidential. When working on secure or shared computers, always log out after accessing electronic cumulative records to protect their security. Paper cumulative records should always be kept in school fireproof cabinets unless staff is directly working with them. Replace checked-out cumulative records nightly, never taking them home or leaving them in classrooms.

ETHICAL RESPONSIBILITIES FOR A CLASSROOM TEACHER (CAPTAIN)

1. **Confidentiality**: A teacher must not reveal confidential information regarding a student, unless for a professional purpose or as required by law.
2. **Advantage**: A teacher must not use professional relationships with students for private advantage.
3. **Protection**: A teacher must protect a student from harm to his or her health, safety, or welfare. A teacher's duty includes reporting any suspicion of abuse or neglect and taking the proper care not to expose a child to inappropriate disparagement or embarrassment.
4. **Truth**: A teacher must faithfully render reports regarding either students or colleagues. A teacher must never knowingly make false or malicious statements about a student or a colleague.
5. **Authenticity**: A teacher must not distort or suppress elements of his or her subject matter. A teacher must not deny a student's access to different viewpoints and must not impede a student's independent action in pursuit of learning.
6. **Integrity**: A teacher must not misrepresent his or her educational credentials or those of another person.
7. **Non-Discrimination**: A teacher must not unfairly deny benefits from (or grant benefits to) a student on the basis of race, gender, personal beliefs, family, cultural background, or sexual orientation.

ROLE OF THE EDUCATION SYSTEM IN A DEMOCRATIC SOCIETY

American education systems arose, in part, as a mechanism to prepare students to become responsible citizens in a democratic society. Historically, decisions regarding schools were made in deference to the common good. The school system is open to every student and every student is entitled to an education that will allow him or her to have a fair opportunity to become a successful adult. As a cornerstone of the American democratic society, schools have sometimes been at the center of controversial social questions. For example, 1954's *Brown vs. Board* Supreme Court decision forbidding segregated schools was a crucial part of the larger civil rights movement. Since 1954, Congress has passed legislation (such as 1973's Individuals with Disabilities Education Act) promising each student a free and appropriate public education. This phrase is particularly meaningful for exceptional students who may not be served well by standard educational offerings. Exceptional students may be entitled to an Individual Educational Program (IEP) that provides access to the general curriculum otherwise unavailable due to disability. Educators at every level (national, state, and local) work in collaboration so that every student can have access to a quality education and the promises of a democratic society.

SUSPICION OF ABUSE OR NEGLECT OF A STUDENT

The exact guidelines regarding the reporting of child abuse or child neglect will vary by state. In many states teachers who suspect abuse or neglect are required by law to report the suspicion to local authorities within a set timeframe (e.g., 48 hours). Reports of suspected abuse are most likely confidential and educators who make a report of suspected abuse in good faith are typically immune from criminal or civil repercussions. Although you may wish to talk about the situation with a mentor or administrator, reporting to an educational superior will not satisfy a teacher's legal reporting requirement. All reports must be made to the proper local authorities (e.g., Child Protective Services).

CLASSROOM FAIR USE OF COPYRIGHTED IMAGES, SOUNDS, AND VIDEOS FOUND ON THE INTERNET

Images found on the internet may be used for in-classroom purposes by a teacher or student. Images found on the internet may not be reposted to the web without permission. No more than 15 images or 10% (whichever is less) of a given collection may be used. Up to 10% (up to a maximum of 30 seconds) of a copyrighted musical composition may be used by educators or students as part of a multimedia presentation. Videos may be used in the classroom for instructional purposes and may not be used for entertainment. No more than 10% of a video or three minutes (whichever is less) may be used.

The Professional Environmnet

Family Involvement

COMMUNICATING WITH PARENTS

Ask individual students' parents which communication methods work best for them; use multiple methods. Though traditional written notes and phone calls take more time, some parents prefer them. Many parents email; others want text messages; some can be reached on Twitter or Facebook; others want classroom blogs, websites, and/or videos. SnappSchool.com and similar online tools enable simultaneous multiple communication methods. Target goals—recruiting more parents to share workplace experiences with students, improving student attendance, etc.—when planning communications. Establishing and communicating high standards and expectations at the beginning of the year and regularly thereafter make parents allies to reinforce your expectations at home: studies find parental expectations among the strongest predictors of student achievement; later communications about problems receive more objective, supportive responses. Communicating about the class, not just their child, helps parents see your viewpoint if some decisions that are not ideal for one student are best for the class. Remember the school also communicates with parents, so avoid duplicating fundraising appeals. But inform and advise them of all school resources, including after-school and summer programs or other services supporting shared goals for students. Measure effectiveness by whether parents return permission slips and/or visit, students come to class prepared; note which methods elicit more responses for future reference.

PARTNERING WITH PARENTS TO INCREASE STUDENT ACHIEVEMENT

While preparing educators with information and training for involving parents, ED's model for parent involvement through parent-educator partnership to enhance student achievement prepares parents by communicating, in appropriate formats and languages, timely accountability data, core subject teacher qualifications, supplemental education services, home and school involvement opportunities, and parental rights and roles. ED also provides training and materials for helping children achieve academically; recruiting and training parent leaders in data interpretation, advocacy skills, and training other parents; involving parents in helping to monitor and evaluate the effectiveness of school policies for parental involvement; facilitating meaningful two-way engagement; and training parent leaders for participating on school advisory boards, school site-based parental advisory councils, and other groups that influence educational policymaking. Educators are informed of parent involvement policies and procedures, opportunities to involve parents, accountability data, and options among supplemental education services available to students. Educators and school staff receive training to prepare parents and other educators; assess needs; create family-friendly schools; identify, recruit, and train staff in parental involvement's value; monitor compliance with parental involvement requirements; evaluate parent involvement policy effectiveness including parent input; engage parents in developing plans for increasing student achievement; and collaborate with parents on advisory boards and site councils.

ENGAGING FAMILIES FROM DIVERSE BACKGROUNDS

In recent decades, education research shows parental involvement and student achievement correlate directly. Multiple studies find that, regardless of background or income, students with involved parents more likely attend school regularly, adapt well, enroll in higher-level programs, achieve higher test scores and grades, display better behavior and social skills, graduate, and pursue post-secondary education. Research reveals three key practices of schools successfully engaging families from diverse backgrounds: recognizing, respecting, and addressing cultural and class differences and family needs; focusing on building trusting, collaborative relationships among families, community members, and teachers; and espousing partnership philosophies with shared power and responsibility. Every Student Succeeds Act's (ESSA) Title I lists parental involvement requirements for Title I schools, other schools, districts, and state education agencies. Immigrant parents may have cultural beliefs of not questioning teachers; low-income, homeless, multi-job, single, and/or LEP parents and those with past negative school experiences care about children's education, but may have difficulty expressing it. They may not know how to engage, feel incapable of making meaningful contributions, or do not feel welcome. The US Department of Education has therefore established a nationwide system of Parental Information and Resource Centers (PIRCs) under the Elementary and Secondary Education Act (ESEA) to provide parents, schools, and organizations with training, technical assistance, information, organizational partnerships, and support regarding child development and school success needs.

HELPING PARENTS UNDERSTAND SCHOOL DATA ABOUT STUDENT PROGRESS

Under federal ED establishment of nationwide Parental Information and Resource Centers (PIRCs), state family centers have produced digital media explaining information related to the Every Student Succeeds Act (ESSA), including on school accountability, testing, school choice, and socioeconomic status. Trainers use these DVDs at PTA, school board, advisory board, school staff, and community organization meetings and site council trainings to reach wider audiences. Some have produced Spanish versions. DVDs are especially useful to inform non-reading parents, and can trigger questions and discussions which PIRC staff and volunteers can address or facilitate. Center staffs ask parent advisory councils and focus groups, including immigrants, to review materials and give feedback whether it is comprehensible and interesting. The American Development Institute's (ADI) PIRC offers workshops helping parents understand school (not student) report card data including demographics, academic performance, and Adequate Yearly Progress (AYP). ED guidelines for teachers to help parents access and understand education-related information include: rather than "reinvent the wheel," look for and distribute existing tools and publications. Design NCLB-related materials that are short, clear, and concise. Ask parent representatives to review drafts of new materials for reader-friendliness before production. Make informational DVDs for group meetings and non-reading parents. Initiate guidance sessions, websites, and workshops to communicate and help parents understand relevant educational issues.

CONDUCTING CONFERENCES WITH PARENTS

A parent-teacher conference is a two-way conversation focused on student learning. A teacher should use concrete examples and avoid abstract assessments of a student. A teacher should seek collaborative solutions to issues that have arisen and should seek to open the lines of communication for future dialogue on improving student learning. A teacher should remain positive and discuss a student's growth and progress. Though some negative aspects of a conversation may be inevitable, a teacher can always pivot back to future positive opportunities and building on a student's previous successes. One of the core aspects of cultural responsive curricula is positive perspectives on students' families. A parent conference is an excellent opportunity to build rapport and establish a collaborative relationship that will positively affect student learning both in the classroom and in the home. A teacher should ask questions of parents and listen actively. A family will be able to provide input into a student's learning styles and background that are not otherwise easily accessible.

Include students in parent conferences when possible. Hearing teacher praise benefits them. For criticisms of performance, study habits, or behaviors, attending students are present to participate in correction plans. Come prepared with test results, work samples, anecdotal observation notes, etc., presenting concrete evidence to discuss with parents rather than vague references. Ask parents to inform you about their child's performance in previous school years. Approach problems positively, focusing on plans for correction with student and parent agreement. Propose any ideas you have for implementing assistance as specifically as possible, including what parents can expect of you in progress reporting and how to stay in communication in the immediate future and throughout the year. Take care not to overextend yourself with phone calls or written reports on just one of many students, which can also irritate busy parents. Impress upon parents that you are a team to recruit their participation, e.g., monitoring children's studying, checking homework, and/or signing your weekly or daily reports. Avoid defending your policies or yourself: reflect on the student and how s/he can best work with existing classroom procedures and rules. Give parents contact information. Regardless of effort required, begin and end conferences with something positive about the student.

MTLE Practice Test

1. At the start of a unit on the life cycle of plants, a nineth-grade teacher instructs her students to write an open-ended response on what they already know in their daily journals. How can the teacher best use this data to guide her instruction?

    a. Use the student responses to create her assessment on the unit
    b. Gauge how interested her students are in the topic
    c. Evaluate which students are the most advanced
    d. Assess each student's background knowledge

2. A teacher has trouble getting students to refocus after lunch. What method should the teacher use to best correct this problem?

    a. Allow students 15 minutes to get back on task after lunch
    b. Hold all students back after class and have them call their parents
    c. Remind students of the rules and expectations when in class
    d. Immediately assign students detention when they misbehave

3. A tenth-grade teacher wants to assign a writing assignment to her class that has a real-world connection. Which of the following writing assignments should she assign?

    a. Allow students to choose a book in the library to write a report on
    b. Have students write a letter to their local school board about what new topic they want taught in schools
    c. Allow students to work in groups to brainstorm an assignment, then have the classroom vote on the best option
    d. Assign students an expository essay on the steps to passing a law

4. Which of the following would be the most effective in helping students take better ownership of their own individual learning processes?

    a. Allow students to choose which of their assignments should be graded
    b. Have students self-grade each assignment to say what grade they think they should receive
    c. Provide checklists and rubrics to students to let them know what is expected on assignments
    d. Have a designated place in each student's binder to record each grade and track their progress

5. Which of the following accurately describes rubrics as assessment tools?

    a. They typically define specific tasks, skills, or behaviors after performance.
    b. They typically guide task performance but do not give criteria for success.
    c. They typically should be explained to students by teachers after assessing.
    d. They typically define and describe general ranges or levels of performance.

6. A special education teacher is working to create an IEP for one of her students. To complete her IEP, she needs to record when the student reached certain developmental and academic milestones. Who is the best person to reach out to in order to get this information?

    a. The student's pediatrician
    b. The student's previous teachers
    c. The school counselor
    d. The student's parent or guardian

7. A student with autism is non-verbal but is in an inclusion classroom with a paraprofessional for support. The teacher is planning a group activity with students. What is an intervention that the teacher or paraprofessional could put in place to support this student?

a. Pair him with another non-verbal student for group assignments
b. Tell the student to listen to other students in his group but tell him he does not have to participate
c. Excuse the student from all group activities
d. Provide a device to the student to assist him with communication

8. In her sociology unit on race and ethnicity, a teacher struggles to maintain respectful conversations among students regarding controversial subjects. Which of the following steps should she implement to address this problem?

a. Direct students to ask their parents what they should say
b. Refer students to administrators when they behave inappropriately
c. Demonstrate what appropriate discussion on the topic sounds like
d. Assign students to write an essay on how to be polite in class

9. A nineth-grade life science teacher wants to see if her students are following proper safety procedures in a lab setting. What is the best way to assess if they are correctly following procedures?

a. Give students a pop quiz on proper lab safety procedures
b. Observe students while they are working on a lab in class
c. Hold a class-wide discussion on how to maintain proper lab safety
d. Have students role-play scenarios demonstrating both proper and improper lab safety scenarios

10. Of the following terms, which one means thinking and learning about one's own thought and learning processes?

a. Schema
b. Transfer
c. Self-efficacy
d. Metacognition

11. An 11th-grade class has a requirement of a year-long project for successful completion of the course. Which of the following strategies would be best for the teacher to implement to ensure that students do not fall behind during the project?

a. Establish mini-deadlines for students to turn in parts of the project to hold them accountable
b. Schedule regular visits to the computer lab during class time for the students to work on their project
c. Teach students how to best collect research for this project
d. Ask students for updates on their progress once a week

12. In an inclusion classroom, a student with profound hearing loss is regularly mocked by students when she speaks. How should the classroom teacher and resource teacher work to solve this issue?

a. Correct inappropriate behavior immediately when it occurs in class
b. Create and put in place a strict no-bully policy for all students in the classroom
c. Move the child back to a self-contained environment for her protection
d. Contact the parents and guardians of all students to explain what is occurring

13. Which of the following selections best specifies the benefits of using a variety of instructional strategies for classroom instruction?

a. Teachers that use a variety of instructional strategies are more likely to be engaged in their classroom
b. Helps keep students from becoming bored in class
c. It serves as data for teachers to document that they have attempted multiple strategies
d. Using multiple instructional strategies helps address the different learning styles of students

14. A 10th grade world history teacher begins a lesson on how to properly answer document-based questions in his classroom. Which strategy is likely to prove most effective in teaching this process to his students?

a. Provide the students with an expected layout for answering all document-based questions
b. Show multiple good models of responses to document-based questions and evaluate what the respondents did well as well as what they could have improved upon
c. Assign students a document-based question, grade it, and return it to them so they can see what they need to improve upon
d. Have students peer review each other's first attempt at a document-based question to learn how others chose to formulate their answers

15. What is the best way that teachers can help make sure that proper ethical behavior related to technology is followed in their classroom?

a. Model appropriate behavior while using technology
b. Continually monitor students while they are using technology in the classroom
c. Give students a list of guidelines that they should follow
d. Give a test on proper ethical behavior to the students

16. During classroom discussions, what is the best way to show that students' opinions and additions to the discussion are respected, appreciated, and important?

a. After a student comments, the teacher asks the entire classroom what they think of their statement
b. Requiring each student to speak at least twice every time a class discussion is held
c. Regularly encouraging students to elaborate on their contributions to the discussion
d. Allow students enough time to formulate responses and prompt them when they experience difficulty answering questions

17. In a probability unit, a teacher assigns multiple word problems nightly for the students' homework. The students complain that the word problems are boring and they do not want to do them. What can the teacher do to help the students become more engaged in the probability unit?

　　a. Excuse the students from homework and only do math problems in class for the remainder of the unit

　　b. Teach a lesson on the importance of word problems and how they will relate to everyday life

　　c. Ask teachers of other subjects for word problems that can be used in her classroom

　　d. Create word problems that better relate to real-world experiences for the students

18. Which of the following can be typically found in permanent student records?

　　a. Contact information for all of the student's family members

　　b. Creative projects by the student from each school year

　　c. A personal goal sheet updated yearly by the student

　　d. Report cards for the student going back to when they entered public school

19. Prior to the start of his first year of teaching, a language arts teacher asks other teachers for advice on how to best organize his class for group work. Which of the following is the best advice for this teacher to take to organize his classroom?

　　a. Make sure all supplies are in a central location for groups to easily access

　　b. Display posters around the classroom about how to properly work and behave in groups

　　c. Organize students into rows and assign them to groups early in the school year

　　d. Arrange desks in groups of four to five and create spaces for students to collect materials and turn in assignments

20. A group of teachers are given a day to plan interdisciplinary units collaboratively prior to the beginning of a school year. What should these teachers do first to ensure that they plan effectively?

　　a. Create an outline of key concepts in each unit to see which concepts overlap between subjects

　　b. Have each teacher discuss what they want to accomplish in the interdisciplinary unit

　　c. Work together to create a detailed summative assessment for the unit that will assess each subject being taught

　　d. Construct a list of what information they want students to learn from this unit

21. What kind of validity indicates how representative a test is of every part or detail of a construct?

　　a. Content validity

　　b. Criterion validity

　　c. Construct validity

　　d. Concurrent validity

22. Which of the following is the best reason for using technology in a lesson?

　　a. It allows students to become more immersed in the content they are learning

　　b. Students can finish assignments faster so that more material can be taught

　　c. It allows the lesson to become more accessible to students of varying abilities

　　d. It gives the teacher an opportunity to create further lessons to use

23. When a teacher asks an oral question to a student in class, what should be the main reasoning for how long to allow the student to formulate a response?
 a. How many students have their hands up to also answer the question
 b. The level of difficulty of the question
 c. How well the student usually performs in that teacher's classroom
 d. How much time the teacher built into the class period for questioning

24. A nineth-grade math teacher spends a week teaching her advanced students a new concept. After giving a quiz, she notices that four students in her class are still having difficulty mastering the subject. What should this teacher's next step be in helping these students learn the material?
 a. Assign the other students an enrichment activity while using targeted instruction with the group of four
 b. Allow the struggling students the opportunity to retake assessments to see if they improve
 c. Assign each of the four students a peer tutor in the classroom to assist them with their work
 d. Assign the students extra homework to see if their work improves in class

25. Upon receiving a quiz back from earlier in the week, a high school student puts his head down on his desk and will not lift it back up. What should the teacher try first to help the student?
 a. Email a counselor to request that they pull the student out of the classroom and discuss the issue
 b. Contact the student's parents after class to inform them that he may be upset about his quiz results
 c. Write a note asking if the student is okay, discreetly give it to them, and return later to read the response
 d. Ask the student to sit back up and assign appropriate consequences if he does not do so

26. During a unit on integers, a math teacher administers a quiz to assess her students. A large proportion of students receive a failing grade. What is the best strategy the teacher should implement to correct this issue?
 a. The teacher should individually conference with each student who failed to ask what they did to prepare for the quiz
 b. The teacher should look at the quizzes to see what common mistakes were made, and work on reteaching the material to the students
 c. The teacher should increase homework and encourage students to study at home
 d. The teacher should ask students for input on what they still need to learn to be successful

27. What is the primary reason teachers should strive to read educational articles and publications related to their own subjects?
 a. It allows teachers to take ownership of their learning so they can model independent study
 b. It enables teachers to identify the professional goals that they need to work on improving
 c. It allows the educator to learn from other professionals in their field to ensure they are teaching current content
 d. It allows educators the opportunity to find new research and studies that they can bring to meetings at their school

28. What is the best way for an educator to utilize tablets in the classroom?
   a. To assist students in completing homework
   b. To help students stay on task
   c. To supplement instruction through activities on the tablet that support the concepts being taught in class
   d. To provide enrichment to students who complete their assignments faster than other students in the classroom

29. Teachers at a school are required to take attendance in every class period. When is the best time for them to take attendance each period?
   a. At the very beginning of the class
   b. Once students have settled down and are working
   c. Immediately before dismissing students for the day
   d. Just after the students leave the classroom, so the teacher does not waste instructional time

30. In a parent-teacher conference to discuss a student's progress, both the parents and the teacher agree that they each need to take steps to support the education of the student. Which of the following could the teacher suggest for keeping track of steps being taken at home and at school?
   a. Request the parents discuss necessary interventions with their child to make them more willing to accept the steps being taken to assist them
   b. Create a spot in the child's daily folder for parents and teachers to communicate regularly about interventions, progress, and problems that may arise
   c. Hold conferences with the parents once a week to discuss the progress that has been made with the student
   d. Suggest the parents hire a personal tutor for the child to implement the interventions and collect data for the student

31. What is the main purpose of formative assessments?
   a. To establish the background knowledge of students prior to beginning a unit
   b. To assess students partway through a unit to establish which content is mastered and which needs to be retaught
   c. To compare data to other teachers and assess the effectiveness of the teacher
   d. To assess students at the conclusion of a unit of study

32. A tenth-grade teacher wants to help her students develop critical thinking skills. Which assignment would best help students develop this skill while in her social studies class?
   a. Ask students to create a law they feel should exist and defend their reasoning
   b. Have students interview an adult who works in government
   c. Have students write a report on the history of their state government
   d. Give an assignment to create a list of laws passed in the last year

33. On the first day of school, a teacher leads her classroom in a discussion of proper rules and procedures to follow in class. She begins with a rule she believes is vital for learning and asks the students to propose new rules and procedures for class with her input and approval. What is the primary benefit of discussing classroom rules in this manner?

a. It encourages students to better be in control of their behaviors while in the classroom
b. It helps students feel like they are contributing members of the classroom environment
c. It serves as an important icebreaker on the first day of school to get to know the students
d. It encourages students to take ownership of their learning

34. A ninth-grade teacher is planning to assign a major research paper to his students. What strategy could he implement that would be most helpful to help his students be aware of the teacher's expectations of this research paper?

a. Have students self-grade their research paper prior to turning in it using the rubric provided by the teacher so they can predict their grade
b. Allow students to create the rubric for the paper so that they are allowed to take ownership of what the requirements should be
c. Discuss and show the students the rubric for the paper in the same class after assigning the paper and allow them to ask questions about the rubric
d. Discuss with students what they want to learn from writing this research paper and create a rubric based on what they hope to learn

35. FERPA regulations allow student records disclosure without consent under which conditions?

a. To any school officials, who need not have specific reasons
b. To schools where students transfer so records are needed
c. To school personnel excepting those related to financial aid
d. To any auditing or evaluating officials with no specifications

36. Which of the following is an example of extrinsic motivation?

a. A student works hard in all classes because his parents give him $20 for every "A" grade he receives
b. A student volunteers to walk dogs at an animal shelter after school because he wants to help animals in tough situations
c. A student wants to audition for the school play because they want to learn how to perform in front of an audience
d. A student works on developing their conversational skills because they want to make friends at their new school

37. An economics teacher assigns students a section to read in the textbook over types of unemployment. Which of the following extension activities could this teacher assign to their students after the reading that would involve the highest level of mastery for the students?

a. Define the characteristics and include examples of the different types of unemployment
b. Write five multiple choice questions to give to another student in the class to evaluate their knowledge on unemployment
c. Create flash cards over important vocabulary words from the reading section
d. Build a compare/contrast diagram to demonstrate how each type of unemployment compares to the other types

38. At the end of a unit on stoichiometry, a high school chemistry teacher wants to assess student knowledge. What is the best summative assessment for the teacher to administer to the students?

a. A pop quiz on stoichiometry
b. A test on stoichiometry
c. A video on stoichiometry and its application in the real world
d. A class-wide review game on stoichiometry and the concepts involved

39. A teacher is trying to help students understand and appreciate the diversity among her students at an extremely diverse school. Which of the following strategies could this teacher implement to meet this goal?

a. Give a planner with the holidays and festivals of the cultures represented in her classroom to each student
b. Decorate her classroom with posters and maps showing the world's diverse cultures and their locations
c. Ask each student to give a presentation about parts of their culture important to them
d. Create a plan to incorporate resources that represent various cultural perspectives into her lessons

40. A teacher is working on improving organizational skills with her students. Part of what she does is to allow five minutes of time at the end of every class for students to record what they were working on carefully into their notebooks and update their student planners with any homework or test information. How does this likely promote student learning and achievement within her classroom?

a. It conveys her expectations that students will be held accountable while in her classroom
b. It helps to make students aware of which skills need more improvement
c. It helps teach important life skills that will hopefully lead to increased academic success
d. It demonstrates to her students that her classroom is a place where they should feel safe to learn

41. Mr. Glenn, a teacher with seven years of experience, has been asked to mentor his first teacher this year. Which of the following will be likely required of him to do as a mentor teacher?

a. Observe the teacher teaching in her class several times a week
b. Providing encouragement, support, and guidance to the new teacher throughout the year
c. Regularly review the new teacher's lesson plans to make sure she is teaching the correct material
d. Reporting to the administrator what struggles the new teacher is experiencing and how the school can help

42. Which of the following scenarios would be appropriate from a developmental standpoint for students within the respective age range?

a. Kindergarteners assembling a puzzle of the United States to learn geography
b. Fifth-grade students raising tadpoles to frogs to learn about the life cycle
c. First-graders using jelly beans to understand addition and subtraction
d. Seventh-grade students researching and writing an independent research paper on an expansive subject

43. A new teacher wants to make her students feel like their contributions during class discussions are important and vital to the flow of the classroom. What can this teacher do to ensure that students understand this while they are in her classroom?

a. Always be sure to ask follow-up questions when students contribute to the discussion
b. Offer extra credit when students participate in class
c. When students speak, allow other students a chance to respond to what the student said
d. Provide appropriate wait time and necessary cues when students are participating in class

44. A student is struggling with finishing her multiplication tests in the allotted timeframe. What could the teacher implement to help the student?

a. Assign the student extra homework
b. Reduce the number of questions this student must complete in the timeframe
c. Have the student stay in class during recess for more practice
d. Isolate the student from other students in the classroom

45. In the middle of the school year, a high school teacher learns that a new student with moderate vision loss will be joining her classroom. What can the teacher do to help the student feel comfortable and safe in her classroom?

a. Set aside a time during the student's first week in class for other students to ask questions about his disability and limitations
b. Arrange a time to discuss any concerns or requests the student may have in private
c. Hold a class discussion on how to make students with disabilities feel welcome in the classroom
d. Allow the student's parents to observe the class any time they desire

46. What is the purpose of a teacher assessing student knowledge prior to the start of an instructional unit?

a. To see what prior knowledge students may have about a topic
b. To see which intervention strategies a teacher may need to implement in a unit
c. To assess student interest in a topic
d. To gauge which students will need the most instructional support in the upcoming unit

47. In a high school classroom, there are multiple English-language learners (ELLs) of differing English proficiencies. How can a teacher best support these students in the classroom?

a. Pair each ELL with a native speaker for all assignments
b. Provide personal dictionaries and extended time to all students
c. Make directions on assignments simpler so that all students can understand the instructions
d. Pull ELLs out of the classroom for more complicated assignments

48. When giving standardized assessments, why is it imperative that teachers read all required directions aloud to their students, even if it may seem repetitive at times?

a. To make sure that all teachers take the same amount of time to administer the assessment
b. So that teachers are aware of all directions that exist for the duration of the assessment
c. To ensure that students are focused prior to beginning the assessment
d. All students should be able to test in similar environments, regardless of their teacher

49. A class is learning about the effect sunlight has on plants. What is the best way for these students to learn and comprehend this new topic?
   a. Go on a walk outside during science class to view plants in the woods behind the school
   b. Have students watch a video on the process behind photosynthesis and how it works
   c. Create a worksheet that teaches the students the process of how photosynthesis works with plants
   d. Have students plant seeds and raise them in the classroom in varying levels of light

50. On the first day of school, a teacher asks her students to create a list of tasks they feel they do well. How can this activity help the teacher throughout the year?
   a. It is a way for the teacher to informally assess her students' abilities and learn about their interests
   b. It serves as a tool the teacher can use to assess each student's background knowledge
   c. It will help the teacher know which students to pair in groups
   d. It helps the students feel confident about what they already know

51. The day before a unit test over the Civil War, a teacher builds in a day to allow her students to review. She wants her students to work together to review the material. Which of the following would be the best way to have her students prepare for the test?
   a. Allow students to decide how they should review for tomorrow's test
   b. Students work in groups of two or three to complete a study guide for the test
   c. Have students watch a video reviewing key battles and moments of the Civil War
   d. Assign students to work in groups to create a concept map over the Civil War unit

52. A teacher is assigning students a group science project to create a plan for keeping water clean in their community. She plans to have students work in groups of four. What would be the benefit to using homogeneous groups for this project?
   a. Students on a higher level will be able to assist lower-level students within their group
   b. The teacher would have the opportunity to assist lower-ability groups, while also enriching the project for groups of higher ability levels
   c. It would make grading the projects more straightforward and would likely cause fewer disagreements in each group
   d. Students in the same groups should be able to assist each other more easily

53. A student has begun struggling in several content areas where previously they did not demonstrate any deficiencies. Which of the following would be the most appropriate in terms of delivering this information to the parents of the child at a meeting?
   a. Create a chart comparing the student's progress to the progress of a typical student in their grade
   b. Ask the parents what they think the teacher should do for their child
   c. Bring multiple samples of the student's work to the parents that demonstrate the areas of concern
   d. Compare the student's work to the work of their classmates to show how the child is struggling

146

54. A first-year teacher wants to improve how well she manages her classroom. Which approach would be most effective in improving her classroom management practices?

a. Ask the principal of the school for the best techniques for classroom management
b. Ask the media center specialist for books and other resources that teach effective classroom management
c. Observe experienced teachers to get an idea of how they manage their classrooms
d. Consult with parents about what they have found effective in managing their own children

55. A high school history teacher has assigned his final research project of the semester. For this project, he sets the requirement of four online sources and three print sources. Over the next few days, several students express their concern over being unable to find the necessary sources to complete their project due to their lack of computer access at home. What can the teacher do to make sure all students have fair access to complete this project?

a. Make and arrangement media center specialists for students to stay after school to gather the necessary research materials for the project
b. Schedule time in your class period for students to go to the media center and computer lab to gather the necessary research
c. Provide clear instructions for the project so that students know what is expected of them
d. Pair students together so that students with access to resources work with students without access to resources

56. A teacher's second period class is proving to be repeatedly disruptive during classroom instruction. Several interventions by the teacher have proven ineffective. The teacher decides to implement a system where every time he must stop class due to a student disruption, a check mark is placed on the board. If there are fewer than seven checkmarks at the end of the week, the students get 20 minutes of free time in the classroom. Why is this intervention likely to be more successful than the teacher's previous attempts?

a. Students will be incentivized to not disrupt the class because they will not want to disappoint their classmates
b. Parents will ensure that their child is not the cause of the classroom not receiving the reward
c. Students will become more concerned with the consequences of their behavior
d. Students will want to show the teacher that they are not the reason class is being continually disrupted

57. An ELL teacher is working on improving the writing skills and confidence of her ELL students. Which would be the best method for providing feedback to her students on a written assignment?

a. Provide positive comments as well as comments on the errors the students made
b. Be careful to comment on only what the student did correctly on the written assignment
c. Use a rubric to grade each student's work, pointing out what they did well and what they should work to correct in the future
d. Note each mistake the student made and tell them how to properly fix the error

58. What is the best reasoning for using collaborative groups in the learning process?

a. It makes students more excited to be in school

b. It increases engagement in the classroom

c. It reduces the amount of time spent grading, so more time can be spent planning lessons

d. It allows students to work with each other to create solutions to problems presented in class

59. What is the proper way for an educator to ensure students with auditory processing disorders understand instructions given in a classroom?

a. Repeat each set of instructions at least twice to make sure students understand what to do

b. Speak louder and slower when giving instructions and check in with the student when it is time for independent work

c. When giving verbal instructions, always include written instructions on the board or in front of students

d. Refer the student to the school counselor to learn new strategies for listening to instructions

60. A senior in high school notices that a classmate, Karis, whom she has known for years, has become quiet and withdrawn from school. The original student approaches her math teacher to let her teacher know her concern. The teacher tells the student that Karis' mother has just died, and Karis is struggling to adjust. Which statement gives a correct assessment of the teacher's response to the student?

a. The teacher's response was ethical because she was stating facts about Karis, not opinions

b. The teacher's response was ethical because it allows the student to help Karis in a time of need

c. The teacher's response was unethical because Karis should be present for this conversation

d. The teacher's response was unethical because it violated Karis' right to confidentiality

61. What is the purpose of a flipped classroom?

a. To have students watch lectures at home and then work on more complex tasks in the classroom

b. Students prepare the materials to teach other students instead of the teacher, while the teacher acts as a facilitator

c. To help students take notes more efficiently

d. For teachers to instruct from behind the students' desks to avoid distraction and so they can focus on the content

62. Which of the following scenarios is the most probable indicator that a 4-year-old might have a developmental disability?

a. The student is having trouble reading at the same level as his peers

b. Student cannot tell their left from their right

c. Their play is largely imagination-based

d. Student is very anxious when away from their parents.

63. What is the relationship between project-based learning and technology?

a. Technology is a fundamental characteristic of project-based learning
b. Technology should only be used in project-based learning after students are in middle school
c. Technology should generally not be used in project-based learning
d. Technology can strengthen project-based learning

64. On the first day of a new unit in math, a teacher gives students a pretest of the unit with 10 questions. All students score at least an 80 percent on the pretest. If anything, what should the teacher do differently after seeing the pretest results?

a. Continue with the theme of the unit, but teach more advanced questions to further challenge students
b. Move on to the next unit since students have mastered this one
c. Reteach the questions that students missed on the pretest so that all students can score 100 percent
d. Do not change instruction for the unit because the teacher is doing a good job already

65. A teacher in a high school is preparing to teach about the Doppler effect, but lacks confidence in her ability to teach the material well. Instead, she shows an educational video about the Doppler effect to demonstrate the concept to her students. Which of the following would be best for the teacher to also do as preparation for this topic?

a. Ask other science teachers for enrichment activities to assign to the students after the video
b. Study the Doppler effect to be able to answer questions and clarify material for her students
c. Prepare an information packet on the Doppler effect to give to students after the video
d. Create a guided worksheet for students to complete as they watch the video

66. An English language learning teacher reads aloud to her students several times a week. One of her English-language learners is struggling to comprehend what she reads out loud. What is a strategy this teacher could implement to help this student, and others like him, in the classroom?

a. Prior to reading, teach key vocabulary words using images or examples
b. Read each paragraph twice while increasing the volume at which she reads
c. Have all students take turns reading out loud
d. Consult with the student to see what he does not understand

67. When having a parent-teacher conference, who should open the conference?

a. The administrator or school counselor should be the one who starts the conference
b. The parents should begin the conference because they know what their child needs best
c. The person who asked for the conference should start the meeting and establish its focus
d. The teacher should begin the conference because it is the teacher's responsibility

68. What is the definition of scaffolding with regards to education?

a. Allow students to choose which assignments to do based on their personal interests and strengths
b. Breaking down words to their prefixes, suffixes, and roots
c. Developing further skills based on what a student already knows
d. Asking students to build their own assignments to help assess other students

69. A new law is passed by the state that changes what will be taught in certain science classrooms. Who is accountable for ensuring that this is carried out in classrooms?

a. The Department of Education
b. The state government
c. The local government
d. Each individual school

70. Which is the best method to teach essential life skills (empathy, communication, self-control, etc.) to students in kindergarten?

a. Correct students who misbehave in front of the rest of the class
b. Quiz students on life skills
c. Punish incorrect behavior
d. Model proper life skills while teaching

71. A first-year teacher implements a large variety of different instructional activities into her classroom. Her methods include videos, debates, lectures, games, and project-based learning assignments. Which of the following is the greatest benefit for her using a variety of instructional methods in her classroom?

a. The teacher will be more enthusiastic while teaching due to the variety of lessons being taught
b. The teacher will easily be able to gather a variety of data on her students' achievement
c. Multiple learning styles of students can be addressed with her daily activities
d. Children will be excited to attend her class, which will lead to higher student achievement

72. In reviewing her lesson plans and test data following the completion of a unit, which of the following should the teacher be most concerned about regarding her students?

a. Multiple students finished the project two days before it was due, and she had to quickly create enrichment activities for them to complete so they would not become bored and distract others
b. Two lessons took longer than anticipated due to student questioning and classroom engagement
c. Several students with documented learning disabilities struggled with the unit and were unable to complete their project
d. ELL students had to use their translators and dictionaries on difficult vocabulary more than they have in the past

73. How can project-based learning help foster student learning?

a. By encouraging students to explore content in a variety of ways
b. By teaching students new content in a methodical approach
c. Allowing students to take ownership of their own learning
d. By introducing students to new knowledge and learning materials

74. Why should a chemistry teacher consider joining at least one science-related organization?

- a. To stay current on knowledge and developments within their field as they relate to education
- b. To acquire necessary professional development hours
- c. To attend several professional development sessions throughout the year to get a break from teaching
- d. To obtain tax write-offs related to membership costs

75. In a teacher's first year at a new high school, a marketing teacher notices that his students come from a wide range of socioeconomic backgrounds. What is the best way this teacher can promote the success of all students in his classroom?

- a. Establish connections in the community so all students are able to obtain internships
- b. Regularly pair students from more affluent backgrounds with students from poorer backgrounds
- c. Ensure all students in the class have the reasonable background knowledge required in the subject
- d. Create a library of resources in the classroom for all students to access as needed to do their work

76. A special education classroom has several students with differences in their physical characteristics and physical development. What is the best way that the teacher can make sure not to exclude any student in activities that they may plan for classroom instruction?

- a. Allow students of differing physical abilities to pair up so those with more coordination can help those with less coordination
- b. Interchange activities between those that account for their physical differences and those that do not
- c. Take care to not plan any activities that require students to leave their desks
- d. Take care to not exclude students when planning activities that require specific levels of coordination

77. A team of teachers notice that one student seems to be continually falling behind their peers in most of their classes. Which of the following strategies should the teacher try first to help support this student and promote engagement in their classrooms?

- a. Use differentiated instructional strategies to help engage the student and meet regularly to discuss the student's progress
- b. In each class, assign a student to help tutor the student each day during instruction
- c. Refer the student for testing to see if the student needs special education services
- d. Provide the student with extra time and a quiet environment to complete important assignments

78. A nineth-grade language arts teacher gives a five-question quiz over grammar using clickers once a week to her students. How could the teacher best utilize the data she can gather from these quizzes?

- a. Use data from the quizzes to reteach the concepts that the students most commonly missed
- b. Preview grammar from upcoming units
- c. Develop future lesson plans that connect grammatical concepts
- d. Create a review sheet for ELL students to review tricky grammatical concepts

79. Which of the following is most important for teachers to keep in mind when attending professional development sessions?

a. Strive to avoid conflict in professional development sessions, stay on schedule with the session

b. Maintain the key focus of how to continually assist lower-achieving students within the school

c. Maintain a focus on student learning and achievement in professional development sessions

d. Work on group collaboration to improve teamwork within the school and community

80. Which of the following is the best step to address the concerns of parents who feel their child is being assigned too much homework in a class?

a. Explain the merits of completing homework on time, and have data ready to present to the parents

b. Listen to the parents' worries, explain the study skills that are taught, and establish a plan to assist the student

c. Ask the parents how much time it takes the student to complete their homework every day

d. Ask a counselor to work with the student to help them learn how to better do their homework

81. While welcoming students into his homeroom class for the day, Mr. Gonzalez notices a student who is typically happy and easygoing seems unusually withdrawn. Later that day, he sees several bruises on the student during recess. Which of the following meets the requirements of Mr. Gonzalez reporting suspected child abuse as a mandated reporter?

a. Mr. Gonzalez shares his concern with the school counselor

b. Mr. Gonzalez shares his concern with his team teacher so they can monitor the student

c. Mr. Gonzalez calls the parents after the school day to ask if his suspicions are true

d. Mr. Gonzalez asks the student if they are being abused at home

82. Which of the following groups of people are likely the most influential on an individual's sense of self during adolescence?

a. Teachers

b. Friends

c. Family

d. Television

83. A first-year high school science teacher has assigned her first group project of the year. What is the best way that she could monitor how well students are understanding and working on the intricate details of this project?

a. Ask each group to hand in a project update sheet at the end of each class period

b. At the conclusion of the project, ask each student to complete a self-assessment survey on how they did and what they think they learned

c. Regularly watch the students from her desk and take notes on how each group is progressing

d. Walk from group to group periodically throughout the class and observe the students working in groups

84. A teacher sends a grade report home with her students every other week. The report includes the student's current grades on each assignment, overall average, a list of missing assignments, and upcoming assignments. What else could the teacher include on this grade report to help parents and students better understand what to expect in the classroom?

    a. Scoring criteria and requirements for upcoming assignments

    b. Current class averages on each assignment so parents can compare their child's progress to other students

    c. Individual goals the teacher feels each student should work to achieve that year

    d. A list of upcoming homework assignments

85. A language arts teacher is working to improve the writing skills of her students in the computer lab. She realizes they are heavily relying on the same words frequently and wants to help them learn how to successfully use the thesaurus tool on their computer. Which of the following would be the most important thing to teach the students about how to successfully use a thesaurus?

    a. Teach students to use a thesaurus and then the dictionary to define new words and make sure they fit grammatically in the sentence

    b. Teach students the purpose of a thesaurus and why it was first created

    c. Assign each student a partner to verify that each word they choose makes sense in the sentence

    d. Encourage students to use the thesaurus on as many words as possible to make their writing more interesting and varied

86. An educational researcher gives the same test to two groups of students, then delivers an instructional intervention to one group, and then gives both groups the same test again. The intervention/treatment group scores much higher this time; the control (non-treatment) group scores essentially the same as the first time. The researcher concludes that barring other factors, the intervention was what raised one group's scores. What type of validity does this illustrate?

    a. Internal validity

    b. External validity

    c. Ecological validity

    d. Population validity

87. What is the best way that a teacher can utilize the data from standardized tests from the previous year?

    a. Seat students with similar deficiencies together in class to make it easier to facilitate learning

    b. Identify the highest and the lowest achievers and enact a plan for the highest achievers to assist the lowest achievers

    c. Identify the achievement gaps of each student and create a plan that addresses the largest gaps

    d. Compare data with other teachers in the grade level to evaluate the best methods for instruction

88. A science teacher wants to allow the students to investigate which parts of the school have the most bacteria. He splits the students into groups to have them brainstorm where they should test for bacteria and how they should report their findings. Which of the following is the most important reason for having students brainstorm how to do this investigation?

a. It assists the students in determining what they still need to learn to conduct this experiment
b. It allows the students to form positive relationships with their peers in the classroom
c. It helps the teacher determine which students understand the purpose of the experiment and which students need more assistance
d. It helps the students take ownership and become engaged in their learning

89. Which of the following modes of representation did Jerome Bruner describe as emerging the earliest in child cognitive development?

a. Iconic representation
b. Enactive representation
c. Symbolic representation
d. They all develop simultaneously

90. A ninth-grade language arts teacher tries to incorporate diagrams, music recordings, pictures, and artwork into their instruction as much as possible. How could this help to develop learning in students with various needs?

a. It promotes individual examination on topics being taught
b. It uses background knowledge of students to help complement what they are learning
c. It makes class more interesting and helps students stay on task
d. It helps create connections to the world via the content being taught

91. In a unit about the Vietnam War, a high school history teacher wants to use the song "Fortunate Son," by Creedence Clearwater Revival to help teach students about the cultural reaction of the war in the United States. Can this teacher play this song for their class?

a. No, because the teacher has not obtained copyright permission to play the song
b. No, because the song is inappropriate to use in an educational setting
c. Yes, because an educator can play a song for instructional purposes under fair use
d. Yes, because fair use allows teachers full rights to use all media over 20 years old for educational purposes

92. How can the department chair of a department within a school show they respect the personal time of other teachers in their department?

a. Stop by for discussion and questions only while the teacher is actively teaching
b. Avoid contacting other teachers after their contract hours have ended when at all possible
c. Ensure all teachers have access to the supplies they want in their classroom
d. Provide extra sick and personal hours when teachers work past their designated contract hours

93. When a high school teacher assigns projects or research papers, she always builds time into her explanation to have a discussion with students about how long they think it will take them to complete the assignment. After the students turn in the assignment, she asks them how long it ended up taking them to complete the assignment. How does this help students in the learning process?

    a. It communicates to students that they are responsible for the work they do in class
    b. It directs students to work more efficiently
    c. It helps students reflect on which assignments were the most difficult to complete
    d. It helps students learn the skill of effectively managing their time

94. Ms. Langston is a dedicated teacher at her school who coaches lacrosse. Due to recent budget cuts, she is struggling to arrange transportation for students after away games. Several times, she has given multiple students rides to their homes. Which of the following is the biggest potential problem she might encounter?

    a. Ms. Langston's personal time is being infringed upon
    b. Knowing where students live is a direct violation of the code of ethics
    c. Other students may accuse Ms. Langston of favoritism
    d. Ms. Langston may be beginning to cross personal boundaries with students

95. One month into the school year, a teacher is working on creating homogenous groups in her classroom. Which of the following would be the best way for this teacher to utilize those groups in her class?

    a. To ensure that low-achieving students are not falling behind in instruction
    b. To instruct small groups of students who are struggling with specific standards in her classroom
    c. To assess the content knowledge of different demographics in her classroom
    d. Use to connect with students who seem uninterested in the current unit in school

96. A class is about to receive a new student in the middle of the school year. This student has cerebral palsy and uses a device for communicating. What could the teacher do prior to the student's arrival to help the student feel more welcome when they arrive in class?

    a. Instruct students to not use their voices for one class day to empathize with the new student's situation
    b. Demonstrate how the device works and how the student will use it to communicate
    c. Assign each student a day of the month where they are assigned to assist the new student
    d. Allow students to play with and investigate a similar device

97. In a classroom debate about student rights in school, a high school teacher asks if students should be allowed to leave campus for their lunch period. She divides her classroom into two groups and assigns each group one side of the discussion. Each group is assigned to come up with seven reasons to support their side and then present their reasons to the class. What is likely the teacher's intended purpose of this activity?

    a. To create assignments in the classroom that are relevant to the students' lives outside of the classroom
    b. To apply what they have learned to the specific content area
    c. To facilitate learning in a diverse classroom with lots of individual opinions
    d. To create a safe learning environment where the students can express their personal opinions

98. A large school has divided its departments into multiple professional learning communities (PLCs) within the school. What should be the main goal of PLCs regarding teacher participation?

    a. Each should be led by the teacher or teachers with the most experience
    b. They should strictly follow the curriculum and guidelines sent from the district's main office
    c. They should strive to listen to and incorporate everyone's opinions and thoughts
    d. They should remain the same throughout the school year for consistency

99. Every year, a social studies teacher teaches her students a large variety of vocabulary words that are new to her students. She wants students to not only learn the definitions, but also have a deep understanding of the concept of the new words. Which of the following activities would work best with achieving this teacher's goal?

    a. When a new vocabulary word is introduced, assist students in creating word maps on the new words
    b. Make sure that each set of desks includes dictionaries so students are always able to look up the meanings of words they are unsure of
    c. Create a list on the wall of new topics so students know they are not expected to have learned them until this year
    d. When speaking in class, use the new vocabulary words as much as possible to ensure a deeper understanding

100. When a teacher is sexually harassed by a coworker at their school, which law is the coworker in violation of?

    a. Fair Labor Standards Act
    b. Title IX of the Educational Amendments
    c. Occupational Safety and Health Act
    d. Title VI of the Civil Rights Act

Answer Key and Explanations

1. D: Option D is correct because asking the students to write an open-ended response will give the teacher a valuable opportunity to investigate what students already know about the life cycle of plants. Option A is incorrect because the teacher should be creating her assessment on what she wants her students to know by the end of the unit. Option B is incorrect because an open-ended response does not indicate how much interest her students would have in the topic. Some students might not know anything yet but will become interested as they learn more. Option C is incorrect because prior knowledge on a topic is not correlated with how advanced a student might be.

2. C: Option C is correct because effective teachers should regularly remind students of expectations in their classrooms so that the students are clear on rules and procedures. Option A is incorrect because it should not take a large portion of class time to redirect students to get them back on task. Option B is not correct because if all students are having problems refocusing, then the issue may be the teacher's methods and the teacher should first try to correct it herself. Option D is incorrect because students should not be assigned detention without prior warnings for most offenses.

3. B: Assigning students the task of writing a letter to their local school board serves as a real-world application to help connect classroom learning to real-world situations. This helps students better understand the purpose of learning and how they can apply what they have learned to potentially create change in the world. Allowing students to choose a book to write a report can be a valuable learning tool, but writing a book report does not necessarily involve a real-world application. Working in groups to brainstorm new class assignments does help students take ownership of their learning, but does not include a real-world connection. Although writing an essay about the steps of passing a law does teach what a certain process in the real-world is like, such an activity is not actually connected to the outside world.

4. C: Providing checklists and rubrics to students is a valuable way to teach students to take ownership of their learning. It helps the students know what is expected so that they can self-check their own work and progress along the way. Students generally should not choose which of their assignments should be graded, nor should they be required to self-grade each assessment prior to turning it in. Having students keep an established place in their binder to track their grades is a helpful way to allow students to monitor their progress, but is not the most effective way to teach students to take ownership.

5. D: As assessment tools, rubrics typically define general ranges or levels of performance (e.g., excellent, satisfactory, or unsatisfactory) and briefly describe characteristics of each. They define specific tasks, skills, or behaviors *before* they are performed to guide students, as well as provide referents afterward for evaluating performance. In addition to guiding task execution, they *do* provide criteria for performing tasks successfully. Teachers should explain rubrics to students so they can follow them in performing tasks, *before* using them to assess student task performance, not after.

6. D: The parent/guardian is the best person to consult for this information. Parents and guardians have been with their children for their entire lives and would have much more information than any other source. They should have access to the student's medical records and will have information from before their children started attending school. Previous teachers and school

157

counselors likely would not have access to most developmental milestones and would likely be missing other pertinent information.

7. D: A device is the best method for helping this student successfully participate in group assignments. Assistive technology can help non-verbal or low-level language students become more independent in the classroom. It can help them form meaningful social interactions in the classroom with other students and can increase their confidence, which will allow them to learn more. Excusing students from group work or pairing them with other non-verbal students does not help the student develop, and may even hold them back from learning new skills.

8. C: Option C is correct because students may have no prior experience or practice on how to have professional conversations about controversial topics. A teacher may need to explain and demonstrate what proper language is when discussing certain topics and issues. Option A is incorrect because parents might not be the most unbiased sources in what proper professional and respectful language is in a classroom. Option B is incorrect because students need to know proper expectations for conversation and discussion in a classroom before getting in trouble for the behavior. Option D is incorrect because a writing assignment without further instruction on expectations is not the proper way to teach respectful language.

9. B: The best way for a science teacher to see if students are following lab safety protocol is by assigning students a lab and observing them working on the lab assignment. This allows for the teacher to see what each student is doing, make corrections when necessary, and help instruct them on details they may not understand. Administering a pop quiz and holding a class discussion on lab safety are not good ways to practically assess if students are following procedures. Role-play could be a good way to demonstrate lab safety scenarios (both good and bad), but observing students in a lab and correcting potentially dangerous behavior is the best way to see if students are following the required procedures.

10. D: Metacognition means thinking about one's own thinking processes and/or learning about one's own learning processes. An example of metacognition is knowing that one learns better by seeing pictures, diagrams, or other visual images than by hearing or reading verbal information, or vice versa, etc. Schema is Piaget's term for a mental construct that one forms to understand the environment. For example, babies form schemas for things they can suck, things that make noise when shaken, etc.; toddlers form schemas for dogs and cats, etc. Transfer involves applying learning to different settings and situations. Self-efficacy is Bandura's term for task-specific self-confidence or belief in one's ability to complete a specific task.

11. A: For students who may still be learning how to manage their time efficiently, establishing mini-deadlines for larger projects is a good way for educators to make sure students are on track to finish the project and are not making major errors. This can help teach students how to effectively plan their time. While regular visits to the computer lab with time to work on certain projects can absolutely be helpful to students, they do not ensure that individual students will not fall behind. Teaching students how to best collect research can also be helpful, but it does not ensure that they will be on track for completing the project. Updates on student progress may not be the best strategy because a teacher cannot determine how the student is progressing with their project without seeing the student's work.

12. B: Creating and enacting a no-bullying policy should be one of the first steps that the classroom teacher and the resource teacher should work together to help improve the classroom environment. This should not only educate the students on why it is inappropriate to tease the child with hearing loss, but should prevent other children from being bullied in the class as well. No-bully policies can be implemented by setting guidelines for appropriate behavior and administering consequences when bullying occurs. Correcting inappropriate behavior is a good step to take, but it is not always appropriate to correct behavior immediately because it may single out students who do not understand what they are saying and how it is inappropriate. Moving the child to a self-contained environment does not allow for the least restrictive environment for the student and is not an acceptable solution. Contacting all parents and guardians to explain what is occurring in class is not a feasible solution without first trying other solutions.

13. D: Using various instructional strategies in a classroom allows a teacher opportunity to address the different types of learners in their room. It also increases the likelihood that the needs of each student in a teacher's class will be met. While using a variety of instructional strategies can keep both teachers and students engaged and interested in class, it is not the primary goal of utilizing multiple strategies in classroom instruction. The same can be said for using multiple instructional strategies as a means for collecting data. While this could be useful for documentation about potential issues in a class, it is not the primary reasoning behind using a variation of instructional strategies.

14. B: Showing students examples of properly constructed document-based questions and then discussing what the writers did correctly is an excellent way for a teacher to convey how document-based questions work. The examples should help the teacher communicate to his students what the final products are that he is looking for regarding these types of assignments. Providing an expected layout is not the best strategy for document-based questions, since they can vary greatly depending on the documents provided for the students to use as references. Giving students an assignment and grading it before communicating the best way for them to answer it is not likely to help the students learn how to properly answer document-based questions. Having students practice writing a document-based question is a good strategy, but instructing students to peer review the essays without including further communication is not likely to teach them all the knowledge they need.

15. B: To ensure that students are using technology appropriately and ethically in a classroom, teachers should continually monitor what students are doing when they have access to technology. This is the best way to ensure that proper ethical behavior is followed in a classroom. Modeling appropriate behavior can help reinforce how to use technology properly, as can lists of guidelines that are provided for students about how to behave. However, continually monitoring students is the best way to make sure that students act appropriately.

16. D: Allowing wait time when questioning students instead of moving on to other students who could answer quickly is a vital way to let students know that their opinions are respected and valued in the classroom. Some students need time to think and reflect before speaking, so giving them that opportunity is an effective way to show students that they matter and are appreciated. Regularly asking students what they think of other students' responses regularly may discourage other students from answering because they do not wish to be critiqued on their contributions to the classroom. Requiring the mandatory amounts of time a student is required to speak in a classroom does not lead to constructive discussions in the class because students will be encouraged to speak even if they do not have anything worthwhile to contribute.

17. D: When students continually show that they are not engaged in their assignments, teachers should make every effort possible to make the content more relevant to the students. A good way to do this is to create problems and assignments that better relate to the real world the students are experiencing. If they can personally connect to the material, they are more likely to see the value in the assignment. Excusing students from homework for the year is not a realistic scenario, and teaching a lesson about the importance of word problems is not likely to be an engaging lesson that the students will connect with. While the teacher could potentially ask other teachers for ideas to write word problems, it is unlikely that teachers who do not teach math would have a significant amount to contribute.

18. D: Permanent student records generally include items such as attendance records, discipline records, and report cards from previous school years. These records allow teachers, counselors, and other members of a school access (when needed) to trends or changes in a student's academic progress. While it may also include contact information for some members of the student's family, it does not include all contact information. It may have a few work samples, depending on the district and the previous educators of the child, but they are not required to be a part of the permanent record, nor are personal goal sheets by the student.

19. D: Arranging desks in groups of four to five is a good start for a first-year teacher who wants his students to work in groups. Additionally, creating designated spaces in the classroom where students know they can find material and turn in their work is extremely helpful for both teachers and students alike. These locations do not necessarily need to be centralized in the classroom, as it is more important that the locations remain consistent throughout the year and that students simply know where they are. Posters could be an added tool for this teacher to consider, but it is not the best advice for having the students work in groups successfully. Groups of desks are generally better than rows of desks for group work because it allows students to more easily communicate with each other.

20. A: Creating an outline of key concepts to see which ones overlap between subjects is the first step teachers should take when planning interdisciplinary units. This will allow the teachers to see which skills overlap that they can target in instruction. While teachers should be able to discuss what they want to individually accomplish in the unit, this should not be the first step. Creating a summative assessment should be one of the first steps for planning the unit, but they should first identify which concepts they want students to learn before planning the assessment. Likewise, constructing a list of what information they want students to learn is helpful, but needs to happen after outlining the key concepts from each subject in the interdisciplinary unit.

21. A: Content validity is how representative a test is of every single component of the construct it measures. Criterion validity is how representative a test is of a certain skill set. Construct validity is how representative a test is of a certain construct it is designed to measure (e.g., if it is meant to measure depression, it should not measure anxiety). Concurrent validity is a subtype of criterion validity and indicates how well a test correlates with an established benchmark test.

22. C: Technology allows opportunity for lessons to become more accessible to students of differing abilities. Using technology in the classroom lets teachers more easily make changes to lessons for more students and allows students the ability to access help easier in lessons, as well as the opportunity to investigate and develop assignments more deeply than without technology. While technology can lead to more engaging content, simply allowing students to use technology in class does not automatically lead to students becoming more immersed in what they are doing. Also, technology can help some students finish assignments faster, but this is not always the case, and technology may increase the amount of time needed to finish certain assignments. While technology can hold students' attention, teachers should be actively monitoring students while they are using technology to monitor, assist, and help students in the learning process.

23. B: Wait time when pausing for students to respond to questions should be largely based on the difficulty of the question that was posed. Students, as well as adults, need time to think to answer many questions, and this wait time should be built into a teacher's schedule when planning instruction. Even if other students know the answer to a question, allowing the original student time to think can be greatly beneficial to that student's success and confidence in the classroom. Students of all ability levels may need to reflect and process questions from time to time. Teachers should always factor in wait time for student questioning into a schedule and should not limit a student's time to think based on how much time was built into that class period.

24. A: When a small group of students have trouble understanding a new concept, a teacher should attempt to help remediate those students. One of the best ways to handle this during class time is to provide an enrichment activity to the students who have mastered the concept while providing additional instruction to the students still working on mastery. Retaking assessments can also be utilized, but material should be retaught before having students retake assessments. Taking the time to try to help students understand concepts is particularly important in math classrooms because concepts tend to build upon each other, and teachers should try to incorporate this into their lesson plans when students are struggling.

25. C: Discreetly passing a note to a student gives the student a chance to communicate to you what they need. They may need support, or they may just need a moment to pull themselves together. If the child is not actively disrupting class, giving them a few minutes to pull themselves together can be the least disruptive way to handle this situation to avoid causing potential embarrassment for the student. Reaching out to a counselor may be a step to take later if the student becomes more upset, but it is best to allow the student to try composing himself if he is not disrupting the class. Contacting the parents is a step that should not be taken without further information from the student about why he reacted in this manner. It is possible that his parents are putting too much pressure on him and contacting them about the quiz may agitate the situation. Asking the student to sit up and punishing him if he fails to comply is not the best way to handle this situation. If he is not being distracting and disrupting instruction, it is best to try to give him a little time and discuss it later. Punishment may escalate the situation and create more problems.

26. B: When a large portion of students receive a failing grade on an assessment, the teacher should take the time to look at common mistakes made on the assessment. The teacher then should work on reteaching the material to the students and administer another assessment to gauge student progress. If most students did not perform well on an assessment, instead of individually conferencing with students to see what they did to prepare, the teacher should first self-reflect to see what they did to get the students prepared for the assessment. While encouraging students to study at home is a good practice for improving student performance, increasing the amount of homework does not guarantee better performance. In fact, it may do the opposite if students' stress levels increase due to the increase in amount of work. Although asking students for input on what they need is something teachers should do, it is not the requirement of the student to know what they need to be successful within a classroom.

27. C: Teachers should continually strive to improve their professional knowledge of the subjects that they teach. It allows them to stay abreast of current topics in the field, as well as any educational studies or changes in the field that may change their day-to-day instruction. It also helps teachers remain leaders in their subjects so that they are up to date on current events related to their field. Continual professional knowledge and development is a characteristic that top-level teachers strive to always be working on because it helps them to remain leaders in the school by knowing what is currently occurring in their field.

28. C: Tablets can best be utilized in a classroom as a tool that can help to supplement instruction. This can include games, apps, programs, and websites students can access that support or reinforce concepts currently being taught in class. While all answer choices for this question are ways that tablets can be utilized in a classroom, using it to reinforce instruction allows for students to hopefully develop a deeper understanding with what they are learning, which will help them retain the information as their education progresses.

29. B: Teachers should strive to take attendance once students are settled down and are working on an assignment or otherwise occupied. This will allow the teacher to take attendance without wasting valuable instructional time since the students are actively engaged in a task. If teachers take attendance at the very beginning of the class before students are settled down, the teacher will waste several minutes of class, which can add up to hours of instructional time lost over the course of a school year. If teachers wait until the end of class or after the class ends, they may forget to take attendance due to getting caught up in their work, or they may forget which students were absent if they wait until the students leave before taking attendance.

30. B: Creating a spot for notes in the child's folder or in another easily accessible place is a strong first step to help support the student's educational journey. This allows the teacher and parents to communicate quickly and easily with each other, and to have a running list of their communications for documentation purposes. This allows both the teacher and the parent the opportunity to mention their concerns, struggles, or successes with each other while they are continually working to help the child. Asking the parents to discuss the interventions with the student away from the teacher does not help the student know that the teacher is on their side and wants to help them. The student should know that everyone is working together to help them be successful. Holding regular weekly conferences is likely not something that the teacher will have enough time in the day for, which is why it is better to try to find faster communication opportunities when possible while still helping the student. Suggesting that the parents hire a tutor is not a step that the teacher should take before attempting a variety of intervention methods to see if something else would work for the student.

31. B: The purpose of formative assessments is to assess students partway through a unit to see which parts of the units the students have mastered, as well as which parts of the unit may need to be retaught. These learning checks give the teacher a chance to see how the class is doing and how each student is doing individually. Formative assessments can be given in a variety of manners, including quizzes, tickets out the door, short essays or paragraphs explaining what was learned, as well as multiple other methods.

32. A: Option A is correct because critical thinking involves analyzing and synthesizing information to reach a solution. By having the student create a law and defend their reasoning, they are actively participating in critical thinking. Option B is incorrect because, while interviewing someone in government will teach the student about how government works, it will not help students develop critical thinking skills. Option C is incorrect because simply writing a report does not work on expanding students' critical thinking skills. Option D is incorrect because creating a list requires a low level of thinking and engagement and does not help advance skills related to critical thinking.

33. B: Allowing students to have input on classroom procedures and rules is a way to allow students to take ownership of their learning and behavior while in the classroom. Having the student contribute to creating the classroom rules and procedures helps students feel like important team members, but that act alone is unlikely to encourage students to be better in control with their behavior. While it does serve as a collaborative activity to help the class begin to work together as a team, this is not the primary benefit of the activity. Finally, this activity does not do anything particular that would encourage students to take ownership of their learning in the classroom.

34. C: The teacher should create a rubric prior to giving instructions to the students regarding their paper. After assigning the paper, the teacher should go through the rubric to show the students specifically how the paper will be evaluated. This should indicate to his students what his expectations are, and also serve as a tool the students can refer to while they work on the research papers. Self-grading their paper prior to turning it in can be a useful tool for students to evaluate how they think they did, but it will not make students aware of the expectations of the paper if they self-grade after the paper's completion. Allowing the students to create the rubric for the paper may allow ownership, but it will not communicate the goals of what the teacher wants the students to learn. Likewise, discussing what students hope to learn from the research paper and then creating the rubric based on those suggestions is not the best way to convey the teacher expectations.

35. B: When students transfer schools, FERPA regulations permit the previous school to provide the new school with student records without consent, since the new school will need the student's records from past schools. FERPA also allows student records disclosure to school officials, but only if they have valid educational interests; to appropriate school personnel related to student financial aid for purposes of determining and awarding aid; and to any auditing or evaluating officials, but only those specified.

36. A: Extrinsic motivation is behavior that is motivated by external rewards like money or grades. Offering a child money based on good grades is a prime example of extrinsic motivation. Extrinsic motivation can also include praise, rewards, and other motivators unrelated to the target activity. The other answer choices in this scenario are all related to intrinsic motivation. Intrinsic motivation is the motivation to complete an action, assignment, or project because of inherent benefit related to the activity, such as feeling accomplished after a successful performance, as in answer C.

37. D: Creating a compare-and-contrast diagram would involve the highest level of mastery for the economic teacher's students. When used properly, compare-and-contrast diagrams can lead to a deeper level of mastery for students. They allow students to critically assess what they have just learned, and make judgements about them that should hopefully create a deeper understanding in their minds. The other answer choices are good ways to help students gather information or assess what they have learned in the reading, but creating a chart where they compare the similarities and differences of the types of unemployment would likely lead to the deepest level of understanding.

38. B: A test on stoichiometry is the best summative assessment strategy for assessing student knowledge at the end of this unit. Summative assessments have the purpose of evaluating how much learning a student has accomplished during a specific unit. These generally take the forms of tests, but can also include essays, research papers or projects, or a variety of other methods. A pop quiz does not allow students an opportunity to study, which is necessary for a proper summative assessment. A video at the end of the unit will do nothing to actively assess how much the students have learned in the classroom, while a class-wide review game may only evaluate the knowledge of specific children in the classroom.

39. D: Using resources to incorporate cultural perspectives into the teacher's lessons is a way to help her students learn to appreciate the diversity at the school. It allows them to learn about different cultures while connecting them to the community where they live. Providing students with planners with the dates of holidays and festivities to help students understand cultural diversity is a potentially costly endeavor for the teacher. It is unlikely for students to learn a great deal from seeing when different holidays are celebrated in their planners. Decorating the classroom with posters and other resources representing the cultures can be a helpful tool for helping teach the students, but it is not as useful as incorporating resources into her lessons to help educate the students. Asking students to give presentations about parts of their culture could be a helpful tool, but some students may not want to talk about their culture or may not know much about the cultures that they belong to.

40. C: Allowing students time at the end of class to organize and secure their belongings is a great way to teach and model proper organizational skills for students. By allowing time at the end of class to secure their belongings and update their planners with important information, this teacher is emphasizing to her students how important it is to both organize and keep track of dates and responsibilities. This should help set a good foundation for the students to implement these skills in other classes so that they have the tools to be successful in school.

41. B: The purpose of a mentor teacher is to provide encouragement, support, and guidance to new teachers or teachers who need to work on developing or improving certain characteristics. Mentor teachers can be extremely useful because their inexperienced mentees can go to them about anything from simple day-to-day operational questions to questions about how to handle student discipline challenges. Mentor teachers may also allow the new teacher to observe their class and learn techniques or procedures that the new teacher had not thought of prior to observing the mentor teacher. Mentor teachers can be extremely advantageous to newer teachers, helping them get a good understanding of what the responsibilities of being a teacher are.

42. C: Option C: First-graders using manipulatives to start learning the concepts of addition and subtraction is a developmentally appropriate activity for students at this grade level. Assembling a puzzle of the United States is not developmentally appropriate for kindergarteners to learn about geography because it is likely far too advanced for most children at this age. Fifth-graders raising tadpoles to frogs is not complex enough for students to learn new material at this age in development. Completing an advanced research paper is likely far too advanced for most seventh-grade students to complete.

43. D: Allowing appropriate wait times for student responses in class is an important way to show students that their opinions are important to the classroom. Additionally, providing cues to students who need help answering a question will let them know that their contributions are appreciated in the classroom. This helps students feel safe and valued, which can improve their self-esteem and motivation in school.

44. B: Option B is correct because the student might be having issues with completing the number of questions in the allotted time. If the teacher reduces the number of questions the student must answer in the timeframe, the student can focus more on getting the questions she has correct. Option A is incorrect because extra homework on top of what the teacher already assigns likely will not help the student be successful. Option C is incorrect because singling the student out from her peers and punishing her may be potentially damaging. Option D is incorrect because the student should not be punished for struggling academically.

45. B: Arranging a time in private to discuss concerns or requests with the visually impaired student is an essential first step in helping the student feel welcome in the classroom. It is likely the teacher has already received a list of accommodations for this student from the teenager's case manager. However, setting aside a time for a conversation with the student can help the teacher learn more about their needs and if there are any extra steps that can be taken to make the student more comfortable and successful. Setting aside time in the class for the student to be asked questions by their peers might be something the student could suggest to the teacher, but it should not be done without the student's approval. The same can be said for a class discussion because it may make the student feel like an outcast. Inviting the parents to observe any time they want is a lot to ask for the teacher, and while the parents should be allowed to observe class if both they and their child feel it would be helpful, it should only be expected on a mutually agreed upon date, and not at any time they wish.

46. A: Administering pretests prior to beginning a unit is a good way to see what the prior knowledge of the subject is for all students in a class. It allows the teacher to see if there are any parts that most students already know, or if there are parts that most students seem to have little background knowledge on. Having this knowledge allows teachers to better plan instructional units while allotting more time in their plan to teach lesser known topics. Administering a pretest should not be used as a method to see which intervention strategies need to be implemented, nor should it gauge which students will need the most instructional support. It also does little to assess student interest, since some students who have never been exposed to the topic before might prove to be those that are the most interested.

47. C: When teaching in a classroom with multiple ELLs, teachers should strive to make all instructions on assignments as simple as possible. Using instructions with simple, understandable language should help ELLs become aware of what is actually required on an assignment. These directions should be free of slang, abbreviations, and colloquialisms that might be hard for students learning English to understand. Pairing ELLs with native speakers is a good strategy to use from time to time, but should not be used on all assignments, nor should pulling students out of class regularly when harder work is assigned. Dictionaries are also helpful as a resource to provide students with extra assistance, but the teacher should first make sure their instructions are easy to understand for all students.

48. D: When giving standardized assessments, it is important that all students have similar testing conditions to prevent some students from potentially being given unfair advantages. This means that testing rooms should have testing proctors read the exact same directions, necessary supplies (such as pencils or calculators) be provided to students as necessary, lighting should remain consistent in every classroom, etc. If these protocols are not followed by some teachers, this may lead to some students not understanding directions or not being able to test in an environment in which they feel comfortable.

49. D: Students should plant seeds and watch them grow in varying levels of light. This practical experience is the best way for students to truly learn about the effect that sunlight has on plants because they will be able to actively see a real-world application of how it works. A nature walk could be helpful enrichment activity for students to learn more and see plants in varying degrees of sunlight, but it will not allow them to see the entire process. While videos and worksheets are other tools that can be used in unison with growing plants in class, they are best used as supplements to the more practical, hands-on activity of students growing their own plants.

50. A: Asking students to create lists of what skills they feel they are strong in allows the teacher to informally assess what students know, as well as learn about her students' interests. This should allow the teacher to use their strengths and interests to better plan instruction and activities in their classroom. Asking students to create a list of strengths is not a formal assessment and should not be used as an all-inclusive tool to assess the background knowledge of a student. While the teacher may be able to use the list of tasks as a way of gauging what students know, it is not the best tool that the teacher can use to create collaborative groups within her class. Although creating a list of tasks that students can perform may increase student confidence temporarily, it is not the ultimate purpose of this activity and is instead a secondary benefit.

51. D: The best way to have her students prepare for the test is to assign students to work in groups to complete a concept map over the Civil War. Students working together to gather data and make connections should activate prior learning to help them focus on both what they have already learned and the connections they have made in the unit. While the other options are all somewhat acceptable methods to review for a test, instructing students to complete a concept map should activate a deeper understanding of the unit to help students retain more information long-term about the Civil War.

52. B: Homogeneous groups place students of similar abilities in the same group, and they allow students to work on improving or enriching certain areas of their knowledge. They provide instructors the opportunity to give extra assistance to students who are struggling or have lower ability. It also provides the freedom to amend group project requirements for certain groups, such as enriching the project for higher-level groups while adjusting the standards for struggling groups. Homogeneous groups are groups of similar ability levels and are intended for students to be able to remain on the same level within the group to prevent higher-ability level students from taking over the group. Heterogeneous groups are groups where higher-level students can assist lower-level students within their group. While students can assist each other in any type of collaborative group, being in a homogeneous group does not make it easier for students to help other students.

53. C: Parents need to be kept up to date with their child's progress in school. When areas of concern arise, teachers should be ready with concrete examples of specific struggles that their child is experiencing. Concrete examples include projects, tests, and written work samples. Charts and grade printouts do not effectively demonstrate what the specific areas of concern are for the student. While parents should be consulted for ideas on how to help their child, it is not the best way to convey that a child is struggling. By comparing the child's work to the work of his classmates, parents may become defensive and upset about the progress of their children. It is generally best practice to not compare the work of specific children, particularly when holding conversations with parents and guardians.

54. C: Observing more experienced teachers can be an extremely useful tool for first-year teachers to improve both their classroom management and their instructional strategies. This allows teachers to see new strategies in action and has the potential of being able to teach much more to a newer teacher than most other methods. Asking the principal for suggestions may result in a few useful suggestions, but it is likely not the most effective method for gathering ideas or strategies. Asking the specialist for books can be an additional tool to utilize for classroom management strategies, but it would not be as effective as observing experienced teachers. Consulting with parents is not an ideal way to develop classroom management strategies because most parents have not been in the classroom as educators and do not know effective strategies for managing large groups of children while teaching them.

55. B: When teachers assign projects that require the use of technology and independent research, they should ensure that all students have reasonable access to the materials they need to complete the project. In this case, if the teacher can schedule time for students to go to the media center and computer lab during class, this would help students gather the materials they need and ensure that all students have a fair chance to complete the project. Asking students to stay after school may be difficult for students who rely on the school bus for transportation or who have other responsibilities after school. Clear instructions should always be given on assignments, but clear instructions will not help students who do not have the means to complete the assignment. Pairing students together for the assignment is likely not what the teacher wants to do for a final research project that he was anticipating students complete alone. It would be best for him to make sure all students have access to the resources they need.

56. A: Students should become motivated to behave due to the added incentive that good behavior in class is rewarded. If students are interested in the reward, they will put pressure on misbehaving students to behave. This is likely to be more effective in difficult classes where the teacher struggles to gain the respect of his students since students will be encouraged to behave by their peers. If parents have not been supportive in getting their own children to behave in class, this incentive is unlikely to change their behavior. Students may be more concerned with the consequences of their behavior, but this is more likely to be attributed to being responsible for the class losing a reward. Some students may want to make sure that the teacher does not think they are the reason that class is disrupted, but students are more likely to seek the approval of those in their peer group.

57. C: Using a rubric is the best method for providing feedback in this situation. A well-constructed rubric allows students to get clear feedback on what elements of the writing process they need to improve, and it also allows them to see where their strengths are. While positive comments and comments on errors can be helpful to students, they should be included with the rubric for the most effective assessment tool. Writing nothing but positive comments will not help the student learn what they should correct on their work, and while it might help their confidence, it will not help them become better writers. While teachers should correct errors, they should be careful not to correct every minuscule error on a struggling writer's papers. Too many markings on the paper could negatively affect a student's self-esteem and make them unmotivated to learn and correct their mistakes.

58. D: Collaborative groups allow students to solve problems together in the classroom. It teaches them to combine their efforts and create solutions that they may have not been able to do while they were alone. Although collaborative groups do have the potential of making students more excited to go to class or to increase engagement in the classroom, those are not the best reasons for using them in the classroom. Additionally, while collaborative groups can lead to less time spent grading, monitoring student cooperation and mediating problems in the groups mean that group activities do not generally lead to extra time for the teacher to plan lessons.

59. C: Providing written instructions as well as auditory instructions is a good practice when educating students with hearing or attention issues. It allows students the opportunity to listen to instruction while providing a reference for them to consult if they do not understand, forget, or need more clarification. Repeating instructions multiple times might help some students, but will likely not help those with auditory processing disorders. Speaking louder and slower might not help either, and asking them if they need help after giving directions singles them out to the class when there are more discreet ways of helping while teaching them how to read and follow directions independently. Referring students to the school counselor is not likely to help them learn to follow directions when they have a diagnosed disorder and may make the students feel as if they are doing something wrong in class.

60. D: When the teacher shared what was causing Karis' change in mood, she violated Karis' right to confidentiality. It is fine if Karis wants to share this information with other students, but that decision is not the teacher's to make. While the teacher can share this information with counselors or other school personnel who could potentially help Karis, it is not acceptable to share this information with students or other members of the community.

61. A: Flipped classrooms allow students to watch prerecorded lectures or otherwise gather information on fundamental concepts that they would usually learn under direct instruction from a teacher. They can be beneficial because they give students the opportunity to re-watch concepts that may be difficult for them and allow the benefit of letting parents see how the teacher is teaching in the classroom. Then, when students return to school, they can work on complex tasks related to the material they learned at home, with the teacher there to reinforce learning. This allows students the opportunity to gain deeper understanding of concepts covered in their educational experience.

62. D: Option D is correct because a child should be able to be away from their parents for periods of time by the age of 4. Option A is incorrect because reading is too advanced for many 4-year-olds and is not a skill that students are expected to have mastered by this age. It is not a developmental concern if students cannot read by this age. Option B is incorrect because this is too advanced for a typical 4-year-old and is the developmental milestone of a 6-year-old. Option C is incorrect because imagination and fantasy are typical at this stage of development.

63. D: Technology is a tool that, when used properly, can strengthen project-based learning in the classroom. When teachers incorporate good technological tools into class, it can greatly strengthen the learning that occurs, and make students more independent. While not all project-based learning projects will use technology, a great number of them are likely to use it at least some for students to gather the necessary materials. With proper supervision and education, elementary school students should be able to use technology in project-based learning just as well as middle and high school students.

64. A: When students show mastery at the beginning of a unit, teachers should still work to teach material on the same topic, but teach more advanced concepts at a higher level. This helps challenge students and keeps them engaged in the material, and it helps students become more proficient at the easier questions while also allowing them to work towards answering the more challenging questions. While the teacher could shorten the unit to move on to harder units, it probably is best that they continue teaching the unit so that students can reinforce their skills to build on their pre-existing knowledge for the next unit. It is important to allow students a chance to learn more advanced material when the planned material may be too simple for them, as it will help increase their confidence and allow students a chance to improve on what they know.

65. B: To best help the students learn about the Doppler effect, the teacher should take steps to learn, comprehend, and be able to teach about the Doppler effect. This might include asking other teachers for clarification about it, watching videos, or reading instructional materials. Enrichment activities are likely not reasonable to give to students after they only watch a video about a new concept. A packet of information could also be helpful to the students, as could a guided worksheet, but the best step the teacher could take is to learn the information so as to help the students learn it as well.

66. A: Students, especially those learning a new language, need to be exposed to new words multiple times to fully comprehend the meaning and usage of the words. By taking the time to teach new words and concepts, the teacher will help to form meaningful connections to the words that should help students learn and retain new vocabulary. Reading the passage multiple times is not likely to influence the student's comprehension since it is unlikely that they will implicitly learn the meaning from a re-reading if they did not know it before. Students can derive meaning from naturally encountering new words, but to do so requires a working knowledge of the majority of the encountered words for context clues. Consulting with the student may help to an extent, but it is likely that an English-language learner would be unable to articulate what they did not understand.

67. C: The person who requested the conference should be the one who starts the conference so they are able to establish the purpose of the meeting. This could be a teacher, counselor, administrator, parent, or (in some cases) even the student. This allows everyone in attendance to know the purpose of the meeting so they are better able to focus their discussion and not waste valuable time. Administrators, school counselors, parents, and teachers can all request meetings, and if they are the ones to request the meeting, they should generally be prepared to be the ones that will open the meeting. If a parent requests a conference, it may still be best for a staff or faculty member to introduce and organize the discussion to help establish clear lines of communication.

68. C: Scaffolding is working to develop further skills based on what a student already knows. Scaffolding works to move students towards a greater understanding and greater independence in their educational progression. Allowing students to choose which assignments they want to do based on their interests and strengths is a good practice to use occasionally, but it is not scaffolding. Breaking down words to learn the roots can be a component of scaffolding in education. While asking students to develop assignments can be a useful tool in education, it is not the definition of scaffolding.

69. C: The local government is responsible for making sure that the new changes will be carried out in schools. This is generally carried out by each individual school district, who passes the changes on to each school in their district. While the state government is responsible for mandating what should be taught in schools, local governments are responsible for ensuring that they are implemented.

70. D: Option D is correct because it is vital for teachers to regularly model how they expect students to act and what they expect students to do in a classroom. Students need guidance on proper behaviors, and modeling is an effective way for them to see those behaviors. Option A is incorrect because it singles out students in the classroom, which might affect both their engagement and how much they enjoy school. Option B is incorrect because quizzes are not always the most effective ways to learn certain skills. Option C is incorrect because punishing incorrect behavior prior to modeling correct behavior is not an effective means of instruction.

71. C: When a teacher uses numerous types of instructional activities, they are making sure to address the multiple learning styles of students in their classroom. While a teacher being more enthusiastic may lead to both the teacher and the students being more engaged in classroom, it is not the primary asset of using multiple strategies. Using a variety of instructional strategies can lead to more data being able to be gathered in a classroom, but it is not the designed benefit of these strategies. Although using a variety of instructional practices may make class more engaging, that is not the greatest benefit for using a variety of instructional methods in a classroom.

72. C: The teacher should be most concerned that several students in her classroom struggled with an assignment so much that they were unable to complete it. When something like this happens in the classroom, a teacher should be willing to self-assess what they may have done incorrectly, or what they could do differently in the future. A teacher should ensure that activities and assignments in their classroom are able to be completed by all students in their classroom, even if some students may need some accommodations due to disabilities or other limitations. The goal of education is to make learning accessible for all students, and that should be one of a teacher's most important goals in the classroom.

73. A: Project-based learning is a meaningful tool that allows students to investigate topics in depth and apply what they know to investigate new material. Students examine content in depth and generally have a choice for how they choose to approach their learning. It is not a methodical approach to learning, but rather is a way for students to learn how to formulate a plan, research, and apply knowledge to real-world topics. While students may have a choice in how they approach the topic, they are not in charge of their own learning because the teacher should act as the facilitator and give guidance. It also is not necessarily introducing students to new knowledge, but instead may be allowing enrichment on topics students are already familiar with.

74. A: It is important that teachers stay current on knowledge and developments in their fields, particularly as they relate to education. This is especially important for teachers in higher-level subjects, like many high school courses. When a high school chemistry teacher joins a science organization, they gain access to publications, studies, and other developments in their field that they may be able to incorporate into their classroom. This may help them provide better instruction and more in-depth discussions in the classroom that can lead to student growth and development.

75. C: This teacher should make sure that all students have the background knowledge necessary to complete the course successfully. In schools where there are large socioeconomic differences, there are likely to be gaps in knowledge between students who have had more advantages in life versus those students who have not been as fortunate. Establishing connections with the community could potentially offer internships to students, but students from lower socioeconomic backgrounds may still experience problems arranging transportation to the internship or having time after school to work at an internship. Regularly pairing affluent students with poorer students is unlikely to do much to promote the success of all students. Ensuring the classroom has a variety of resources for students to consult can help the students to be successful, but it is more important to make sure that all students have the prior background knowledge required to be successful in class.

76. D: When classrooms include students at different levels of physical abilities, it is important for the teacher to make sure not to accidentally exclude students from activities because of their ability level. Their ability level could include both physical and mental limitations that should be accounted for when planning instruction. This does not mean that teachers should not plan any activities that require coordination, but rather that they should account for any accommodations the students may need, which may include pairing some students with paraprofessionals for certain activities. While occasionally a teacher might choose to pair up students of differing physical ability levels, they should not solely rely on that as a means of accommodation. Additionally, interchanging activities is a good plan, but it is not a way to ensure that student needs are always addressed, nor is never planning any activities that allow students to move around the classroom.

77. A: Using differentiated instructional strategies to help engage the student is a strong way for a teacher to try reaching the student and helping them learn. Additionally, meeting with the student (and potentially the student's parents) to discuss how they are doing helps the student keep up with the progress they are making in the classroom. This will hopefully help to keep the student from being discouraged when they fall behind. Assigning a daily student-tutor could potentially harm the student's self-esteem. If the teacher's interventions do not work to help the student succeed in their classroom, then the student should be potentially referred to others at the school for testing. This should not be done until the teacher has tried multiple strategies and gathered documentation on the student. Although providing the student with extra time and a quiet environment might be a good strategy to put in place, it can also be isolating for the student, especially if they are not a part of the IEP.

78. A: The teacher can best use this data to evaluate what topics and themes her students in general are having trouble learning. By utilizing this data from the clickers, it should be relatively easy for the teacher to see the common questions that were missed, which allows for the opportunity to reteach certain concepts. The benefits of using technology like this allow for information to be gathered and analyzed quicker than standard quizzing methods in a classroom.

Mometrix

79. C: When teachers attend professional development sessions of any kind, it is vital to remember that student learning and achievement should generally be the focus of the sessions. The goal of such sessions is to take away something from the session that they can bring to the classroom to improve what they do. This could include improving how they speak to their students, new instructional or assessment strategies, or any other of a wide range of topics. While these sessions may cut into time that teachers would prefer to spend working on other tasks, these sessions are important for the continuing education of teachers and other staff within a school.

80. B: Parents need opportunities to express their concerns when something is not working for their child in a classroom. Teachers should strive to be empathetic to parental concerns and attempt to work out resolutions to problems that can work for all involved. Explaining why homework is important and providing data to the parents likely will not make a difference in the stresses they are experiencing at home with their child. Asking their parent how long it takes their student to complete homework will likely come up in the conversation, but the question itself does not work to address the problem that the family is experiencing. A counselor could be a useful tool to help the student next if the strategies the parents and teacher discuss prove to be ineffective.

81. A: Mr. Gonzalez should share his concerns with a school counselor. Mr. Gonzalez is a mandated reporter, and a school counselor is a person at the school he can share his concerns with. Once Mr. Gonzalez shares his concerns, it is then the counselor's obligation to investigate further. This may include contacting the police, talking to the student, or contacting DFPS. Mr. Gonzalez should not go to his team teacher since they would have the same obligation to report their concerns to the counselor or an administrator at the school. He should not contact the parents after school because this could cause further harm to the student if the child is being abused. Mr. Gonzalez should not ask the child if they were abused because that is better handled by people who have been trained in how to ask sensitive questions, and it is best to not make the child relive potentially traumatizing events more than is absolutely necessary.

82. B: Option B is correct because friends and peer groups are the most influential on children during adolescence. Adolescents look towards their friends for examples on what to think, how to act, and what to do. Option A is incorrect because while teachers are influential, they are not the most influential in this age group. Option C is incorrect because family is the most influential during the younger years of childhood, but they are not the most influential later. Option D is incorrect because television is passive and does not influence children in adolescence like their friend group.

83. D: To best monitor her students' progress on the project, the teacher should walk through the classroom regularly to observe her students closely. This will allow her to hear individual conversations, check the actual work being completed, and ensure that all students are participating in each group. If a mistake occurs, walking around the classroom allows the opportunity to catch and correct it early. While a project update sheet might be occasionally helpful for longer projects, it might not be enough to catch issues with student understanding of the project. A self-assessment survey that occurs after the project will not help to see if students are learning while completing the project in class and should not be used for that purpose. Watching students from a desk does not allow teachers to clearly hear conversations in the classroom and will not allow for proper monitoring of student work.

84. A: Sending home data that helps make parents and students more aware of criteria on upcoming assignments is the best option that the teacher could also send home with her students. This makes both students and parents more aware of the upcoming work and what will be expected of the students. Class averages on assignments may make some students lose confidence in their ability to do well in school and should be avoided in many situations. While the teacher can include

171

goals that they think students should achieve that year, it is better to have students create goals for themselves so that they are more attached to the goal and therefore more likely to work towards achieving them. While a list of upcoming homework assignments could be helpful to parents and students for planning, it will not help parents and students better understand what is occurring within that teacher's classroom.

85. A: When teaching students how to effectively use a thesaurus, teachers should ensure that they teach students to verify the meaning of words suggested in the thesaurus so that they fit within the context of the sentence. This can be a challenging skill for some students to acquire, and it may take a bit of time for all students to feel comfortable with using a thesaurus correctly. While teaching about the history of the thesaurus might help some students learn more about them, it is unlikely to be much help in this situation. Assigning each student a partner may help for peer revision, but it is better in this situation to teach students how to be self-sufficient. While encouraging a student to use a thesaurus to improve their writing is good, encouraging students to use them on as many words as possible is likely not a good strategy.

86. A: When a test (or an experimental research design) shows cause and effect, it has internal validity. External validity is whether or how much a test's results (or research effect) can be generalized to larger populations, other settings, measurement variables, and/or treatment variables. External validity includes ecological validity, i.e., how impervious a test or effect is to environmental influences, and population validity, i.e., how representative of the population the sample tested is and whether the sampling method used is acceptable.

87. C: The best way that a teacher could use standardized test data in her classroom is to use it to analyze gaps in learning that their students may have. They could potentially identify common gaps among the students and identify which students struggled more on specific standards than other students. It allows for the teacher to have an opportunity to plan out what she wants her students to improve upon in the upcoming year and enact a plan to see them achieve.

88. D: By allowing the students time to brainstorm where they feel the most bacteria can be found in their school, students can take ownership and become better engaged in the learning process. By discussing this in groups, the students can choose where they want to investigate, which should lead to further discussion and excitement in the groups about where they should test the bacteria. Allowing the students to brainstorm where to test does not help students determine what they still need to learn to conduct the experiment, since they may be unaware of what the teacher wants them to do after brainstorming is complete. While positive relationships may form in the group discussions, it is not the intended purpose of having the students brainstorm in groups for this activity. Group work is frequently a time when teachers can monitor their class and see which students understand the work they are performing; this is not necessarily the case in a group brainstorming session. Some students may be quieter than others while brainstorming but still understand the purpose of the assignment.

89. B: Bruner named enactive representation, i.e., muscle memory retention of motor response information, which he described as emerging in infancy. He named iconic representation (a), i.e., information based on visual imagery, which he said emerges between one and six years old. He named symbolic representation (c), i.e., encoded storage of information via symbols, which he said emerges around seven years and older. Since he described these as developing sequentially and not simultaneously, (d) is incorrect.

90. D: Integrating multiple types of media into a unit helps to promote understanding and growth for a variety of learners. Utilizing multiple types of media into one's instruction helps accommodate students with disabilities, English-language learners, and the students' various learning types. It also can help students form connections with the real world by connecting what they have learned with how it applies to life outside school, which can help increase their comprehension as well as their connection to the material.

91. C: Under the fair use doctrine, educators can use certain copyrighted works in the classroom for educational purposes. Playing a song in class is one of the allowed items under the fair use doctrine. Teachers need to ensure that materials they are using in the classroom are not infringing on copyright laws, and the fair use doctrine provides guidance as to what teachers can use. Media specialists, curriculum chairs, and other leaders in the school should also be able to provide guidance on what resources can be used by teachers without violating copyright laws.

92. B: Many teachers work numerous hours outside of their contract hours. It is important for leaders at the school to respect the time of teachers. Department chairs, administrators, and other leaders should make every effort to avoid contacting other teachers after their contract hours have ended if at all possible. There will be emergencies that will come up where contact after work hours may be necessary, but leaders should strive to keep that to a minimum if possible. It is important to keep a work-life balance to avoid teacher burnout, and this is one way that those in charge of a school can help to maintain that work-life balance.

93. D: By asking students to predict how long it will take them to complete an assignment, and then asking students how long it actually took to complete an assignment, this teacher is helping students develop their ability to manage their time. This skill can be used by students in all their classes and in the outside world. Asking students to do this is a good way to make them take responsibility for their learning and hopefully enhance each student's understanding of how much time it might take them to complete assignments in the future.

94. D: When Ms. Langston allows students into her personal vehicle and transports them home, numerous problems could occur. These problems vary from potentially getting in an accident where she would become liable for what happens to students, to violating district rules, to potentially opening herself up for a false claim from the students. Teachers generally need to talk with the district or school, fill out paperwork, and get parental permission before transporting students. In some districts, teachers are almost never supposed to be responsible for transporting students. Mrs. Langston needs to check what her district-specific requirements are so that she does not unknowingly violate any code of ethics.

95. B: Homogeneous groups allow teachers to provide extra targeted instruction for students who are struggling on specific concepts. Grouping these students together for specific instructional help is likely to help them catch up when they fall behind on certain concepts. These groups do not have to remain the same for all subjects or for the school year; the teacher can change them around as student needs change. Homogeneous groups are useful tools that teachers can implement to help create balance and avoid large gaps in knowledge among students in a classroom.

96. B: Demonstrating how the device works and explaining how the student will use the device to communicate will help potentially ease the child's entrance into the classroom. Students should have fewer questions and be more willing to engage with the student if they know more about what to expect. Instructing students to refrain from using their voices for a day trivializes the struggle the student deals with for his life and is not the best activity to have in class to help this student feel welcome. While it may be helpful to assign a helper to the student, the student might not want his peers helping him in class and it would be better to ask the student privately if that is something he might like. Allowing students to play with a similar device may help them learn how it works, but they may need more explanation and instruction to understand and empathize with the student who uses the device.

97. A: Creating a way to link activities that directly connect to relevant parts of students' lives is a vital way to promote engagement and learning in a classroom. Students are more likely to feel connected to the material since it directly affects both their school and opinions they may have about the topic. It is not known for sure based on the description of the question if this is an application to what they have already learned. The classroom may be diverse, but this activity is not geared specifically towards helping learners in a diverse classroom. While this activity should be done in a classroom where students feel safe to express their opinions, this ideally has already been established by the educator and is not the specific or intended purpose of the activity.

98. C: Professional learning communities (PLCs) should strive to listen to and incorporate all members' opinions and thoughts while in the community. The purpose of PLCs is to collaborate, share skills and knowledge, and work to improve both the skills of the teachers in the community and the teachers in the school, as well as improve student performance. PLCs do not necessarily have to be led by the teachers with the most experience, nor do they have to generally follow guidance from the district office. They also do not have to remain consistent throughout the year and can change as the school year progresses.

99. A: Word maps, which are ways to visually organize concepts, are good ways to introduce new vocabulary words and concepts to students in a classroom. Word maps provide a way for students to clearly detail a new vocabulary word and its definition, and also a way to create connections to both the word and the definition. This allows for the students to have a deeper understanding of the new concept, and to ideally form a connection with it so they can build permanent connections in their mind to the vocabulary word. Dictionaries, word walls, and using new vocabulary words regularly can all be helpful in the classroom, but for students to have the best chance to learn new vocabulary, they need to have an opportunity to work with the word and form their own connections to it.

100. B: Title IX of the Educational Amendments was a law created in 1972. The purpose of this law was to prevent discrimination on the basis of sex in any federally funded education program or activity. It provides extra funding from the federal government to help prevent discrimination and to implement programs to help keep people protected.

How to Overcome Test Anxiety

Just the thought of taking a test is enough to make most people a little nervous. A test is an important event that can have a long-term impact on your future, so it's important to take it seriously and it's natural to feel anxious about performing well. But just because anxiety is normal, that doesn't mean that it's helpful in test taking, or that you should simply accept it as part of your life. Anxiety can have a variety of effects. These effects can be mild, like making you feel slightly nervous, or severe, like blocking your ability to focus or remember even a simple detail.

If you experience test anxiety—whether severe or mild—it's important to know how to beat it. To discover this, first you need to understand what causes test anxiety.

Causes of Test Anxiety

While we often think of anxiety as an uncontrollable emotional state, it can actually be caused by simple, practical things. One of the most common causes of test anxiety is that a person does not feel adequately prepared for their test. This feeling can be the result of many different issues such as poor study habits or lack of organization, but the most common culprit is time management. Starting to study too late, failing to organize your study time to cover all of the material, or being distracted while you study will mean that you're not well prepared for the test. This may lead to cramming the night before, which will cause you to be physically and mentally exhausted for the test. Poor time management also contributes to feelings of stress, fear, and hopelessness as you realize you are not well prepared but don't know what to do about it.

Other times, test anxiety is not related to your preparation for the test but comes from unresolved fear. This may be a past failure on a test, or poor performance on tests in general. It may come from comparing yourself to others who seem to be performing better or from the stress of living up to expectations. Anxiety may be driven by fears of the future—how failure on this test would affect your educational and career goals. These fears are often completely irrational, but they can still negatively impact your test performance.

> **Review Video: 3 Reasons You Have Test Anxiety**
> Visit mometrix.com/academy and enter code: 428468

175

Elements of Test Anxiety

As mentioned earlier, test anxiety is considered to be an emotional state, but it has physical and mental components as well. Sometimes you may not even realize that you are suffering from test anxiety until you notice the physical symptoms. These can include trembling hands, rapid heartbeat, sweating, nausea, and tense muscles. Extreme anxiety may lead to fainting or vomiting. Obviously, any of these symptoms can have a negative impact on testing. It is important to recognize them as soon as they begin to occur so that you can address the problem before it damages your performance.

> **Review Video: 3 Ways to Tell You Have Test Anxiety**
> Visit mometrix.com/academy and enter code: 927847

The mental components of test anxiety include trouble focusing and inability to remember learned information. During a test, your mind is on high alert, which can help you recall information and stay focused for an extended period of time. However, anxiety interferes with your mind's natural processes, causing you to blank out, even on the questions you know well. The strain of testing during anxiety makes it difficult to stay focused, especially on a test that may take several hours. Extreme anxiety can take a huge mental toll, making it difficult not only to recall test information but even to understand the test questions or pull your thoughts together.

> **Review Video: How Test Anxiety Affects Memory**
> Visit mometrix.com/academy and enter code: 609003

Effects of Test Anxiety

Test anxiety is like a disease—if left untreated, it will get progressively worse. Anxiety leads to poor performance, and this reinforces the feelings of fear and failure, which in turn lead to poor performances on subsequent tests. It can grow from a mild nervousness to a crippling condition. If allowed to progress, test anxiety can have a big impact on your schooling, and consequently on your future.

Test anxiety can spread to other parts of your life. Anxiety on tests can become anxiety in any stressful situation, and blanking on a test can turn into panicking in a job situation. But fortunately, you don't have to let anxiety rule your testing and determine your grades. There are a number of relatively simple steps you can take to move past anxiety and function normally on a test and in the rest of life.

> **Review Video: How Test Anxiety Impacts Your Grades**
> Visit mometrix.com/academy and enter code: 939819

176

Physical Steps for Beating Test Anxiety

While test anxiety is a serious problem, the good news is that it can be overcome. It doesn't have to control your ability to think and remember information. While it may take time, you can begin taking steps today to beat anxiety.

Just as your first hint that you may be struggling with anxiety comes from the physical symptoms, the first step to treating it is also physical. Rest is crucial for having a clear, strong mind. If you are tired, it is much easier to give in to anxiety. But if you establish good sleep habits, your body and mind will be ready to perform optimally, without the strain of exhaustion. Additionally, sleeping well helps you to retain information better, so you're more likely to recall the answers when you see the test questions.

Getting good sleep means more than going to bed on time. It's important to allow your brain time to relax. Take study breaks from time to time so it doesn't get overworked, and don't study right before bed. Take time to rest your mind before trying to rest your body, or you may find it difficult to fall asleep.

> **Review Video: The Importance of Sleep for Your Brain**
> Visit mometrix.com/academy and enter code: 319338

Along with sleep, other aspects of physical health are important in preparing for a test. Good nutrition is vital for good brain function. Sugary foods and drinks may give a burst of energy but this burst is followed by a crash, both physically and emotionally. Instead, fuel your body with protein and vitamin-rich foods.

Also, drink plenty of water. Dehydration can lead to headaches and exhaustion, especially if your brain is already under stress from the rigors of the test. Particularly if your test is a long one, drink water during the breaks. And if possible, take an energy-boosting snack to eat between sections.

> **Review Video: How Diet Can Affect your Mood**
> Visit mometrix.com/academy and enter code: 624317

Along with sleep and diet, a third important part of physical health is exercise. Maintaining a steady workout schedule is helpful, but even taking 5-minute study breaks to walk can help get your blood pumping faster and clear your head. Exercise also releases endorphins, which contribute to a positive feeling and can help combat test anxiety.

When you nurture your physical health, you are also contributing to your mental health. If your body is healthy, your mind is much more likely to be healthy as well. So take time to rest, nourish your body with healthy food and water, and get moving as much as possible. Taking these physical steps will make you stronger and more able to take the mental steps necessary to overcome test anxiety.

> **Review Video: How to Stay Healthy and Prevent Test Anxiety**
> Visit mometrix.com/academy and enter code: 877894

Mental Steps for Beating Test Anxiety

Working on the mental side of test anxiety can be more challenging, but as with the physical side, there are clear steps you can take to overcome it. As mentioned earlier, test anxiety often stems from lack of preparation, so the obvious solution is to prepare for the test. Effective studying may be the most important weapon you have for beating test anxiety, but you can and should employ several other mental tools to combat fear.

First, boost your confidence by reminding yourself of past success—tests or projects that you aced. If you're putting as much effort into preparing for this test as you did for those, there's no reason you should expect to fail here. Work hard to prepare; then trust your preparation.

Second, surround yourself with encouraging people. It can be helpful to find a study group, but be sure that the people you're around will encourage a positive attitude. If you spend time with others who are anxious or cynical, this will only contribute to your own anxiety. Look for others who are motivated to study hard from a desire to succeed, not from a fear of failure.

Third, reward yourself. A test is physically and mentally tiring, even without anxiety, and it can be helpful to have something to look forward to. Plan an activity following the test, regardless of the outcome, such as going to a movie or getting ice cream.

When you are taking the test, if you find yourself beginning to feel anxious, remind yourself that you know the material. Visualize successfully completing the test. Then take a few deep, relaxing breaths and return to it. Work through the questions carefully but with confidence, knowing that you are capable of succeeding.

Developing a healthy mental approach to test taking will also aid in other areas of life. Test anxiety affects more than just the actual test—it can be damaging to your mental health and even contribute to depression. It's important to beat test anxiety before it becomes a problem for more than testing.

> **Review Video: Test Anxiety and Depression**
> Visit mometrix.com/academy and enter code: 904704

Study Strategy

Being prepared for the test is necessary to combat anxiety, but what does being prepared look like? You may study for hours on end and still not feel prepared. What you need is a strategy for test prep. The next few pages outline our recommended steps to help you plan out and conquer the challenge of preparation.

STEP 1: SCOPE OUT THE TEST

Learn everything you can about the format (multiple choice, essay, etc.) and what will be on the test. Gather any study materials, course outlines, or sample exams that may be available. Not only will this help you to prepare, but knowing what to expect can help to alleviate test anxiety.

STEP 2: MAP OUT THE MATERIAL

Look through the textbook or study guide and make note of how many chapters or sections it has. Then divide these over the time you have. For example, if a book has 15 chapters and you have five days to study, you need to cover three chapters each day. Even better, if you have the time, leave an extra day at the end for overall review after you have gone through the material in depth.

If time is limited, you may need to prioritize the material. Look through it and make note of which sections you think you already have a good grasp on, and which need review. While you are studying, skim quickly through the familiar sections and take more time on the challenging parts. Write out your plan so you don't get lost as you go. Having a written plan also helps you feel more in control of the study, so anxiety is less likely to arise from feeling overwhelmed at the amount to cover.

STEP 3: GATHER YOUR TOOLS

Decide what study method works best for you. Do you prefer to highlight in the book as you study and then go back over the highlighted portions? Or do you type out notes of the important information? Or is it helpful to make flashcards that you can carry with you? Assemble the pens, index cards, highlighters, post-it notes, and any other materials you may need so you won't be distracted by getting up to find things while you study.

If you're having a hard time retaining the information or organizing your notes, experiment with different methods. For example, try color-coding by subject with colored pens, highlighters, or post-it notes. If you learn better by hearing, try recording yourself reading your notes so you can listen while in the car, working out, or simply sitting at your desk. Ask a friend to quiz you from your flashcards, or try teaching someone the material to solidify it in your mind.

STEP 4: CREATE YOUR ENVIRONMENT

It's important to avoid distractions while you study. This includes both the obvious distractions like visitors and the subtle distractions like an uncomfortable chair (or a too-comfortable couch that makes you want to fall asleep). Set up the best study environment possible: good lighting and a comfortable work area. If background music helps you focus, you may want to turn it on, but otherwise keep the room quiet. If you are using a computer to take notes, be sure you don't have any other windows open, especially applications like social media, games, or anything else that could distract you. Silence your phone and turn off notifications. Be sure to keep water close by so you stay hydrated while you study (but avoid unhealthy drinks and snacks).

Also, take into account the best time of day to study. Are you freshest first thing in the morning? Try to set aside some time then to work through the material. Is your mind clearer in the afternoon or evening? Schedule your study session then. Another method is to study at the same time of day that you will take the test, so that your brain gets used to working on the material at that time and will be ready to focus at test time.

STEP 5: STUDY!

Once you have done all the study preparation, it's time to settle into the actual studying. Sit down, take a few moments to settle your mind so you can focus, and begin to follow your study plan. Don't give in to distractions or let yourself procrastinate. This is your time to prepare so you'll be ready to fearlessly approach the test. Make the most of the time and stay focused.

Of course, you don't want to burn out. If you study too long you may find that you're not retaining the information very well. Take regular study breaks. For example, taking five minutes out of every hour to walk briskly, breathing deeply and swinging your arms, can help your mind stay fresh.

As you get to the end of each chapter or section, it's a good idea to do a quick review. Remind yourself of what you learned and work on any difficult parts. When you feel that you've mastered the material, move on to the next part. At the end of your study session, briefly skim through your notes again.

But while review is helpful, cramming last minute is NOT. If at all possible, work ahead so that you won't need to fit all your study into the last day. Cramming overloads your brain with more information than it can process and retain, and your tired mind may struggle to recall even previously learned information when it is overwhelmed with last-minute study. Also, the urgent nature of cramming and the stress placed on your brain contribute to anxiety. You'll be more likely to go to the test feeling unprepared and having trouble thinking clearly.

So don't cram, and don't stay up late before the test, even just to review your notes at a leisurely pace. Your brain needs rest more than it needs to go over the information again. In fact, plan to finish your studies by noon or early afternoon the day before the test. Give your brain the rest of the day to relax or focus on other things, and get a good night's sleep. Then you will be fresh for the test and better able to recall what you've studied.

STEP 6: TAKE A PRACTICE TEST

Many courses offer sample tests, either online or in the study materials. This is an excellent resource to check whether you have mastered the material, as well as to prepare for the test format and environment.

Check the test format ahead of time: the number of questions, the type (multiple choice, free response, etc.), and the time limit. Then create a plan for working through them. For example, if you have 30 minutes to take a 60-question test, your limit is 30 seconds per question. Spend less time on the questions you know well so that you can take more time on the difficult ones.

If you have time to take several practice tests, take the first one open book, with no time limit. Work through the questions at your own pace and make sure you fully understand them. Gradually work up to taking a test under test conditions: sit at a desk with all study materials put away and set a timer. Pace yourself to make sure you finish the test with time to spare and go back to check your answers if you have time.

After each test, check your answers. On the questions you missed, be sure you understand why you missed them. Did you misread the question (tests can use tricky wording)? Did you forget the information? Or was it something you hadn't learned? Go back and study any shaky areas that the practice tests reveal.

Taking these tests not only helps with your grade, but also aids in combating test anxiety. If you're already used to the test conditions, you're less likely to worry about it, and working through tests until you're scoring well gives you a confidence boost. Go through the practice tests until you feel comfortable, and then you can go into the test knowing that you're ready for it.

Test Tips

On test day, you should be confident, knowing that you've prepared well and are ready to answer the questions. But aside from preparation, there are several test day strategies you can employ to maximize your performance.

First, as stated before, get a good night's sleep the night before the test (and for several nights before that, if possible). Go into the test with a fresh, alert mind rather than staying up late to study.

Try not to change too much about your normal routine on the day of the test. It's important to eat a nutritious breakfast, but if you normally don't eat breakfast at all, consider eating just a protein bar. If you're a coffee drinker, go ahead and have your normal coffee. Just make sure you time it so that the caffeine doesn't wear off right in the middle of your test. Avoid sugary beverages, and drink enough water to stay hydrated but not so much that you need a restroom break 10 minutes into the test. If your test isn't first thing in the morning, consider going for a walk or doing a light workout before the test to get your blood flowing.

Allow yourself enough time to get ready, and leave for the test with plenty of time to spare so you won't have the anxiety of scrambling to arrive in time. Another reason to be early is to select a good seat. It's helpful to sit away from doors and windows, which can be distracting. Find a good seat, get out your supplies, and settle your mind before the test begins.

When the test begins, start by going over the instructions carefully, even if you already know what to expect. Make sure you avoid any careless mistakes by following the directions.

Then begin working through the questions, pacing yourself as you've practiced. If you're not sure on an answer, don't spend too much time on it, and don't let it shake your confidence. Either skip it and come back later, or eliminate as many wrong answers as possible and guess among the remaining ones. Don't dwell on these questions as you continue—put them out of your mind and focus on what lies ahead.

Be sure to read all of the answer choices, even if you're sure the first one is the right answer. Sometimes you'll find a better one if you keep reading. But don't second-guess yourself if you do immediately know the answer. Your gut instinct is usually right. Don't let test anxiety rob you of the information you know.

If you have time at the end of the test (and if the test format allows), go back and review your answers. Be cautious about changing any, since your first instinct tends to be correct, but make sure you didn't misread any of the questions or accidentally mark the wrong answer choice. Look over any you skipped and make an educated guess.

At the end, leave the test feeling confident. You've done your best, so don't waste time worrying about your performance or wishing you could change anything. Instead, celebrate the successful completion of this test. And finally, use this test to learn how to deal with anxiety even better next time.

> **Review Video: 5 Tips to Beat Test Anxiety**
> Visit mometrix.com/academy and enter code: 570656

Important Qualification

Not all anxiety is created equal. If your test anxiety is causing major issues in your life beyond the classroom or testing center, or if you are experiencing troubling physical symptoms related to your anxiety, it may be a sign of a serious physiological or psychological condition. If this sounds like your situation, we strongly encourage you to seek professional help.

Thank You

We at Mometrix would like to extend our heartfelt thanks to you, our friend and patron, for allowing us to play a part in your journey. It is a privilege to serve people from all walks of life who are unified in their commitment to building the best future they can for themselves.

The preparation you devote to these important testing milestones may be the most valuable educational opportunity you have for making a real difference in your life. We encourage you to put your heart into it—that feeling of succeeding, overcoming, and yes, conquering will be well worth the hours you've invested.

We want to hear your story, your struggles and your successes, and if you see any opportunities for us to improve our materials so we can help others even more effectively in the future, please share that with us as well. **The team at Mometrix would be absolutely thrilled to hear from you!** So please, send us an email (support@mometrix.com) and let's stay in touch.

> **If you'd like some additional help, check out these other resources we offer for your exam:**
> http://MometrixFlashcards.com/MTLE

Additional Bonus Material

Due to our efforts to try to keep this book to a manageable length, we've created a link that will give you access to all of your additional bonus material.

Please visit http://www.mometrix.com/bonus948/mtlepedsec
to access the information.